ATE   DUE

D0820644

PG 3443 R566 1980
Ripp, Victor.
Turgenev's Russia

TURGENEV'S RUSSIA

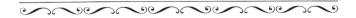

TURGENEV'S RUSSIA

FROM

Notes of a Hunter

TO

Fathers and Sons

BY Victor Ripp

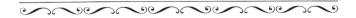

Cornell University Press

Ithaca and London

OCT 1 8 1984

DOUGLAS COLLEGE LIBRARY

This book has been published with the aid of a grant from the Hull Memorial Publication Fund of Cornell University.

Copyright © 1980 by Cornell University

All rights reserved. Except for brief quotations in a review, this book, or parts thereof, must not be reproduced in any form without permission in writing from the publisher. For information address Cornell University Press, 124 Roberts Place, Ithaca, New York 14850.

First published 1980 by Cornell University Press.
Published in the United Kingdom by Cornell University Press Ltd., 2–4 Brook Street, London W1Y 1AA.

International Standard Book Number 0-8014-1294-3
Library of Congress Catalog Card Number 80-15534

Printed in the United States of America

Librarians: Library of Congress cataloging information appears on the last page of the book.

For my mother

Contents

Contents

Preface

〜〉〜〜〜

Though it may seem odd to say of a writer renowned for his lucid style, there is a "Turgenev problem." A major source of the problem is precisely that style. On the one hand, the meanings of Turgenev's fiction are so accessible, the questions his characters raise and the values they endorse so easily comprehensible, that commentary seems superfluous; on the other hand, if we stop with these readily accessible meanings it is hard to account for the broad political significance that contemporaries attributed to his work. *Fathers and Sons* is concerned with some of the political issues troubling mid-nineteenth-century Russia—though less explicitly than one might expect of a novel regularly cited as a momentous political statement—but Turgenev's other novels appear to be largely about private desires and domestic arrangements.

Some critics have tried to give political weight to Turgenev's literary corpus by alluding to his role in the history of Russian progressivism. It cannot be done. His disagreements with his contemporaries about Russia's relationship to the West and about the emancipation of the serfs are indeed evidence that he was concerned about politics; but he never devised an explicit program or led a coherent movement. If he is an important figure in Russian political history, the proof must be discovered in his fiction. Trying to establish the significance of his fiction by alluding to his political activity is not only to turn things upside down but to build an argument on a very skimpy foundation.

To be sure, many critics have begun with a consideration of

9

Turgenev's literary career before moving on to other questions. It is a favored approach among both Soviet and Western scholars, though the conclusions usually differ. Both groups make his career a symbol of the liberal tradition that was snuffed out in 1917, but whereas Soviet scholars use the opportunity to show the irrelevancy of liberalism to Russia's needs, Western scholars indicate regret that the values Turgenev espoused were not allowed to develop fully. Turgenev thus becomes a touchstone for distinguishing between liberalism and radicalism, and he fills the role fairly well, for two reasons. He depicted characters who can easily be placed along a political spectrum, so that their actions appear as ideologies in motion; and contemporaries, who, of course, noticed this element of his works, used him as a weapon in their political debates.

The eagerness to establish the battle lines between radicalism and liberalism has, however, obscured other political aspects of Turgenev's work. Obviously, the idea of two monolithic camps confronting each other can hardly do justice to the complexity of Turgenev's fictive worlds, not to speak of Russian political reality. In exploring Turgenev's historical significance, then, I will discuss not only the differences dividing radicals and liberals but also the underlying assumptions they shared. Progressive politics in nineteenth-century Russia was part of a cultural system that it will be necessary to define.

Though the cultural implications of Russia's political battles have generally been ignored by literary scholars, they have lately received renewed attention from American historians, notably Nicholas Riasanovsky in *A Parting of The Ways* (Cambridge, 1976) and Abbott Gleason in *Young Russia* (New York, 1980). They have emphasized the importance of the concept of *obshchestvo* (literally, "society"), an alliance of individuals holding diverse political beliefs but united in their resistance to the encroaching influence of the central government. *Obshchestvo* plays a considerable role in my analysis: Turgenev, I shall argue, was one of its chief spokesmen. Though he did not pay much explicit attention in his fiction to the aims of *obshchestvo*, he did explore the attitudes that underlay them. It was his particular genius to translate the political issues of his era into depictions of men and women engaged in the tasks of daily life.

Preface

In trying to make sense of the Russia in which Turgenev's fiction is set, I have introduced materials from several areas—among others, pedagogy, the women's rights movement, and journalistic debate about the social consequences of the emancipation of the serfs. Because these topics are not usually considered in criticism of Turgenev, my interpretations of his fiction are somewhat unconventional. I have discovered no single true meaning; I believe, however, that a critical perspective that includes a detailed analysis of the key cultural issues of Turgenev's time will shed new light on his literary efforts, and in turn will illuminate Russian culture.

The organization of what follows is meant to reflect this double aim. In Chapters 1–4, I try to show that Turgenev's decision to stop writing sketches and try his hand at novels was simultaneously an aesthetic and a political choice. The experience of writing *Notes of a Hunter* taught him that contemporary Russian life could be confronted only from certain perspectives; in learning about his literary capacities, he learned about politics. The second part (Chapters 5–9) traces the consequences of this new knowledge. In Chapter 5, I define the novelistic structure that Turgenev devised to describe the political situation after 1856. Chapters 6–8 show that *Rudin*, *Nest of the Nobility*, and *On the Eve* not only resolve problems broached by his earlier writings, but raise problems of their own, which Turgenev had to explore. The concluding chapter, on *Fathers and Sons*, is an attempt to explain Turgenev's position in the progressive movement after the national crisis caused by the emancipation of the serfs brought *obshchestvo* to the brink of collapse.

Though I have included both interpretations of the four novels that Turgenev wrote during 1856–1861 and discussions of the areas of Russian culture that the novels addressed, my point is not that the novels reflected something that can be called "Russian reality." Nineteenth-century Russia is not an easily discernible empirical fact but a totality of shifting relationships and symbolic meanings, and Turgenev's novels are aspects of this totality. Yet, in their best moments, they also make the relationships and meanings vividly clear.

I am grateful to the International Research and Exchange Board for making it possible for me to spend a year in Leningrad, where I

Preface

did much of the research for this book. The Soviet Studies Committee of Cornell University generously extended financial support for the typing of several versions of the manuscript. I would especially like to thank Ann Rosalind Jones, who patiently pointed out many lapses in my style and my argument. The editors of Cornell University Press have also been very helpful. Lastly I would like to acknowledge my debt to the late Rufus Mathewson, who first aroused my interest in Turgenev.

In transliterating Russian, I have followed System II of the transliteration chart in J. Thomas Shaw, *The Transliteration of Modern Russian for English Language Publications* (Madison, Milwaukee, and London, 1967), pp. 8–9, with the exception that I have used the more common English form -sky for the ending of Russian surnames, rather than -skii.

In translating passages from *Notes of a Hunter*, I have used Bernard Guerney's version, *The Sportsman's Sketches* (New York, 1965), as a model but have introduced emendations where I thought necessary. All other translations are my own.

Part of Chapter 3 appeared, in different form, in the *Slavic Review*, 38 (March, 1979). Part of Chapter 4 appeared in an earlier version in *Literature and Society in Imperial Russia, 1800–1914*, ed. William Mills Todd III, © 1978 by the Board of Trustees of Leland Stanford Junior University, published by Stanford University Press.

VICTOR RIPP

Ithaca, New York

Part One

THE PATH TO THE NOVEL

1.

Introduction

⟨~⟩⌒⟩⌒⟨⟩

Ivan Sergeevich Turgenev came to literary prominence in the late 1840s, with the publication of the sketches that constitute *Notes of a Hunter*. It was a bleak moment in Russian history. Nicholas I, who had gained the throne by crushing the Decembrist Uprising, pursued regressive policies throughout his reign (1825–1855), imposing censorship, curtailing education, and in general extending bureaucratic controls: the government's alarmed reaction to the European disturbances of 1848, which was to institute a period of administrative terrorism, was only the natural culmination of its previous course. It is also true, however, that the last years of the reign of Nicholas I opened the way to social and political liberalization. The machinery of repression began to show signs of strain just when it was most fully operating. The most telling portents of breakdown appeared in the area of economics, where it was becoming increasingly clear that the rigid feudal system could not sustain the nation's material well-being. But the intellectual life of Russia also was on the brink of change. If a sense of purposelessness still pervaded the culture, it was a purposelessness that made individuals irritable and eager for remedy, instead of merely plunging them into despair. Thus, Russian writers of the period were expected to confront social and political issues, and most did.

Though *Notes of a Hunter* fulfilled the demands that were placed on literature more effectively than any other contemporary work, Turgenev's preeminence was never secure. That was because his fame seemed partly an accident of history, the result of a cultural vacuum. Gogol had ceased to be productive, Dostoevsky's career had been interrupted by exile to Siberia, Tolstoy's thoughts were just beginning to turn to literature. Turgenev seemed to be Russia's leading writer by default; but though contemporaries treated him with less awe than Russians have usually accorded writers they consider natural genuises, they accepted him as the chief literary spokesman of their society, He retained this status until the early 1860s, altering his method and perspective as the society evolved.

Turgenev maintained his preeminence more by wisely exploiting his shortcomings than by insisting on his merits. His manner of vague affability made him unfit to be a charismatic leader, and indeed many contemporaries questioned his intellectual energy. Turgenev regretted his reputation, but he rarely resorted to self-justification. In his most expansive moods—which were the ones he usually carried into his fiction—he realized that his difficulties were more than merely personal. He argued that his flaws were an aspect of Russian history. The charges against his character were, in fact, widespread. Thus, though Dostoevsky's famous caricature of him as Karmazinov, the fatuous novelist in *The Devils*, is at points unfair (statements from Turgenev's fiction are paraded as his personal credo) and everywhere ungenerous (since Turgenev had helped Dostoevsky financially in a moment of great need), the assertion that Turgenev was a poseur in itself provoked no indignation. That possibility was perhaps to be rebutted but hardly to be dismissed out of hand. Herzen, on first meeting Turgenev, compared him to Russia's most famous fraud, the hero of Gogol's *Dead Souls:* "A Khlestakov, educated, clever, superficial, with a desire to express himself and fatuité sans borne."[1]

Even confirmed friends felt they had to comment on Turgenev's sincerity. Pavel Annenkov, who was close to Turgenev for some forty years, wrote: "There arose the general opinion that he [Turgenev] was a man who never spoke a sincere word or had a sincere feeling. Turgenev's aims were clear. . . . He intended to cause a literary effect and to achieve a reputation for originality."[2] Annenkov raises the question of Turgenev's insincerity only to explain it away. Still, it is striking that a friend would mention such a topic.

1. Quoted in Leonard Schapiro, *Turgenev, His Life and Times* (New York, 1978), p. 31. I am indebted to this book for its illuminating analysis of Turgenev's career.
2. P. V. Annenkov, *Literaturnye vospominaniia* (Moscow, 1960), pp. 381–382.

Annenkov's remarks are about a young man in his twenties, but Turgenev remained highly self-dramatizing. One observer commented how even in later life Turgenev would be "taken by amazing fantasies. . . . He would ask for permission to crow like a rooster, then climb onto the windowsill and would indeed crow inimitably well and stare at us with immobile eyes. At other times he asked permission to imitate a madman."[3] Though some people prized his energy and charm, others found his social performances, like the ones referred to above as well as less extreme diversions, disingenuous. Indeed, his exhibitions of high spirits alternated with moods of deep despondency, in a way that called both attitudes into question. Tolstoi insisted that Turgenev only played at life, whether he was speaking of the difficulties of life in general or his in particular: "As soon as Turgenev arrives it is one and the same thing: 'tra-ge-dy, tra-ge-dy.' "[4]

The most notorious attack on Turgenev was made by Ivan Goncharov. The author of *Oblomov*, once a good friend, came to believe that Turgenev was plagiarizing his works in progress, which the two men often discussed.[5] The charge certainly was the result of Goncharov's paranoia; indeed, Goncharov also believed that Turgenev was passing the plagiarized plots to his literary friends abroad. Since Turgenev's friends included Flaubert, Henry James, Maupassant, the Goncourts, and George Sand, Goncharov was implying that his work was the source of much of nineteenth-century European culture. Though the affair was bizarre, it is noteworthy that it was Turgenev who became the object of Goncharov's suspicions, and that at the meeting of Russian literary figures who were brought together to arbitrate the dispute, Turgenev defended himself in-

3. N. A. Tuchkova-Ogareva, "Ivan Sergeevich Turgenev. 1848–1870," in *I. S. Turgenev v vospominaniiakh sovremennikov*, ed. V. V. Grigorenko (Moscow, 1969), I, 235.

4. Quoted by B. M. Eikhenbaum in his introduction to *Turgenev v zapisiakh sovremennikov*, ed. A. Ostrovsky (Leningrad, 1929), p. 7. One other appraisal of Turgenev's character is worth mentioning, since it bears the endorsement of three people. "According to [Granovsky], no one had so truly defined Turgenev as A. K. Tiutcheva, who apparently only told him to his face, 'Vous n'avez pas d'épine dorsale au morale' [sic]," in E. M. Feoktistov, *Za kulisami politiki i literatury 1848–96* (Leningrad, 1929), p. 2.

5. The episode is analyzed in a good introductory essay by B. M. Engel'gardt in *Goncharov i Turgenev: po neizdannym materialam pushkinskogo doma* (Petersburg, 1921).

eptly, with the result that he was not fully exonerated. Even when innocent, Turgenev projected an air of being less than forthright.

Nevertheless, there were few actions in Turgenev's life which evoked the charge of deceit. Specific acts were never the main issue. Rather, it was his character, the inclinations underlying his behavior, that troubled many people. Such a focus gave the issue a terrible tenacity. Once enough people have rejected a person's sincerity, merely to insist on it may appear only another, more subtle form of insincerity. Even seemingly admirable actions may fail to alter the judgment. Thus, although Turgenev's progressive stance in this highly politicized period was generally respected, suspicion persisted that here, too, he was only posturing. Certain of his actions appear indisputably courageous—for example, his obituary for Gogol, then in official disfavor, which earned him two years of exile on his estate—yet contemporaries refused to credit them as the actions of a man fully committed to his ideals, in the manner, say, of Herzen or Granovsky.

The opinions of Turgenev's contemporaries did not amount to outright condemnation, but they did create a daunting moral atmosphere. More than for most people, his actions were an object of skeptical scrutiny, his every word an opportunity to discover fakery. Not surprisingly, much of his fiction shows a distinct nervousness about putting too much of himself at risk. He desperately needed some sort of strategy that would defuse contemporaries' judgment of him, but the one he found, which was to show that his character exemplified the nation's dilemmas, was itself risky. It was not a heroic period, and wrapping oneself in the mantle of history meant identifying with very uncertain values.

The most prominent historical circumstance influencing Turgenev was his social pedigree. He was born in Orel, in 1818, to parents belonging to the wealthier segment of the nobility.[6] Any sensitive individual who gains advantage from accident of birth may well feel guilt; being born into the Russian nobility could lead one to suffer

---

6. I shall use the term "nobility" when referring to the Russian *dvorianstvo*. Because the Russian estate has no exact European counterpart, various translations have been attempted—for example, Turgenev's novel *Dvorianskoe gnezdo* has been rendered as *Home of the Gentry* by Richard Freeborn and *A House of Gentlefolk* by Constance Garnett.

from the feeling even without reaping the benefits supposedly caus-
ing it. At first glance, noble status appears an undiluted good. The
nobility had privileges denied the rest of the population, such as
exemption from taxation and army service, the right to own land,
and—no small thing in a country skirting barbarism—freedom from
corporal punishment. Turgenev accepted and enjoyed being a
nobleman. He took pride in his provincial estate near Orel, he
participated in regional assemblies of nobles, he supervised the
peasants working on his land. More important, he several times
argued that the nobility could play a privileged political role.[7] Only
the nobility, he claimed, could resist the central government's oppressive influence and provide an alternate vision for Russia to follow. The incorporated status of the estate, as well as the common
background and occupations of most of its members, gave the nobility the self-consciousness to be an independent political force. Allegiance to the nobility, while reasonable—indeed, precisely *because* it was reasonable—caused much anxiety. The capacities that
seemed to promise it a pivotal role proved to be empty forms,
undercut by the exigences of Russian life. Belonging to the nobility,
for all the advantages it brought, was like sitting in a well designed
vehicle that curiously refused to move.

In part the problem was the composition of the nobility. From a
legal point of view it was an open estate; the rank could be acquired
by fulfilling certain requisites and lost by defaulting on certain obligations. From an economic point of view, the nobility included
heterogeneous elements, ranging from the very rich to noblemen
who lived no better than their impoverished peasants. What
seemed on paper a well defined group was actually shifting, incohe-
sive, and therefore unable to engage in concerted action.

But the composition of the Russian nobility of this period is less
important to understanding its ambiguous role than the way it
functioned vis-à-vis other political forces, especially the central gov-

---

7. Turgenev expressed this view explicitly in his unfinished article "Neskol'ko
myslei o sovremennom znachenii russkogo dvorianstva," in *I. S. Turgenev, Polnoe
Sobranie Sochinenii i pisem* (Moscow and Leningrad, 1960–68), *Sochineniia*, XIV,
299–304. Hereafter quotations from Turgenev's collected works and letters will be
marked directly in the text, with the reference "*P*" for letters (*Pis'ma*) and "*S*" for
works (*Sochineniia*).

ernment. The relationship of the nobility to the government was often of petitioner to grandee. The government's brute strength had much to do with the nobility's supplicatory stance; so also did the history of Russian autocracy—the tsar's office, unlike that of many of his Western counterparts, was not the result of a compromise among rivals; he was consequently beholden to no group. But the nobility's role was also a question of cultural psychology. The nobility had great difficulty even imagining an independent purpose.[8]

The issue of state service illustrates the limits of the nobility's political energy. At one time obligatory, state service (military or civil) was not required of the nobility after the Imperial Manifesto "Concerning the Granting of Freedom and Liberty to the Entire Russian Nobility" in 1762. Nevertheless, in the nineteenth century the bureaucracy of the central government was still largely staffed by noblemen. By continuing to enter state service, the nobility pointedly slighted local administration, which officially was in its hands. In England organs of district government provided a political base for the gentry; the Russian nobility considered local administration a second-rate occupation. Service in the central government seemed the only worthwhile game in town; if one wanted to engage in Russia's political life, one played. Even those who were repelled by the government's policies often found they could not ignore its unique capacity to certify every individual Russian's existence. As one writer put it, "Not to serve in Russia—means not to be born; to leave the service—means to die."[9] Typically, Turgenev served. His term was short (1842–1844), his performance desultory, and he was in the most progressive department, the Ministry of Internal Affairs.[10] Still, it must be said, the bureaucracy seems a strange train-

8. An interesting account of how this attitude came into being is given by Marc Raeff, *Origins of the Russian Intelligentsia* (New York, 1966). For a comprehensive examination of the Russian nobility, its history, rights, and functions, see A. V. Romanovich-Slavatinsky, *Dvorianstvo v Rossii ot nachala XVIII veka do otmeny krepostonogo prava* (Kiev, 1912).

9. The remark, by A. V. Nikitenko, is quoted in M. Aleksandrov, *Gosudarstvo, biurokratiia i absoliutizm* (St. Petersburg, 1910), p. 108. Consider also N. Turgenev's observation that individuals who did not serve in the government were "en dehors de la nation officielle ou légale." It is quoted in Richard Pipes, *Russia under the Old Regime* (New York, 1974), p. 125.

10. Turgenev's state service is analyzed in detail by Iu. G. Oksman, "I. S. Turgenev na sluzhbe v Ministerstve vnutrennikh del," *Uchenye zapiski Saratovskogo universiteta*, LVI (1957), 172–183.

ing ground for a writer who would shortly set about proclaiming the corruption of the status quo.

Turgenev was not behaving hypocritically, nor were the many contemporaries who served with him. Rather, the widespread acceptance of state service even among those who despised state policy gauges the difficulty Russians of the period had in conceiving of autonomous political action. Hypocrisy implies a morally dubious choice; in Russia the idea of choice itself was in question.

The main problem facing progressives in the middle of the nineteenth century was not working for change or even finding a means to denounce the evils of the existing order; such activities had to be preceded by a feat of the political imagination. It was first necessary to envision a genuine alternative to what existed: an area apart from the pervasive influence of the central government. Russia's political landscape was virtually barren of elements normally constituting civil society. There was no fully free press, no independent judiciary or legal profession (or any other well organized profession, for that matter), no powerful church, even very few private associations that might propagate new or eccentric ideas. Also, there was nothing resembling a rising, commercially active middle class, the agency that forged civil society in Western Europe. Indeed, there appeared to be only one social entity with any force: the government. Because individuals had nowhere else to turn in order to regulate everyday life, the government's influence was not only powerful but pervasive. Like an army that relies not merely on superior weaponry but on sheer numbers to overwhelm an objective, the Russian government in the nineteenth century seemed to encroach on every aspect of social intercourse. As Turgenev put it, "The government sphere, especially in Petersburg, subdued and seized everything for its purpose" (*S*, XIV, 15).

It follows, incidentally, that Russia did have a notably large standing army. Citizens of the empire were continually reminded of governmental authority by the uniforms they saw everywhere.[11] Some historians have argued that contemporaries overestimated the

---

11. B. M. Eikhenbaum, *Lev Tolstoi, kniga pervaia, 50-ie gody* (Leningrad, 1928), notes that Tolstoi, in planning to publish a military journal, could speak as if the whole male population were in uniform. See page 161. I am in general indebted to this book for its brilliant analysis of the same period I am discussing, but most of my conclusions differ from Eikhenbaum's.

capacity of a government wracked by inefficiency and corruption to impose its will.[12] The government may indeed have been weaker than it looked—the point is debatable—but it was everywhere one looked, and that proved decisive. Its sprawling presence was enough to persuade most Russians of its great strength. Up to the middle of the nineteenth century, individuals who wanted to escape its encompassing sway seemed to have no choice except political quiescence or fruitless indignation.

The uncertain lot of Russian noblement and noblewomen was not, however, only a matter of their weakness vis-à-vis the government; many, Turgenev included, suffered because of their ambiguous relationship to a social group they dominated. Like virtually all Russians of their station, Turgenev's parents owned serfs. Witnessing the barbarous treatment of serfs on his mother's estate—some were flogged on whim, others punished by being enlisted into the army for a twenty-five year term—revolted Turgenev. As an adult, he formulated principles, political as well as humanitarian, to support his feelings. Nevertheless, he could not escape his background so easily. There is no reason to doubt his sincerity, but serfdom was too deeply ingrained in the life of a Russian nobleman to be extirpated by mere disapproval, no matter how passionate.[13] It is worth noting that Turgenev was able to express his legendary generosity—the warm hospitality and the readiness to help friends in financial need—only after he inherited his mother's wealth, including her serfs. Can one fully renounce a social system that makes one a *better* person?

At one point Turgenev controlled some two thousand serfs. He made sizable financial concessions to them—such as permitting a rent system of obligations (*obrok*) instead of the more burdensome one of required labor (*barshchina*)—and he sought as well to provide health and educational facilities. Perhaps more important, beginning with a memorandum he wrote while serving in the Ministry

---

12. S. Frederick Starr, *Decentralization and Self-Government in Russia, 1830-70* (Princeton, 1972), makes a good case for such a view: "The overriding importance which contemporaries assigned to the mushrooming bureaucracy readily became a historian's shibboleth, admitting of no challenge and requiring no proof" (p. 10). But I am here concerned precisely with "assigned" meanings, not with a statistical reality.

13. For a succinct and lucid account of the economic situation of the nobility, see Pipes, *Russia under the Old Regime*, pp. 171-190.

of Interior Affairs, he often spoke out publicly against the injustices the peasantry suffered.[14] Some of his last thoughts on his deathbed were about the peasant school he had established. The peasants responded to his affection and sympathy by declaring him an inordinately good master (*barin*);[15] which is to say that all his efforts left him very much a part of a social apparatus that he knew was evil.

Even one of Turgenev's most forthright attacks on serfdom, his statement of how he came to write *Notes of a Hunter*, is permeated with ambiguity. The statement is worth considering in some detail, for in a short paragraph, he manages to suggest in condensed form many of the social pressures that he described more discursively in his fiction.

> I could not breath the same air, could not stay side by side with that which I had grown to hate.... In my eyes the foe had a definite visage, and a known name: serfdom. Under that name I gathered and concentrated all that I had decided to contend against to the bitter end, that with which I had resolved never to make peace; that was my Hannibalic Oath, and I was not the only one who took it [at that time]. That is precisely why I left for the West—to carry it out better. I could never have written *Notes of a Hunter*, of course, had I remained in Russia. [S, xiv, 9)

The statement distorts the facts of his life in several ways. First, he did not, as he implies, begin the *Notes of a Hunter* cycle in a subversive spirit. He wrote "Khor' and Kalinych," the first sketch in the cycle, almost off-handedly, at a moment when he was consider-

---

14. Though it is equivocal on the terms of emancipation, the memorandum leaves no doubt that he wanted serfdom abolished. See "Neskol'ko zamechanii o russkom khosiastve i o russkom krest'ianine," S, I, 459–474. However, I. I. Vekslar, *I. S. Turgenev i politicheskaia bor'ba shestidesiatykh godov* (Leningrad, Moscow, 1935), argues that throughout his life Turgenev supported proposals concerning the peasantry which would ultimately bring economic advantage to his own class: thus in favoring the easing of internal passport restrictions and the lessening of the freed serfs' redemption payments, he was most interested in creating a mobile labor force.that would promote capitalism.

The attempt to define Turgenev's politics has obsessed Soviet scholars, the dominant approach being to explain away his suspect liberalism in order to salvage his literary achievements. Much has been written to no purpose. The best book on Turgenev's politics is Henri Granjard, *Ivan Tourguénev et les courants politiques et sociaux de son temps* (Paris, 1954).

15. N. M. Gut'iar, "Turgenev, krestianskii vopros," *Turgenevskii sbornik* (Kiev, 1907), pp. 160–205.

ing whether to give up a literary career altogether; he only wanted to help some friends whose newly acquired journal needed contributions. Certainly there was no solemn moment when he took a Hannibalic Oath. Second, the immediate reason he left for the West in 1846, and the reason he spent much of his life abroad thereafter, was romantic, not political: he wanted to be near the French opera singer Pauline Viardot, the great love of his life. In this passage he is substituting national events for personal ones. That is probably not uncommon and is certainly understandable, for what better gives a meaning to erratic individual experience than fitting it to the contours of history? The obviousness of the effort, however—full of jagged pieces that will not match—suggests how poorly Russian history accommodated the urges of a man like him.

Turgenev's rhetoric, designed to make his equivocal assertions more persuasive, does no more than reveal his ambiguous posture. A single image governs the passage: that of an antagonist both noxious and powerful. He calls this foe serfdom, but he immediately adds that serfdom is a symbol of something else. The "definite visage and known name" point to some larger entity, which Turgenev does not, or will not, define. Persumably he has in mind the elements that supported and sustained serfdom: Russia's economic and social backwardness, the policies of the government—and the attitudes of the nobility. For though the nobility increasingly admitted that serfdom was unprofitable and had always granted that it was morally reprehensible, as a group the nobility was by no means ready to accept emancipation. In this context it makes sense that Turgenev would resort to symbols, that his style became less descriptive and more evocative, for if he had been precise, he would certainly have had to explain how he managed to escape the complicity that dogged other members of his serf-holding class. The combative tone of his Hannibalic Oath follows directly from that predicament: Turgenev wants to endow a complex moral dilemma with the aspect of a pitched battle. For that battle he adopts a curious strategy: he removes himself to a distance of several thousand miles from his foe. In fact, his definition of evil makes the strategy appear wise. Evil is not merely powerful in Russia, but pervasive, and just being in Russia means he must breathe the air of corruption. He retreats, vowing attack.

24

Introduction

The Hannibalic Oath, for all its self-congratulatory air, expresses great uncertainty. Its apparent daring is really only nervous irritability aroused by the complexity of Russian life. Turgenev, in striving to paint a picture with clearly defined villains and heroes, is disguising many political contradictions, not the least of which is his own role. The oath is a remarkably skewed document; but the distortion is exemplary, born of a genuine effort to find an explanation for the morally uncertain position of Russia's progressive nobility.

Though Turgenev's sensitivity to moral issues endows his career with historical meaning, not all the consequences were benign. For one thing, his awareness of his ambiguous position in Russian society often made him appear tentative. It is an unusual feature in a major writer. There is no joy of innovation in his works, nothing that approximates Dostoevsky's audacious insistence that he, Dostoevsky, was bringing a "new word" to Russia. Turgenev continually relied on his literary predecessors and contemporaries for guidance, and his view of his place in literary tradition is almost irksomely self-effacing. "We are all writers of the interregnum," he said, "the epoch between Gogol and a great future leader" (*P*, III, 32).

At its worst, Turgenev's modesty degenerated into an unappealing willingness to forgo responsibility. In 1855 he joined Grigorovich and Druzhinin, two writers of immeasurably lesser talent, in writing a farce called *School for Hospitality*, a work notable only for its vivid caricature of the critic Chernyshevsky. Though in itself innocuous, the episode shows how ready Turgenev was to view literature as a group endeavor, something approaching a hearty and comfortable conversation among friends. (In this instance he deeply regretted his bonhomie: Grigorovich unexpectedly published *School for Hospitality* as a short story, retaining its scurrilous elements.)[16] Throughout his career, Turgenev circulated his manuscripts among his acquaintances, asking for criticism and incorporating advice, seemingly content to be relieved of the burden of hard literary decisions. Annenkov remarked of his friend, "He enjoyed

16. *Shkola gostepriimstva* appeared as a short story in *Biblioteka dlia chteniia*, CXXXIII (1855), 12–76. Grigorovich's account of the episode is in his *Literaturnye vospominaniia* (Leningrad, 1934), pp. 227–239.

any kind of discussion of his works, listened to it with the submissiveness of a schoolboy, and displayed a willingness to make changes."[17]

Turgenev also habitually reused material that he had first created for other contexts. Phrases from letters and occasional pieces turn up unchanged in the fiction, often stripped of their original emotion.[18] By the same token the novels show a noteworthy replication of a single basic structure, as if once having found a serviceable vehicle, he saw no reason for further tinkering. There seems to be, all too often, a determination to reduce the risks inherent in writing fiction.

Turgenev's caution shows up perhaps most visibly in a style occasionally so elegant that it fails altogether to come to grips with its purported subject. His prose can be wondrously supple and luminous, especially in comparison with other Russian master novelists like Gogol, Dostoevsky, and Tolstoi, who wrote prose that was in various degrees jagged and nervous. Unfortunately, suppleness and luminosity are qualities that can promote the evasiveness to which Turgenev was inclined. He often appeared content to stay on the surface of things instead of getting close to the bone: "The sky was speckled with stars; they seemed to look, with quiet attention, at the distant earth. . . . One could feel some sort of desire in [the air], some sort of thrill," he writes in the story "Three Meetings" (S, v, 235). When the young Tolstoi, considering a writer's career, evaluated the literature of the day, it was passages such as this which most exasperated him: they seemed imprecise and facile.

Turgenev would probably have agreed that his prose was sometimes inadequate to its task, though he might have added that every author has such moments. At the end of his story "Spring Torrents" there is a statement that sums up one of his most persistent beliefs about literature—a belief that fortunately his practice often belied:

> I will not attempt to describe the feelings experienced by Sanin [the protagonist] on reading the letter. There is no adequate expression

17. Quoted in Richard Freeborn, *Turgenev: The Novelists' Novelist* (Oxford, 1960), p. 30. Freeborn presents excellent discussions of the formal properties of Turgenev's novels; however, his remarks about the connection of the works with their cultural context seem to me uninspired.

18. B. M. Eikhenbaum advances this argument in "Artistizm Turgeneva," *Moi vremennik* (Leningrad, 1929), pp. 93–100.

for such feelings; they are deeper and stronger—and more indefinite—than any word. Only music can communicate them. [S, XI, 156]

One feels no gratitude for the information that another art form exists which can capture the hero's emotions, only irritation that Turgenev has abdicated his responsibility to describe them himself. Similar passages in other works suggest that the quicksilver energy of his style, so well suited to render the colors and shadings of the natural world, disguises a desire to will away the complexity of human affairs.

Turgenev's elaborately wary explanations of his characters' experience derive from a view he held of his own life: existence was a series of tasks that appeared more baffling, the closer they were examined. While still in his twenties, he began to suggest that his energy was already spent. Beginning almost with his first published work and continually throughout his career, he hinted that he was on the verge of giving up literature, because he had already accomplished all that lay within the scope of his talent. In 1856 he wrote to Tolstoi, "Shall I add that I am much older than you. . . . All your life is directed toward the future, mine is wholly behind me" (P, III, 13). Despite the unctuous tones of the aging patriarch, he was only ten years older than Tolstoi, and at thirty-eight some of his very best work was still to come.

Turgenev's world weariness was reflected in his recurrent references to impending death. They begin to appear early in his life, much too early to be realistic, and they appear even more bathetic in retrospect when we know that he lived to the age of sixty-five. Their characteristic form is revealing: "death resolves all" (*smert' vse primiriaet*). That is, death is viewed not so much as the cessation of intellectual and physical experience as an escape from life's dilemmas.

When Turgenev's world-weary attitude seeps into his fiction, the effects are disastrous. The theme of missed opportunity, which he often showed could yield a bracing knowledge, then becomes only lugubrious. He seems to deny his characters even the chance of happiness, so eager is he to depict states of regret and loss. His evocation of a happier past becomes empty posturing. The nostalgia is for something no effort was made to secure in the first place. Turgenev can be a very exasperating writer.

27

It is important, I think, to admit his shortcomings—and not only because by facing up to an author's occasional lapses, we learn to appreciate his more characteristic successes. Taking Turgenev's life all in all, it is possible to argue that the lapses were more revealing of his real personality than the successes, which had to be assiduously devised. Thus, as we shall see, his best fiction, especially his novels, are vehicles of self-denial, or at least represent an advertisement of those of his traits with which he was least comfortable. When he speaks in his own voice, the insincerity and self-pity that contemporaries noted become most evident. When he immerses his natural self in a milieu of social influences and allows feelings to be structured by politics, he simultaneously exposes the contradictions of Russian society in the middle of the nineteenth century and presents a forceful and sympathetic account of his personal dilemma.

2.

The Author's Voice

Turgenev first began to think of himself as a writer in 1843, with the publication of *Parasha*, "a story in verse." It was a period when Russian critics were increasingly calling on writers to produce novels, and indeed Turgenev several times expressed a desire to answer the call. His first novel, *Rudin*, was not to appear until 1856, however. In the thirteen-year interval he wrote many sketches, plays, short stories, and essays: since he sometimes seemed to regard literature as a hobby rather than a vocation, his output was about what one would expect, substantial if in no way extraordinary. Nevertheless, his failure to write a novel during these years remains noteworthy. He did, after all, become a novelist eventually, and a highly successful one. Why did he delay fulfilling his destiny?[1]

The widely held view that Turgenev was too irresolute to occupy himself seriously with social issues suggests one answer to the question: in Russia the novel had a distinctly social orientation, and Turgenev resisted committing himself to the genre. Indeed, there is ample evidence of an attraction to pure aestheticism; when he was addressing someone who shared this inclination, he often gloried in

---

1. The question has perplexed many critics. Richard Freeborn, *Turgenev: The Novelists' Novelist* (Oxford, 1960) notes that Turgenev hesitated even after he had ostensibly decided to become a novelist: "If, then, one can give any direct answer to the question: why did Turgenev spend four years with the problem of the novel?, it must be that he had not, until 1855, sufficiently deepened his understanding of human nature and human life, of human destiny and the world of nature to permit him to embark on what he called a 'large work'" (p. 41). Freeborn's comment, it seems to me, is not an explanation but a casting of the question in new terms.

his detachment from contemporary politics. Thus in a letter to his friend and confidante Countess Lambert, he wrote: "You are right to say that I am not a political activist. . . . I never did and never will occupy myself with politics: the business is alien to me and uninteresting—and I pay attention to it only to the extent that is necessary for a writer who has been called upon to paint pictures of contemporary life." (*P*, v, 120).

Similarly, in his *Reminiscences of Literature and Life* (1869), a memoir covering most of his career, he devotes himself to proving that he was above any party. In a typical anecdote he relates how, shortly after the publication of *Fathers and Sons* (1862), an acquaintance accosted him on Nevsky Avenue and blamed "his nihilists" for fires that had recently been sweeping Petersburg (*S*, xiv, 98). The acquaintance was probably misinformed, since it is now considered likely that the fires were set by police *agents provocateurs*, and he certainly misconceived the nature of literature, since fictional characters do not magically enter the general population. Nonetheless, Turgenev was aghast. His ability to maintain a fitting distance between literature and life had been put into doubt. Indeed, he had always scorned works that seemed too closely tied with the contemporary scene. In a letter in 1857 he completely dismissed Shchedrin as being a "tendentious" writer (*P*, iii, 92). Turgenev went on in the letter to say that "the public now requires things coarse and spicy," but he, for one, clearly had no intention of satisfying such appetites.

If such comments by Turgenev help to explain his hesitancy to become a novelist, they raise another question: how did he *ever* come to write the novels he did? Though, unlike Shchedrin, he never treated the "coarse and spicy" aspects of Russian life, neither did he remain on the Parnassian heights he sometimes claimed as his true home. Ultimately, indeed, he was proud that his novels had social weight, even if he remained slightly uncomfortable with what he had wrought. In the preface to the *Collected Novels* published in 1880, he remarked that his aim in writing these works "was to embody in appropriate characters that which Shakespeare calls 'the body and pressure of time'" (*S*, xii, 303). In his novels, he did capture a particular era, the essence of a particular span of history; but the solemn invocation of Shakespeare also reflects his persistent desire to climb above the hurly-burly of contemporary life to a place in a timeless tradition of great art.

The sense of strain in Turgenev's career, as if in writing novels he undertook a task he did not like and for which he felt unsuited, is all the more evident because of his sensitivity to the relationship between the author and his work. That an author is responsible for his work is obvious; but not all authors are equally concerned about the burden. One not unreasonable question—is an author fit, quite apart from talent or insight, to write his book?—often does not get asked. Turgenev did ask himself this question, repeatedly and anxiously, as one might expect of a man whose personality was constantly under scrutiny by his contemporaries.

Turgenev's conception of an author's role was shaped by his early interest in German Romantic philosophy. That he had studied Hegel in Germany in the late 1830s and early 1840s was an important factor in the way his novels were received in the post-Crimean War period. His education stamped him as a "man of the forties," a member of a generation that accepted the power of speculative thinking in a way that the succeeding generation, "men of the sixties," did not. In his novelistic practice he was in fact only an ambivalent champion of his own generation, and he more than once created sympathetic characters who represented men of the sixties. Nevertheless, his intellectual heritage was not simply baggage he could set aside. Even if being a man of the forties was largely a matter of cultural symbolism, he would have had no choice but to accept the role, however he played it out.

But German philosophy also had more than symbolic importance for Turgenev. He had studied it with fervor, as is clear from a letter he wrote to his friend Granovsky concerning the lectures of Karl Werder which he was attending in Berlin:

> Werder has reached the point of distinguishing *Grund* from *Wesen*—and I can say that I experienced at least *l'avant goût* of that which he calls *die speculativen Freuden*. You will not believe with what interest I listen to his lectures, how desperately I want to comprehend the aim, how sad and happy I am simultaneously when each time the ground, on which you think you are standing steadfastly, collapses underfoot—that has happened to me with *Werden, Dasein, Wesen*, etc. [*P*, I, 174–175]

To a twentieth-century reader these remarks may smack of parody. The invocation of that series of arcane intellectual categories, especially when combined with the poor student's befuddlement, summons up the worst excesses of the German tradition. But Turgenev undoubtedly was a believer, as in a religion. In Berlin he was certain that he was at the fount of true knowledge, and after returning to Russia, he set out to pursue an academic career as a professor of the philosophy of history, that key subject for the Romantics. In 1842 he took the written examination for a Master's degree at St. Petersburg University (Moscow University, where he was enrolled, was not staffed to test him in his chosen subject). It helped that the examiners had themselves been greatly influenced by current German philosophy. Their questions, from "Describe the meaning of pantheism, in its academic and natural manifestations" to "Give a brief account of ancient Greek history," seem breathtaking in their scope, but they were of the sort that yielded easily to the philosophical idiom Turgenev had recently grown familiar with. Responding to these broad questions with supremely confident generalizations, he was passed.[2]

Turgenev, however, soon changed his mind about an academic career. He never submitted, apparently never even began, the dissertation required to complete the Master's degree. The written examination had revealed to him both his own limitations and those of his subject. As he wrote to Alexandra Bakunina: "I announce to you that I have passed my philosophy examination in brilliant fashion—that is to say I babbled on about various generalities—and pleased my professors no end, although I am certain that all specialized scholars (historians, mathematicians, etc.) could not but inwardly despise both philosophy and me; and indeed *I* would despise them if *they* did not despise me" (*P*, 1, 224; italics in original).

Subsequently, he grew even more wary of German philosophy: the intricate terminology that he had tried to master now appeared to him to encourage thinking that was imprecise, even fatuous. He

2. A consideration of Turgenev's performance on this examination, as well as the questions and Turgenev's answers, may be found in A. N. Egunov, "Pis'mennye otvety Turgeneva na magisterskom ekzamene," *Turgenevskii sbornik*, ed. A. C. Bushmin (Moscow, 1966), II, 87–110.

would surely have applauded his friend Herzen's satirical description of Moscow intellectual circles, where one "went not just for a walk, but to give himself over to the pantheistic feeling of his identification with the cosmos."[3] Yet though Turgenev became distrustful of the excesses of German philosophy, he did not dismiss all the issues that it addressed. Scornful of vaporizing disguised as intricate argument—and certain that he himself was incapable of endowing such arguments with philosophical rigor—he used German philosophy tentatively but persistently. It served as a map scaled to show the contours of continents instead of one detailing the intricate topography of a region.

Thus Turgenev was less interested in the central epistemological question of Romanticism—how does a creatively thinking subject perceive an external object?—than in its psychological derivative: the desire of man, who feels himself erratic and incomplete, to comprehend the stability and serenity he sees in the world around him. German philosophers beginning with Kant had shown the logical necessity of such a desire. It was easy to be persuaded that man was not at all a being capable of solving every task by the use of his reason, as had been confidently proclaimed during the Enlightenment, but rather was a very perplexed and uncertain creature, eager to find meaning outside himself. Turgenev especially had to be impressed by an argument emphasizing man's fragmented psychology. It fit his own situation, as a man who had been described as lacking a steadfast and coherent personality. The issue figures in his literary activity in two ways. First, many of his characters live with a stark awareness of personal insufficiency that is relieved only by the harmony they perceive in nature. Second, he considered himself an author of only fugitive talent, who was obliged to struggle to create a coherent fictive world.

When Turgenev came to intellectual maturity at the end of the 1830s, he was most attracted to Hegel and Hegel's followers; by the

---

3. Quoted in Martin Malia, *Alexander Herzen and the Birth of Russian Socialism* (New York, 1965), p. 203. Malia's influential book has promoted the belief that Romantic philosophy in Russia was mostly a combination of confused logic and vague aspirations. A more judicious account of that intellectual tendency is Iu. V. Mann's *Russkaia filosofskaia estetika* (Moscow, 1969).

middle of the 1850s he had been drawn to Hegel's fiercest critic, Schopenhauer.[4] Such a radical shift may suggest ignorance or at least cultural faddishness, but it is probably more attributable to the level of Turgenev's interest in philosophy. Though Schopenhauer attacked Hegel's interpretations, he conceded that Hegel began by asking the right questions; these were the same basic questions that fascinated Turgenev. A long, speculative letter to the German writer Bettina Arnim, from the period of Turgenev's greatest enthusiasm for philosophy, nicely lays out his frame of reference: though the concepts were variously rearranged over his career, they remained essentially the same.

The crux of his vision is, simply, that man requires the world. In nature (by which Turgenev meant not only flora and fauna but everything that is not human), the "vital spiritual principle" reveals itself most fully (*P*, 1, 212). For man to comprehend truth, he must move outside himself. Man's inherent character, however, makes such a move most difficult. Man is an egoist, content to remain within the limits of his own personality. Egoism thus implies a moral flaw, but to Turgenev (and to his contemporaries trained in German Idealism) it is also a philosophical fact. Man *must* begin with a sense of himself, for he has no means of acquiring knowledge except through his own faculties. But if egoism is the unavoidable first step, it should not be the last: man should not fall into the dead end of solipsism. In the letter to Arnim, Turgenev shows that he is acutely aware of the danger, and he suggests a way to avoid it: man may overcome his isolation by modeling himself on the principles of the external world. Then as he comes to understand himself, he will understand the universe also: "Just as multifaceted and infinite as are the images of nature, so also should be the thought of man. . . . Nature is a *unified* miracle and a whole world of miracles; so also should each man be" (*P*, 1 213; italics in original). As he comes to resemble the ideal found in nature, man begins to realize his own potential. And, more importantly, though the split between

---

4. Schiller had a particular influence on Turgenev, especially during his formative years. See T. P. Den, "Turgenev i Schiller," *Schiller: Stat'i i materialy*, ed. P. M. Samarin (Moscow, 1966), pp. 78–89. For an excellent account of Schopenhauer's influence on Turgenev, see Sigrid Maurer, "Schopenhauer in Russia," unpublished diss. (University of California, Berkeley, 1975).

man and the world is not truly bridged, the problem loses its urgency.

Such a view of man's relationship to the world leads easily to an authorial stance that Turgenev often assumes: the author as celebrant of nature's mysteries, devoted to describing its seasonal rhythms and the endless variations of its species. The model that man must emulate is detailed and glorified. But at moments, Turgenev's rapturous attitude toward nature understandably wavers. In evoking nature's bounty, he shows a realm that is complete and self-sufficient; the world seems to work perfectly well without man. Instead of serving as a model, nature seems to oppress man by leaving no role for him to play in the universe. Thus Turgenev's admiration of nature always has another side to it—the anxiety that man may prove beside the point. Even in the letter to Arnim, most of which consists of charges of man's unworthiness in comparison to nature, Turgenev insists that the whole scheme ultimately depends on man: "Is it for nothing that everything spiritual concentrates itself in one bright point that we call 'I'? What would nature be without us—what would we be without nature? The one and the other are unthinkable" (*P*, I, 213).

Turgenev's long review (forty-three pages in the Collected Works) in 1845 of a recent translation of *Faust* provided him with an opportunity to elaborate the themes of his letter to Arnim, now referring them more specifically to literature. Of Goethe he says, "The first and last word, the alpha and omega of his whole life was, as it is for all poets, his 'I', but in that 'I' you find a whole world" (*S*, II, 223). "*Faust* is a purely human—or more precisely a purely egoistical—work" (*S*, I, 224). Goethe's great achievement was to depict the power of individual consciousness. In *Faust* man is an embattled, hesitant creature, but *his* actions, not those of some unseen force, determine humanity's fate. "For Goethe (as for Kant and Fichte), the last word of everything earthly is the human 'I'" (*S*, I, 224).

If the *Faust* review is similar to Turgenev's earlier statements, it also introduces a crucial difference. Turgenev fills the abstract categories of the ego and the world with specific content. He says of Goethe, "he imagined himself on the heights of contemplation, regarding everything earthly from the heights of his cold, antiquated egoism" (*S*, I, 239). Though Goethe depicts "the passionate multiplicity of the human world," he himself "withdraws to the shelter of undifferentiated, calm substantiality" (S, I, 230). Goethe is to be admired for asserting his "I"—"he was true to himself, he did not betray himself" (S, I, 239)—but he has in the process revealed that his "I" is deeply flawed.

The world also takes on a definite shape. It is no longer generalized "nature," but society. "We know that the cornerstone of man is not himself alone, an indivisible unit, but humanity, society, with its own eternal, unshakeable laws" (S, I, 235). Moreover, Turgenev's "society" is his own nineteenth-century Russia. In the review's most quoted passage, he says: "As a poet, Goethe had no equal, but we now need not only poets. . . . We have come (and at that, unfortunately, not completely) to resemble people who at the sight of a beautiful painting depicting a beggar cannot admire 'the artistry of representation,' but rather are sadly disturbed by the thought of beggars existing in our time" (S, I, 238).

Written at a time when he was most fully under the influence of his friend Belinsky's passionate determination to correct Russia's iniquities, the passage shows Turgenev's quickening sympathy for his country's misfortunates. But it also marks out a formidable impasse in his thought, one whose implications would dog him for most of his career: man needs the world in order to escape from the insularity of his own mind, but the world he confronts is not invariably good. By his new definition of the world as Russian society, he casts grave doubt on the ideal he had previously endorsed: *this* world is not a repository of truth, not a harmonious model for man to emulate. Merely to glance at Russian society, at injustice and poverty existing side by side with privilege and wealth, was to view a scene of glaring contradictions.

In the *Faust* review, Turgenev considers the options of an author confronting a world whose values are degraded. Goethe, who was blessed with an enduring self-confidence, was able to maintain an air of dispassionate wisdom even as he depicted pain and anguish. In a clumsy but expressive phrase he says that Goethe "resolves all contradictions through the a priori harmony in his classically calm soul" (S, I, 225). The phrase indicates a laudable resistance to the pervasive discord of the world; it also indicates, as Turgenev makes clear, an insensitivity to the suffering of humanity. In any case, most writers lack "a priori harmony," Turgenev says, offering Byron as an example. When Byron describes the disorder of the world, he reveals himself as sympathetically affected. Byron projects a "bitter and uncertain turbulence" (S, I, 225). That, in fact, does not make him an ideal for Turgenev, who sees him as "haughty" and "limited." Byron's stance exposes the cruelty of Goethe's wisdom; but in his feverish attention to existing evils, Byron fails to pay sufficient attention to the condition of his own soul, thus losing the chance to attain Goethe's sense of wholeness. There has to be a middle ground between detachment and all-consuming confrontation.[5]

It is remarkable that Turgenev's analysis includes no suggestion that the individual can change the world. Society remains evil, presumably following "its own eternal, unshakable laws." Just as remarkably, Turgenev does not suggest that the world changes the individual essentially. The personalities of Goethe and Byron remain at their respective stages of development. Turgenev's is a curiously tense vision: the world and the individual exist in intimate juxtaposition, influencing each other continually, but both retain their inherent features intact. In such a universe of fixed entities, the only choice seems to be in finding an optimum location: the best an author can do is orient himself properly to the world, avoiding the extremes that Goethe and Byron represent.

Turgenev's belief in the unchangeability of both the world and the individual made his call for a literature of social awareness a very uncertain rallying cry. It is not hard for a writer to refer to social issues—during most of Turgenev's career, a writer was almost obliged to do so. But to explore such issues from the viewpoint of one's unalterable limitations and prejudices is something else again. Indeed, Turgenev was setting a standard that had to be particularly

5. Turgenev is following contemporary theory. Belinsky defined the ideal, speaking of Gogol, in this way: "Here we understand not the subjectivity which in its limitations or onesidedness distorts the objective reality depicted by the author, but the deep, pervasive, and humane subjectivity which reveals in the artist a man with a fiery heart, a sympathetic soul, spiritual personal independence—the subjectivity which does not permit him to be alienated by apathetic indifference to the world he depicts, but forces him to pass through his living soul the appearances of the external world, and to breathe the living soul into them." V. G. Belinsky, *Polnoe sobrainie sochinenii* (Moscow, 1956), VI, 217–218. Although the idea of the author's participation in his work was current, Turgenev adopted it idiosyncratically, as we shall see.

daunting to himself. His vacillating personality, driven by uncertain enthusiasms and sudden depressions, hardly seems like a sturdy enough foundation on which to create a lasting work of fiction. It is no wonder that his writing often seemed to him an erratic, almost uncontrollable activity. As he put it to Tolstoi, "No matter which way you turn, if you don't have a big, healthy talent, it's like a lottery each time" (*P*, III, 210).

Notes of a Hunter was the work that brought the issue of the author's role to a head. Some of Turgenev's earlier efforts had met with critical approval, but hardly with enthusiasm. The *Notes of a Hunter* cycle, which began to appear in 1846, established his reputation; and publication of the sketches in collected form in 1852 made him Russia's most acclaimed working writer. Fame, however, also imposed responsibility. *Notes of a Hunter* was therefore subjected to intense scrutiny, by its author as well as by its readers.

In terms of the aesthetic satisfaction it offers, the work is arguably the best thing Turgenev ever wrote. In each sketch he covers just enough ground to illuminate his subject, no more and no less. He seems always in control, a master craftsman who knows the resources of his tools and the peculiarities of his material. But in terms of Turgenev's view of himself as an artist in Russian society, *Notes of a Hunter* was not a fully satisfying work. Rather, as I shall try to show, it is full of gestures begun and not completed, paths perceived but not followed. Evident throughout the cycle is the anxiety of an author unable to reach an ideal he clearly sees. In fact, the resulting tension generates an interest for the reader at least equal to that which derives from Turgenev's talent for describing peasant customs and detailing the beauty of the countryside. He himself, however, had to be apprehensive about what he had written.

Turgenev's dissatisfaction with *Notes of a Hunter* began toward the end of the 1850s and came to a climax when the sketches appeared for the first time in collected form. He might reasonably have regarded this event as certification of his talent; instead he minimized and denigrated his creation. Even when he expressed pride, he colored it with irony. Thus, in a letter to Annenkov, he writes: "I am happy that the book [the 1852 collected edition] has come out: it seems that it will constitute my little bit added to the *treasury of Russian literature,* to use the style of textbooks" (*P,* II, 64; italics in original). In later years he would see *Notes of a Hunter* as a singular achievement, artistically and politically, of which he could be fiercely proud. But in this letter, so arch in its style, he seems mainly concerned with noting the distance he feels between himself and his creation.

At other times in the early 1850s, Turgenev's distaste for the work was even more pronounced. In a letter to I. S. Aksakov he described the style of *Notes of a hunter* as "strained and stiff" (*P,* II, 98). Since the prose of the sketches is strikingly lucid and free of any striving for effect and was acclaimed for these qualities even by contemporaries who criticized other elements of the work, his comment suggests his inability to locate the source of his own dissatisfaction. Indeed, when later in the same letter he tells how he hopes to become a better writer, his stated goal is not improving his prose but rather refining the sensibility that underlies it. In subsequent works, he says, he will avoid "playing the coquette and the smart aleck" (*umnichat'*). Coyness must yield to directness; only then will the author appear to the reader without distortion. His belief that *Notes of a Hunter* is somehow not expressive of his true self explains a great deal about his ambiguous attitude toward it; and the more praise the work received, the more Turgenev felt alienated from it. "I truly can assure you," he writes to Aksakov, "that it seems to me that this book was not written by me, so distant do I feel from it" (*P,* II, 99). And to his friend Feoktistov he writes, "It now seems to me as if my *Notes* were written by a stranger" (*P,* II, 97).

Turgenev's feeling that he had not projected his personality into *Notes of a Hunter* is especially remarkable in one respect. Incidents from his own life figure prominently in it, more so than in any of his other fiction. The sketches are all recounted in the first person singular, and the narrator quickly reveals himself as a nobleman, an avid hunter, the owner of an estate in Orel province. Given the presence of still other facts from Turgenev's life, it is hard not to see the work as autobiographical.[6] And yet, its author believed, his real self failed to emerge.

6. The most comprehensive discussion of *Notes of a Hunter,* including its autobiographical implications, is S. E. Shatalov, *Zapiski okhotnika Turgeneva* (Stalinabad, 1960).

That is an extreme predicament. To present oneself directly has the merit of honesty; but what if the result is a personality that is invisible to the reader's eye? A turning in upon oneself that discovers only emptiness is a terribly dispiriting movement: undertaken as a courageous search for authenticity, it ends by questioning the value of authenticity. As Turgenev said in a letter to Annenkov, written around the time of the publication of *Notes of a Hunter:*

> To break oneself and to throw off from oneself the various petty qualities that for the most part one has painstakenly assumed—that is like removing bread from butter—it is possible; to alter oneself is impossible. It is good for that individual to concentrate himself who can again find in his core a true nature—a complete nature—because he is that nature.... Another will concentrate himself and will abruptly become simple, clear, transparent—like a cipher. [*P*, II, 123]

Turgenev's comment appears especially bleak because he seems to be saying not merely that some men discover themselves to be ciphers, but that they discover that the state is inalterable. The syntax and diction of the letter hint at an eternal condition. As Turgenev had indicated in his review of *Faust,* a writer can do no more—though he should do no less—than express who he is. Given his belief in the iron finality of biological and psychological traits, it is not surprising that the experience of writing *Notes of a Hunter* made Turgenev consider retirement from literature: he had tried to speak directly in his own voice and the result had been only a trumpeting of his insufficiency.

There is another side to Turgenev's vision, however, one that is more promising. Though a man cannot change his nature by altering a few habits—an animal that sheds its skin is still that animal—there is room to maneuver. Indeed, the *Faust* review, for all its insistence on the permanence of personality, suggested that a range of strategies were available to an author: the ego stays the same, but the face that it shows to the world crucially affects its capacities. Writing to a young acquaintance who was undecided about a career, Turgenev underscored his belief that men can influence their destinies to some degree: "You must make *yourself*, make a man of yourself—and as to what will become of you and where life will lead you, that you must leave to your nature" (*P*, II, 238, italics in original). Some areas of choice apparently exist which are not controlled by "nature." The trick, clearly, is to define them. To a significant degree, *Notes of a Hunter* is a working through of this problem. The work is a proof of the insufficiency of Turgenev's natural impulses, but it provided him with important knowledge. He discovered aspects of his personality which he could emphasize if he wished to make his voice heard; more specifically, he realized that the political components of his life, which he preferred not to think about, would have to be scrutinized and defined.

3·

World Views
and Literary Forms

In 1877 Turgenev declared himself a "basically unreconstructed Westernizer" (*P*, X, 349), referring to the group of men who had hoped to introduce the ideas and institutions of European liberalism into Russia. Indeed, throughout his life he warmly endorsed the concept of a society built on civil rights, insisting that only juridical guarantees could give men social dignity. He was also typically liberal in distrusting grand and inflexible political schemes; he believed that life was so varied that justice required ad hoc adjustments. It followed that he often sought the middle political ground. He was not willing to risk bloodletting and chaos in the name of high principle if almost as much could be gained through peaceful compromise. These beliefs appear to place him firmly in the liberal tradition, but he is not so easily classified. The difficulties derive not only from his own idiosyncracies but from the peculiarities of the system he lived under: in mid-nineteenth-century Russia the concept of politics, liberal or other, was problematical.

Political philosophy existed, much of it imported from Germany, but ideology, in the sense of a vision that mapped a political path from what was to what should be, was rare, acquired against great odds. The constraints on the Russian political imagination is the unstated theme of Turgenev's *Notes of a Hunter*. Though he once claimed for it the force of a political manifesto, which supposedly induced Alexander II to emancipate the serfs, in the end the work is an illustration of how political positions in Russia were rendered incoherent and ineffectual.

World Views and Literary Forms

The fragmented political perspective that a reader senses in *Notes of a Hunter* is in part the result of its genre. Because *Notes of a Hunter* is a cycle of short sketches, there is hardly time for Turgenev to develop a clearly defined position; with each sketch he must lay his argument out anew. But of course the question must then arise, why did he choose to write in such a limiting form? In fact, the incoherence and incompleteness of the narrator's vision is less a flaw in Turgenev's method than one of his topics. Perhaps it came to him unexpectedly as he worked on the cycle, but he embraced it. Thus the beginning of each sketch, with the narrator setting out from his home along different paths, is both a simplistic device to get the narrative in motion and a sophisticated irony. The geographical variety does not disguise—is not supposed to disguise—the fact that the same moral and social questions recur, at the same level of intractability. For all its movement from locale to locale, *Notes of a Hunter* hovers in place.

Because the connection of *Notes of a Hunter* with contemporary social thought is a matter of its form as well as its content, it is worth noting that the sketches began to appear at a time when a new literary genre was gaining favor in Russia—the physiological sketch. As is implied by the name (and by the title of one of the first popular collections of these sketches, *The Physiology of Petersburg*), authors of physiological sketches greatly admired the natural sciences, and the empirical method in particular. They aimed at finding an equivalent in literature. A detached authorial pose, a distrust of abstractions, and an attitude of critical scrutiny constituted their manner. Most important, however, was the concept of the "type," which informed practically every physiological sketch. The central character of a physiological sketch was portrayed not in terms of individual destiny but as a representative social figure. In describing, say, a journalist, an organ grinder, or an army officer in the Caucasus, the author claimed to be describing one member of a group that could be found in the existing population.[1] At the extreme, the impulse was statistical. Indeed, physiological sketches often appeared in collected form, since that seemed a good way to reproduce the aggregate structure of the whole society.

1. A. G. Tseitlin, *Stanovlenie realizma v russkoi literature* (Moscow, 1965) traces the sources of the physiological sketch in France and remarks on its development in

The Path to the Novel

The rationale of the physiological sketch fit the Westernizers' perspective. The sketches seemed to offer an artistic correlative to their emphasis on the individual. Turgenev summed up the group's basic belief when he said, "Let me be an atom but my own matter; I do not want salvation but truth, and I expect it from reason not grace.[2] His statement does not necessarily imply a world where men are isolated from one another, though the image of the atom strongly suggests the possibility. Turgenev's atom is guided by reason, hence is capable of appreciating the benefits of social harmony. But the statement does reveal suspicion of any view that construes society as an abstract entity with a life and logic of its own: society, to Turgenev and the Westernizers, is an aggregate of individuals moved by particular needs and fulfilling particular functions.

The first sketch in *Notes of a Hunter*, "Khor' and Kalinych," is in many ways an excellent example of the physiological sketch.[3] Not surprisingly, the sketch appeared in an issue of *The Contemporary* that also included one of the key programmatic statements of the Westernizers, Konstantin Kavelin's, "A Glance at the Juridical Life of Ancient Russia." Together, Kavelin's and Turgenev's efforts composed a most persuasive argument: theory buttressed by dramatized experience. It is not extravagant to say that "Khor' and Kalinych" represents the beginning of an extended gloss on Kavelin's claim that "an individuality which is conscious of its unlimited and uncontingent worth is the necessary condition for any spiritual development of a nation.[4]

Russia. A less exhaustive, more theoretical, approach is taken by Iu. V. Mann, "Filosofiia i poetika 'Naturalnoi shkoly,'" *Problemy tipologii russkogo realizma*, ed. N. L. Stepanov (Moscow, 1969), pp. 241–305.

The examples of social types used in physiological sketches are from the works of, respectively, Panaev, Dal', and Lermontov.

2. Quoted by Andrzey Walicki, *The Slavophile Controversy*, trans. Hilda Andres-Rusiecka (Oxford, 1975), p. 172. Walicki's book, which focuses on philosophical sources, is the best book in any language on the Slavophile-Westernizer debate. For a greater emphasis on Turgenev's particular role, see Henri Granjard, *Ivan Tourguénev et les courants politiques et sociaux de son temps* (Paris, 1954).

3. Turgenev's connection with the Natural School was often remarked by contemporaries. See, e.g., Belinsky's comparison of Turgenev to Dal', in *Turgenev v zapisiakh sovremennikov*, ed. A. Ostrovsky (Leningrad, 1929), p. 78.

4. Konstantin Kavelin, "Vzgliad na iuridicheskii byt drevnei Rossii," *Sovremennik*, No. 1 (1847), IV, 499. On the connection between Kavelin and Turgenev, see V. A. Kovalev, "*Zapiski okhotnika* i 'zapadnicheskaia' publitsistiska 1846–1848 gg," *Uchenye zapiski Leningradskogo pedagogicheskogo instituta*, VII (1937), 127–165.

The very first paragraph of "Khor' and Kalinych" immediately establishes Turgenev's Westernizer perspective:

> Whoever may have chanced to make his way from the district of Bolkhov to that of Zhizdra has, most probably, been struck by the sharp contrast between the breed of men in Orel province and that in Kaluga province. The Orel muzhik is of no great stature: he is squat; he eyes you from under his brows, lives in a wretched hut of aspen wood, performs forced labor (*barshchina*) for his master, doesn't go in for trading, eats poorly, wears bast sandals. The Kaluga muzhik pays quitrent (*obrok*) to his masters, dwells in spacious huts of pine, is tall of stature, eyes you boldly and cheerfully, is clean shaven and white of face, trades in butter and birch tar and, on Sundays, goes about in boots. [S, IV, 7]

In this passage the reader is invited to consider contrasts. The naming of a characteristic of one group of men is balanced by the assertion of a contrary characteristic in the other group. There is a social comment implied by this rhetorical scheme: the Russian peasantry is not homogeneous and constant, but rather consists of individuals, men who squeeze some pleasure from their meager circumstances as well as men who yield to despair. Turgenev's reference to *barshchina* and *obrok* helps to emphasize such a claim, since it reminds the reader that although the prevailing system burdened all peasants, there were gradations apparent in the degree of oppression.[5] Throughout *Notes of a Hunter* he insists on the variety of the peasants' experience. He depicts not only the common field muzhik but also house serfs, serfs who have managed to set up businesses of their own, serfs who act as willing agents for their tyranical masters, serfs who are expert in crafts and skills. The world of *Notes of a Hunter* is always bleak, but Turgenev renders his subject so intensely that bleakness is variegated. His ability to impart a particularity to each of his characters, even those one expects to have been crushed to insipid flatness, gives his work a tone that would have appeared progressive at any time; because he was writing when it was common to treat peasants as stock characters or to ignore them altogether, *Notes of a Hunter* was perceived by some contemporaries as an outright attack on the status quo.

5. Serfdom obligated peasants either to perform labor on demesne land (*barshchina*) or to pay the landlord a fixed amount of cash or produce yearly (*obrok*). Of the two alternatives, the *obrok* was generally preferred, since landlords required so much labor that the peasants had no time left to tend to their own crops.

But—in a turn of mind that is typical of *Notes of a Hunter* and gives the book its peculiar power—Turgenev's ringing allegiance to the principle of individualism soon leads to difficulties. Although the value of individualism is never questioned, his narrative begins to disclose a vast gap between the abstract principle and its practical application. The effect is all the more chilling because his manner is so controlled and purposive; he expertly handles the literary method that many contemporaries believed projected the shape and detail of each Russian man's and woman's experience, but the result is only to expose the method's dubious premises.[6] The idea that human society is an aggregate of separate units creates unexpected pitfalls. As he proceeds, the narrator's self-confidence occasionally veers toward arrogance, and his generosity seems condescension— not from a lack of good will, it seems, but from the logic implicit in the way he views the world.

The difficulties become evident almost immediately after the opening of the sketch. The narrator describes the title characters, two peasants he has encountered while out hunting. "The two friends," he remarks, "did not resemble each other in the least. Khor' was a sedate person, practical, with a head for administration, a rationalist. Kalinych on the contrary belonged to the category of idealists, romantics, лd people who are exalted and enraptured" (S, IV, 14–15). The description goes on for another full page, the characteristics of one man set off against those of the other. Khor' is well off and ambitious, Kalinych leads a hand-to-mouth existence; Khor' has a large family, Kalinych is alone in the world; Khor' feels most at ease in society, Kalinych in nature. The narrator succeeds in rendering the peasants as two distinct creatures. At the same time, however, he hardly seems capable of acknowledging that Khor' and Kalinych are individuals, such as would fit Kavelin's definition.

The length and microscopic detail of his description betrays the desperate hope that an accumulation of traits will add up to a man. And his use of the same contrastive scheme as in the sketch's opening passage suggests he may only be parading a rhetorical facility

6. Peter Demetz, "Balzac and the Zoologists: A Concept of the Type," in *The Disciplines of Criticism*, ed. Peter Demetz (New Haven, 1969), pp. 398–418, provides an excellent discussion of some of the conceptual difficulties surrounding the genre of the physiological sketch.

instead of sympathetically responding to the two peasants. When the narrator remarks, on observing Kalinych's affection for Khor', "I confess I had not expected such tender gestures from a peasant" (S, IV , 14), he adds a final ambiguity to his already uncertain posture. The sentence attributes still another individualizing feature to Kalinych's figure, and it is a particularly humanizing one; but the same sentence reduces the peasant to the level of the exotic. Turgenev reveals the other side of the Westernizers' focus on the individual: a mechanical objectivity, which has the effect of deadening sympathy even in the midst of celebrating the uniqueness of each man.

Turgenev was himself both naively committed to his procedure and aghast at its effects. As he put it in a letter to Annenkov, in which he complained of the dead end into which he felt he had written himself: "I've long enough tried to extract from human characters their essences—*triple extraits*—in order to pour them into little glass vials—smell if you please, respected reader—uncork and smell. Doesn't it smell like a real Russian type? Enough, enough" (P, II, 77).

The writing of *Notes of a Hunter* induces a strange reaction in Turgenev. His dismay comes not from a sense of failure but from a feeling of having succeeded all too well. Even though he has captured the very "essence" of characters, he finds his achievement inadequate. The governing image of his letter to Annenkov helps to explain his dissatisfaction. The comparison of writing to a mechanical operation shows that Turgenev feels he has committed himself to a style that precludes any true emotional involvement on his part. He has created, he notes, only Russian types; and his tone underscores his awareness that this is something less than individualized Russian men. The accumulation of concrete and persuasively rendered detail, for which *Notes of a Hunter* is justifiably famous, has evidently been bought at great sacrifice.

Turgenev's doubts reflected a general tendency. Though there was widespread enthusiasm for literary works that dispassionately recorded Russian life, seemingly giving it a statistical solidity, the approach also inspired unease.[7] Was a stark, almost scientific man-

7. Turgenev's sketches were themselves evoking an increasingly skeptical response. Feoktistov wrote to him, "Let us talk of your last 'tales of a hunter' [sic],

ner the only alternative to pomposity and extravagance? As one critic complained, many writers "while asserting the absurdity of romanticism go to the other extreme and see in Gogol and all contemporary literature the daguerreotypization of reality, in which they place the whole secret of art."[8] Instances in other art forms that seemed to show an indulgence of a merely empirical impulse, such as the Flemish School of painting, were invoked as cautionary examples.[9] Turgenev himself, when criticizing *Faust* for the degrading depiction of the "people" (*narod*) as a "stupid mob" that "played a pitiful role," had compared Goethe's manner to that of Teniers and van Ostade (*S*, I, 228–229).

Indeed, as early as 1847, even as he was fully engaged in writing the sketches that would be hailed for their precise and naturalistic rendering of peasant life, Turgenev grew suspicious of such literary methods. In a letter in December of that year he criticized a story by George Sand, whom he usually admired, by declaring, "Art is not daguerreotype" (*P*, I, 292). In a review of an Ostrovsky play, also in 1847, he was even more emphatic:

> Especially in the depiction of these two characters the false method we spoke of above becomes particularly apparent. This false manner consists of an exhaustive presentation, detailed in the extreme, of all the parts and bits of each character through a speciously fine psychological analysis, which consists mainly of having the characters repeat those same basic words that in the opinion of the author express their distinctiveness. We do not wish to say that these words are uncharacteristic, but art must not merely repeat life; and all those endless details smooth the form and the sharpness of depiction. [*S*, V, 390]

In *Notes of a Hunter* Turgenev was not much concerned with depicting psychology through dialogue, or with psychology at all for

---

'Kas'ian' was liked by everyone, 'Bezhin Meadow' also, though less than 'Kas'ian'— but should I tell you the general opinion about them in certain Moscow circles? Everyone says: 'Enough.' The tales are very good, the last ones pleased everyone a great deal, but everyone finds that you are extending them too far and that it is time for you to try something else. To tell the truth, I am not altogether opposed to that opinion because I very much want to read some long story [*povest'*] by you." See *P*, II, 418, n. 3.

8. Quoted in Tseitlin, *Stanovlenie realizma v russkoi literature*, p. 105.

9. The connotations Teniers' work acquired in this period are mentioned by L. P. Grossman, "Rannii zhanr Turgeneva," *Sobranie sochinenii* (Moscow, 1928), II, 49.

that matter, but his main point about Ostrovsky does apply to his own procedure. The desire "merely to repeat life" was very strong in his work at this point. It was remarked on by contemporaries, and even his close friend Annenkov felt he had to call attention to Turgenev's unfortunate readiness to grant objective reality a power of its own which the writer need only record: "Turgenev often falls into the fault of overelaboration (*pererabotka*): the technique that gives an object mathematical precision but robs it of life."[10]

Annenkov's comment is accurate, but by itself it presents a distorted picture. Turgenev was very conscious of the shortcoming Annenkov describes. Like a workman who continually makes adjustments for the imbalance or erratic cut of his tools, Turgenev wrote *Notes of a Hunter* in his "old manner" while at the same time calling into question its assumptions. Thus the most prominent evidence of his attraction to a technique that "merely repeats life" is doubtless the position of the narrator: he always moves to the periphery of the action, so that the peasant life he records can flow naturally, without the intrusion of an alien element. But it is also the narrator's position that most clearly reveals Turgenev's unease with his technique. He makes the narrator's self-effacement such a rigorous necessity that it appears as a striking exertion; the narrator's intricate devices to place himself off stage constitute a declaration of his hovering presence. In "Bezhin Meadow" and "Ermolai and the Miller's Wife," the narrator feigns sleep near a campfire while tumultuous events occur right beside him. In "The Office," he allows himself to be quickly shunted to an out-of-the-way room where he will not interfere in a drama of cheating and cruelty. In "The Tryst," his stance as a detached observer even veers toward farce as he hides in the bushes near a forest clearing in order to spy on the emotional rendezvous of a dandified valet and his peasant girl lover.

The heavy-handed machinations of the narrator call the ideal of objective reporting into question even as he seems to endorse it. The view that an observer's mere presence can distort experience does justice neither to the complexity of life nor to the humanity of the observer. The narrator is reduced to silence, his existence made

10. P. V. Annenkov, "O mysli v proizvedeniiakh iziashchenoi slovesnosti," *Sovremennik*, XLIX, No. 1, p. 4.

an embarrassing excess; life is reduced only to meanings that can easily be perceived at a distance. In the sketch "Prince Hamlet of Shchigrov Province," Turgenev has the title character remark, "I would rejoice to take lessons from it—from Russian life, that is—but then it keeps silent, the darling" (S, IV, 282). That Turgenev could put these words into the mouth of his character suggests that he saw his predicament. He knew that "the darling" would not disclose its secrets easily, that the true meanings of Russian life did not lie on the surface waiting to be picked up.

Why, if an empirical perspective suited Turgenev so badly, did he employ it even tentatively? Why, indeed, were the Westernizers in general attracted to a literary method that projected the ideal of individualism only problematically? In part the answer to these questions is simply that men are often willing to suffer an unfortunate implication or two if they can carry their main point; but there is a more historical answer also. The Westernizers' position was never a fully sovereign program. It was conceived and acquired its meanings as polemic with the Slavophiles. Turgenev and his friends used ideas as cultural weapons. An empirical perspective, with its air of hard common sense, was very effective against an opponent who constructed myths explaining the nation's birth and insisted that the nation represented a transcendent community. Even more important, empiricism was the Westernizers' way of drawing out the individualistic implications of German philosophy—a critical necessity, since their Slavophile opponents invoked the same philosophy as authority for their own quite different ends. Precisely because the two groups did share certain assumptions, the Westernizers vigorously employed every means to prove the disagreements.

Regarding many substantive issues, the disagreements were clear. That the Slavophiles set great store by the Russian peasant commune; that they scorned societies based on juridical guarantees, insisting that men should live together in mutual trust; that they interpreted Russian history to prove a national distaste for politics—these and many other ideas appeared thoroughly wrong-headed to Turgenev and his friends, and they tried to demolish the Slavophile position by bringing contrary evidence to bear. But the Slavophiles' basic assumption was more troubling, because it was finally a variation of their own. The two positions were dependent, as mirror images are dependent. To insist, as the Slavophiles vehemently did, that the social community is logically prior to the individuals composing it was to reverse exactly the Westernizers' most cherished belief. The Slavophiles' position constituted a thorough rearrangement of the Westernizers' intellectual furniture, but they kept the same pieces.

In his 1852 review of the Slavophile S. T. Aksakov's *Notes of a Hunter with a Rifle* (*Zapiski ruzheinogo okhotnika*—a title whose similarity to Turgenev's great work symbolizes the complex cultural linkings of the period), Turgenev begins to reveal the curious intimacy of the disagreement of Westernizers and Slavophiles. Commenting on Aksakov's understanding of nature as a realm of harmony and instinctual cooperation, he obviously felt compelled to offer a qualification: "Doubtless [nature] is one vast sturdy whole—each point in it is connected with every other—but its striving is simultaneously in the direction where each individual point, each separate unit in it, exists only for itself, would consider itself the focus of the universe, would subsume all that surrounded it to its own aims, would reject the independence of [all that surrounded it], and would master this for its own purposes" [*S*, v, 415].

Significantly, Turgenev directly admits the plausibility of Aksakov's world view; his own is only an elaboration of it, an addition. On one level, to be sure, he uses Aksakov's picture of undifferentiated wholeness and coherence to highlight his own vision of the world as an aggregate of differences; but he does not thereby reject Aksakov's description. Rather, by some unexplained intellectual maneuver, he manages to assert that the two visions, though absolutely contradictory, can coexist. Turgenev's logical uncertainty reflects the condition of the Slavophile-Westernizer polemic in general.

Literature occupied a special place in the polemic. Discussions of Russian folk poetry, of Gnedich's translation of *The Iliad*, of Lermontov's *Hero of Our Time* turned into fierce confrontations. An interpretation in the Westernizers' journal *The Contemporary* would immediately evoke a rebuttal in the Slavophiles' *The Moscovite*, which would be rebutted in turn. It has long been noted that censorship tended to make literature appear especially important during this period: issues that could not be discussed publicly elsewhere could be introduced covertly into literature by ingenious authors. But the role of censorship should not be exaggerated. Slavophiles and Westernizers did not consider literature merely a substitute for other, better, but unavailable forms of exposition. Each group was certain that literature could uniquely explain its position, thus defining the real differences with its opponent. In fact, their literary arguments did mark out areas of disagreement; but literature is no magical beacon capable of penetrating every cultural fog, and the Slavophiles and Westernizers often fell into blind embrace as they tried to push apart.

For Turgenev, as for most Slavophiles and other Westernizers, the literary issues of the day crystallized around the figure of Gogol. The third paragraph of "Khor' and Kalinych" begins by describing a Kaluga landowner who is a "passionate hunter and consequently an excellent fellow" and concludes, after a very long itemization of the man's shortcomings, with the statement that "with the exception of these few and insignificant shortcomings, however, Polutykin was, as already mentioned, an excellent fellow" (S, IV, 8). The playing at logic, the adherence to syntax while emptying a phrase of its sense, is Turgenev's homage to Gogol. Turgenev did not, however, remain for long under the spell of Gogol's style. And even less did Gogol's personality exert any lasting influence. Turgenev has left an account of Gogol's brief tenure as a professor at St. Petersburg University, while he was himself a student there, which is very mocking—especially the anecdote, probably apocryphal, of how Gogol concealed his ignorance at an oral examination he was conducting: "He sat, [jaw] tied up in a handkerchief, supposedly because of a toothache—with a completely hangdog expression—and did not open his mouth" (S, XIV, 76). But Turgenev fully credited Gogol as a cultural force. Thus when Gogol died, Turgenev's grief assumed a strikingly combative tone. In a letter to Pauline Viardot, he wrote, "For us he was more than a writer: he showed us what we were. In many respects he was a continuation of Peter the Great" (P, II, 47). The invocation of Peter, the arch villain of Slavophile mythology, because the presumptive source of all European tendencies in Russia, was not innocent.

Though the letter to Viardot indicates the clear belief that Gogol's career could be placed in the service of Westernism, Turgenev was not always confident that the matter was so simple. The Slavophiles could be expected to resist. A letter to the Slavophile Ivan Aksakov, also written at the time of Gogol's death, reveals Turgenev in a much more uncertain state of mind: "I will say to you without exaggeration that for as long as I can remember nothing has made such an impression on me as Gogol's death—everything that you say about it is said directly from the soul. This strange death—an historical event—cannot be understood at once; this is a secret, a heavy, threatening secret—it is necessary to try to unravel it" (*P*,II, 49).

By calling it strange, Turgenev is summoning up the circumstances of Gogol's death, which included inanition, lurid religiosity, the burning of manuscripts. But as his aside about history makes clear, Turgenev also has in mind another sort of strangeness: Gogol's significance for Russia remains a secret. If Aksakov has said many correct things about Gogol (in a statement that Turgenev is here responding to), much remains to be considered before Gogol's meaning can be fixed. Indeed, the many highly elusive passages in Gogol's work, combined with his often mysterious personal pronouncements, made him susceptible to various interpretations. His work became something of a cultural trophy, the appropriation of which would attest to the correctness of one's own position.

The debate about Gogol's meaning was made to center directly on the issues of individualism and wholeness, the critical concepts of Westernism and Slavophilism. To the Westernizers, Gogol was the main source of the Natural School, which was responsible for the popularization of the physiological sketch. With strokes of genius he had revealed the fragmentation and contradictions of society; his works teemed with striking and varied "types," thus proving that Russia was an aggregate of individuals. Gogol's own opinion of what he was doing seemed, at times, to support such conclusions. In a letter to his friends A. C. and V. G. Danilevsky from abroad, in which he made one of his surprising requests for help in finding material, Gogol wrote:

> If God grant you a remarkable talent and, when you go into society, you know how to note its humorous and dull aspects, then you might compose some "types" for me; that is, taking some of those who can be called representatives of their class or of their sort of people, you

could embody in the individual that class which he represents, bearing the designations, for example, of "Kievan social lion," "provincial *femme incomprise*," "bureaucrat-European," "bureaucrat-traditionalist," and so forth.[11]

The Slavophiles, however, insisted with equal fervor on another aspect of Gogol's activity. In reviewing *Dead Souls*, Konstantin Aksakov claimed that Gogol presented a world of harmony and wholeness. The work, Aksakov argued, was an epic (an interpretation that was supported by Gogol subtitling it a *poema*: a long work with epical qualities). If *Dead Souls* lacked some of the formal features of the genre—and it is hard to see reflections of Homer in the adventures of a petty swindler among equally petty landowners—that was less important than Gogol's resurrection of an epic vision. Gogol projected the sense of "a world where rivers splash and murmur as they did in Homer, where the sun rises and nature glows in all of her beauty and man is alive; a world that is whole, which reveals to us the profound inner content of our ordinary lives, in which one spirit connects all phenomena."[12]

The interpretations of Gogol by the Westernizers and Slavophiles could not have been more different. Nevertheless, the use of one author to support diametrically opposed positions indicates a curiously intramural quality to the debate. In trying to push themselves apart, each of the two groups had taken hold of the opposite end of the same club; the more vigorously each tugged at the weapon that was intended to repel the other, the more did he become tied to his adversary. In a letter to Konstantin Aksakov, who of all the Slavophiles had insisted most strenuously on the epical quality of *Dead Souls*, Turgenev wrote: "But I know that this precisely is the point on which I differ with your view of Russian life—I see the tragic fate of the people, a great social drama full of conflict, where you see the serene shelter of the epos" (*P*, II, 72).

Especially considering Turgenev's usual graciousness, the tone of the letter is uncompromising. He says that to see the world in one way is to be unable to see it in another. One faces a decisive choice, not a set of adjustable possibilities. To accept serenity and shelter is

11. Quoted in Tseitlin, *Stanovlenie realizma v russkoi literature*, p. 25.

12. K. S. Aksakov, "Neskol'ko slov o poeme Gogolia *Pokhozhdenie Chichikova ili mertvie dushi*," reprinted in S. A. Vengerov, *Sobranie sochinenii* (St. Petersburg, 1912), III, 219.

to ignore completely the social drama of Russia. Though he is speaking of literary forms, he is, of course, also making a political judgment. The judgment is at once valid and misleading. The Slavophiles *were* politically quiescent; but though Turgenev's ability to see "the tragic fate of the people" implies energetic resistance to evil, it is energetic only in comparison with the contemplation of "serenity and shelter." Indeed, Turgenev and the Westernizers in general were politically active only in comparison with the Slavophiles. The Westernizers finally accepted the role of all intellectuals in the 1840s, engaging in feverish arguments on the margins of Russian life. Circumstances constrained them from more purposeful activity, but their deluded view of their political energy may also have delayed the alteration of circumstances.

In fact, the Westernizers did not have anything that could be called a political program. They only interpreted more vigorously the same philosophical scheme that the Slavophiles employed. Turgenev's performance on his Master's exam begins to suggest how easily that scheme lent itself to various emphases. In answer to a question about Greek culture, he had argued that the classical epic projected a sense of harmony and wholeness, and he had done so in terms no less enthusiastic and sweeping than Aksakov had applied to *Dead Souls*.[13] To be sure, a contemporary epic was a special case. In the middle of the nineteenth century, the individual ego existed apart from the whole in a state of "alienated reflection." A contemporary author who wrote an epic would necessarily have ignored present reality—though not necessarily the future, since the Westernizers believed that the alienated individual would eventually be reincorporated into a new, more complex harmony. The stages of an abstract philosophical scheme, as much as concrete political events, determined Russia's course. Even Belinsky, who among the Westernizers most fiercely resisted the claim that *Dead Souls* was a work "whose content is the substantiality of the Russian people," asserted that such a "substantiality" was possible in the future.[14]

13. Egunov, *Turgenevskii sbornik*, esp. pp. 107–108. "[The heroes of an epic] were not allegories—they were too vital for this, but it seems to me that in these heroic figures, with all the naiveté of those times, was reflected the whole man, just as he was."
14. Belinsky, *Polnoe sobranie sochinenii*, VI, 419–420. For an instance of Turgenev's acceptance of Belinsky's authority on literary matters see *P*, I, 264, where he calls him "my father and commander."

Substantiality and fragmentation, collective harmony and the alienated ego, wholeness and individuality—the concepts are antagonistic but also complementary. Thus in a curious way the Westernizers needed the Slavophiles. Slavophilism had to be exposed for its excesses and errors; but it was not to be entirely demolished, since nothing else provided such an excellent opportunity to define the strengths of Westernism. The debate often had the appearance of a bitter domestic quarrel: both participants wanted absolute victory, but neither wanted the other to leave entirely. The situation had to be especially disconcerting to Turgenev. Of all the Westernizers, he maintained closest contact with the Slavophiles, meeting with some regularly and keeping up a lively correspondence with others. More important was Turgenev's deep attraction to the ideal of harmony. The ego alienated from collective harmony may have been a philosophically necessary stage of development, but he instinctively resisted it. He wished, with an intensity that subverted rational belief, that the individual could find immediate accommodation in some sort of spiritual or political community. As an historian of the Slavophile-Westernizer controversy has written, Turgenev "felt the burden of his own individualism and was tempted by the charms of lost spontaneity and 'immediate harmony'; his work represents both the ceaseless self-flagellation of a Russian Hamlet and the effort to find balm for his tormented soul."[15]

In a letter to Pauline Viardot explaining the circumstances that inspired one of the sketches in *Notes of a Hunter*, "The Singers," Turgenev wrote: "The childhood of all nations is similar and my singers remind me of Homer... the competition [that he witnessed] took place in a tavern and there were many original personalities that I tried to draw à la Teniers. Devil take it! What grand names I cite at the slightest excuse" (*P*, I, 401–402).

Tugenev's modesty in saying that the "grand names" are too illustrious for his purposes disguises a more significant aberration of literary taste. Invoking Homer and Teniers—respectively the acknowledged symbols of the possibility of transcendent harmony and the reality of existing strife—to describe one work was distinctly

15. Walicki, *The Slavophile Controversy*, p. 359. Turgenev even wavered on the crucial issue of the genre of *Dead Souls*. In an 1852 review he wrote, "*Dead Souls* is really a poem—if you like, an epic poem..." (*S*, V, 373).

anamolous. In fact, throughout *Notes of a Hunter*, Turgenev allows his point of view to slide about in unexpected ways. Konstantin Aksakov even greeted one sketch as a wonderful representation of the Slavophile ideal. Turgenev hurriedly wrote to him, disabusing him of the notion, but Aksakov's interpretation is not surprising.[16]

Turgenev's openness to Slavophilism reenforced the view of him as irresolute. Some contemporaries, however, realized that Turgenev's seeming irresolution was actually a remarkable sensitivity to cultural currents.[17] He allowed ideas to flow freely through him, so that what was by others kept apart in the interest of clarity, was in him brought abruptly together. The result was sometimes intellectual confusion, but as often there was the discovery of knowledge where none had thought to look. *Notes of a Hunter*, certainly, offers bracing criticism of Westernism precisely because it is made from within the perspective of Westernism. That is, the book is not simply a frontal attack, though there is plenty of scathing satire of the Westernizers' customs and intellectual fashions. Turgenev explored not only the content but the structure of Westernizer thought, including the turn of mind which grew from the relationship to Slavophilism.

The second sketch in the cycle, "Ermolai and the Miller's Wife" is a good example of the complexity of Turgenev's approach. While out hunting with his peasant companion Ermolai, the narrator encounters Arina, the miller's wife, and this reminds him of her previous history. When she was a twenty-year-old serf girl, Arina had been denied the permission of her master to marry, because he feared that her performance as the lady's maid might suffer. When Arina persisted in her pleas, her master only became angrier; and when in desperation she became pregnant out of wedlock, Arina was treated not only as a criminal but as an ingrate for rejecting her master's greater wisdom. Her hair was cropped and she was packed off to an isolated village, while her lover was drafted into the army for the usual twenty-five year term. These are shocking facts, but Turgenev is not simply condemning social injustice. Rather, he explores the

---

16. For an account of this incident see S, IV, 537.

17. A. A. Grigor'ev, "I. S. Turgenev i ego deiatel'nost': po povodu romana Dvorianskoe gnezdo," *Russkoe slovo*, No. 4 (1859), 1–134, is an especially sympathetic interpretation of Turgenev's ambiguous focus.

concept of moral choice, which must underlie genuine condemnation.

The world depicted in "Ermolai and the Miller's Wife" demands a declaration of preferences, if only because its aspects are so distinct. The tale of Arina's dismal history is bracketed by an opening and closing very different in tone and substance. The sketch begins with a description of a "night watch," a sort of hunting technique:

> A quarter of an hour before the setting of the sun, in the spring, you enter a grove with a gun but without a dog. You search out a spot for yourself at the edge of the woods, examine the percussion cap of your gun and exchange winks with your companion. The quarter of an hour passes. The sun has set, but it is still light in the forest; the air is clean and transparent; the birds chatter away; the young grass gleams like an emerald. You wait. [S, IV, 21]

The style here is remarkably confident, lacking any sense that the author is striving after effect. Indeed this is an excellent example of how Turgenev's prose occasionally achieves a condition of almost perfect transparency, and in this instance the reason is clear enough: all the meaning that is necessary purportedly adheres in the subject matter itself—in a way, in fact, that is not far removed from the perspective insinuated by an epic. Turgenev gives us a natural world which is fully self-sufficient, which projects a feeling of harmony that requires no further comment.

This natural realm stands distinctly apart from the social realm, which is marked by fractiousness and cruelty. It is as if the world had been carefully surveyed; two areas have been demarked which, though they border on each other, carry on no commerce. The picture is bracing in its clarity; but it also raises important moral issues, since it seems that to take advantage of the world's potential for harmony, one must forget about prevailing injustice.

The concluding paragraph fixes the narrator's position:

> A flock of ducks swept by over our heads, whistling, and we heard them settling down on the river, not far from us. By now it had grown dark, and it was beginning to get cold; a nightingale was shrilling sonorously in a grove. We burrowed down in the hay and fell asleep. [S, IV, 32]

The passage shows how context can determine meaning. Though the words seem only to reaffirm the narrator's original enjoyment of

innocent nature, the intervening story gives to the passage a reso-
nant sadness. The birds in the last passage shrill as the birds did at
the beginning of the sketch; now, however, they are not only natural
phenomena but vivid symbols, of a harmony that is notably missing
in Arina's life. The perfection of nature can no longer be enjoyed in
blithe ignorance of human affairs. The narrator at the end of "Ermolai and the Miller's Wife" has managed to give his experience a
shape by holding the disparate aspects of the world in mind at the
same time.

The narrator's considerable achievement does not disguise a
moral flaw, however, and it is one with important implications for
Westernism. The narrator's ability to comprehend the difference
between the natural and social realm depends on a stringent con-
templativeness. He ignores or glosses over events that may upset
his complex vision, like a chemist who rigorously excludes all but
the key elements of an experiment. As a result, the moment in the
sketch that is potentially most explosive proves strangely tranquil,
its emotions muffled by the narrator's unease in the face of the
unexpected. At a social gathering, he encounters Arina's cruel master; he feels scorn, but he maintains a detached appearance, saying
nothing that will let the tyrant know his true feelings. That is, he
sympathizes with Arina, but refuses to engage himself in her plight:
his participation would blur the clear outline of evil that he holds in
his mind's eye. Of course, the narrator could not have substantially
eased Arina's lot—Turgenev's point is not the need for action, but
the difference between passive and active understanding. The narrator everywhere leaves the world as he finds it, so that all issues
appear well defined. His position at the end of the sketch, therefore,
while knowing and sensitive, is only a form of sophisticated acquiescence.

Like the narrator of "Ermolai and the Miller's Wife," the Westernizers defined their world by envisioning distinct realms, a corrupt
reality and a projected ideal; but, also like the narrator, their stance
was essentially contemplative, since they largely failed to show how
Russians might move from one point to the other. The Westernizers
came under fierce criticism after the Crimean War, by men like
Chernyshevsky and Dobroliubov, for not matching their high principles with action. That was to a degree an unfair charge; like

Turgenev's narrator, the Westernizers were effectively blocked from altering society by the weight of an oppressive regime—but it is also true that, like the narrator, the Westernizers presented a false image. Invoking the Slavophile position as a contrast, the Westernizers pictured themselves as politically progressive, on the verge of action. In fact, to be outraged by existing social arrangements, instead of discerning an underlying harmony in the world, is still very far from action. Locked in intricate debate with the Slavophiles, the Westernizers rarely considered the particularities of Russia's on-going political life. All they did was occasionally to enliven their philosophical discussions with contemporary examples.

4.

Russian Reality

In *Notes of a Hunter* Turgenev refrains from condemning men like the Westernizers, with their merely abstract ideal of social justice, but neither does he excuse them. On the one hand, he depicts an existing order of such strength that the individual's efforts to promote change are severely limited. On the other hand, the permanence of evil in the world of *Notes of a Hunter* is as much the result of the individual's failure to imagine change as the result of brute oppression. Turgenev shows characters who are bewitched by the values of the status quo.

His most telling evidence of the failure of the political imagination is the status of serfdom.[1] Peasants as well as noblemen regard the institution as if it were some marvelous perpetual motion machine that should run down because of its design, but doesn't. The awe they feel at the spectacle seemingly keeps them from summoning any true resistance, however accurately they gauge the cruelty and injustice of the effects. "Raspberry Spring" is probably the sketch that offers the most sustained analysis of how serfdom induces moral passivity. While out hunting, the narrator decides to escape the mid-day heat by retreating to the tree-lined banks of a cool spring. There he encounters three peasants. They represent three different responses to the pressures of Russian reality. One peasant, Vlas, has come to Raspberry Spring on his way home after walking to Moscow

1. The classic work detailing the condition of serfdom in the period immediately before the Emancipation Act is P. A. Zaionchkovsky, *Otmena krepostnogo prava v Rossii* (Moscow, 1954), to which I am indebted.

(some three hundred miles) to apply for relief from an exorbitant *obrok* obligation. He has got no relief, no sympathy. And though the consequence of this is probably starvation, Vlas shows no surprise that his master has taken not the slightest interest in his plight, that in fact he had Vlas chased from his presence immediately. Masters are supposed to behave in such a way.

This is Turgenev's first of three insights into the psychological mechanism sustaining serfdom: even to those it most oppresses, it appears reasonable. Serfdom was clothed in the trappings of legality. It was not slavery, which depended on force and terror, but was rather part of a rationalized system that supposedly apportioned benefits to all. If the disadvantages to the serf were obvious—he could not own property, he was obliged to perform labor on his master's land or pay him a tax, he could be bought, sold, mortgaged, or given away—the law mentioned benefits also. A landowner was required to provide his serfs with a strip of land they could cultivate for themselves, he was obliged to arbitrate disputes, to open his grain reserves in time of famine, to refrain from "excessive" punishment. Such benefits appear ludicrously paltry, but it made considerable difference to the peasant, as exemplified by Vlas, that technically at least he was not dependent on his master's whim; he was part of a logical, though unfair, scheme.

The second peasant, Stepushka, at first seems to be in a better position than Vlas. By some remarkable oversight he has been allowed to fall outside the system of serfdom altogether. He has slipped through the bureaucratic grid, so that it is even doubtful, as the narrator notes with amazement, "if he was actually listed in the government census of serfs." But in the event, Stepushka's situation is not enviable. "Every human being," the narrator remarks, "has some sort of status in the social situation, has some sort of connection; every domestic is issued, if he gets no wages, at least a so-called 'flour allotment.' Stepushka received no subsistence aid whatsoever, he was not related to anybody; nobody was aware of his existence" (S, IV, 35). In the summers he sleeps in a cubbyhole in the back of the henhouse, in the winters in the entry to the bathhouse; and his days are wholly taken up with scavenging for food.

This is Turgenev's second major insight into the workings of serfdom: it was not only legal, it was encompassing. There was virtually no life in Russia except within the prevailing system. In removing himself from accountability to the government, Stepushka removes himself as well from the only means in Russia by which men acquire social status and a measure of security. In fact, in escaping direct oppression, Stepushka comes close to losing all traces of humanity. The encompassing nature of serfdom suggests why, when peasants did manage to mount a rebellion, it was often carried out in the name of the tsar. The sanctity of the system was not challenged, only specific abuses of it. In general, though serfdom came into existence in Russia gradually and haphazardly, once in place it functioned efficiently in a crucial respect: men had great difficulty imagining an alternative way to live.

The last peasant, nicknamed Fog, is a liberated serf of almost seventy, and his response to serfdom is perhaps the most striking of the three. Fog had in the past served as a sort of major domo to a rich count, organizing a vast manorial estate so as to provide the maximum of pleasure and luxury for his master. He entered upon his duties so wholeheartedly that even now, years after, Fog still rhapsodically recounts the manner of life the count enjoyed, he still itemizes, with something approaching love, the various appurtenances of his master's pleasure: the numerous hunting dogs kept on silk leashes, the servants decked out in red caftans with gold braid, the marvelous snuffboxes, canes, wigs, and colognes. To sum up his memories of his master, Fog remarks, "When he set out to give a banquet—O Lord, Sovereign of my life—the fireworks would begin and so would the pleasure jaunts" (S, IV, 39). That parenthetical expression is terribly revealing; for in such an expression of spontaneous enjoyment and undistanced enthusiasm, Fog reveals how fully his pleasures depend on pleasing the count.

This is Turgenev's third insight regarding serfdom: serfdom does not oppress all peasants equally. In certain cases, such as that of Khor', who is able to acquire his own business, there are rewards for extraordinary effort. In other cases, such as Fog's, the rewards are given almost randomly. In general, however, serfdom allows peasants to believe they have a chance to work out their own destiny, instead of having to accept the common dreary fate. (It helped that the details of how much serfs could legally hope to achieve was obscure. Even Turgenev, famed as an expert on peasant affairs, was unsure of all the laws. Only after studying the issue carefully does he write to Annenkov, "An enserfed individual does *not have* the right to acquire property except in the name of his master" [*P*, II, 103; italics in original].) The incremental differences in injustice seem to lighten the degradation all peasants suffered. Fog, for example, is so exhilarated by his proximity to wealth that he forgets completely his actual status—and forgets also that he should think of satisfying his own desires as well as his master's.

The climax of the sketch comes when Vlas recounts how his master drive him away when he applied for help. The peasants are confronted with the incontrovertible cruelty of slavery; and the stifling heat, which previously helped to explain their lackadaisical behavior, now seems to suggest that such an atmosphere of purposelessness cannot long continue. But Fog responds with only token sympathy, then returns to his fishing; Stepushka at first seems ready to remonstrate, but after a few disconnected words sinks into confusion and silence—a sequence of gestures befitting a man who is apparently free but actually powerless; and even Vlas himself proves curiously incapable of comprehending what he is saying, telling his story "with a mocking smile, as though it were someone else he was talking about" (*S*, IV, 41). Thus the climax, instead of altering the situation the rest of the sketch has built up, only recapitulates it in a more intensive fashion. The evidence of great evil suggests there should be change; but there is none, because the evil is of a nature that prevents men from thinking of alternatives. The values of the status quo appear as pervasive as the heat, as correct as the sun.

Throughout *Notes of a Hunter*, Turgenev describes a complete lack of comprehension of one's own interests, a comprehension that is the prerequisite of politics. When a character manages to rise above the common level of degradation, it is not by ignoring and still less by combatting the prevailing order, but rather by accepting it most fully: men scramble to secure a more elevated place in the hierarchy of power, content to be oppressed if they can oppress others. In "The Tryst" a valet transforms a farewell meeting with his peasant girl lover into a vicious encounter, rebuffing her expressions of love in the haughty manner that he believes his superior position entitles him to. In affected and dandified tones, like a master speaking to an underling, he tells her, "Anyway, you've got no education—so you must obey when you're told to do something" (S, IV, 265). In "Ermolai and the Miller's Wife," Ermolai routinely exploits Arina's misfortune for his own sexual pleasure, pointedly oblivious to the social process that has degraded them both, if in different degrees. In "The Steward," the title character curries favor with his master, a real tyrant who is restrained only by his wish to appear a progressive: the steward carries out the master's cruel impulses for him, unconscionably maltreating the peasants under his control.

Indeed, Turgenev elaborates such a convincing logic to explain why men are kept from experiencing their own impulses and enacting their own preferences that any exception to the rule seems a most remarkable feat. The sketch "Lone Wolf" is one of the few aberrations in the dismaying larger pattern. It is the story of a peasant serving as a forester for his master. The man is wonderfully conscientious and dedicated; no bribes or threats can compromise him. Even the hatred of his fellow peasants, who in their desperation must steal from the forest if they are to survive, does not deter him. In one sense the Lone Wolf is an honorable man, strictly conforming to the ethical code that comes with his job; but this sense of honor also directly causes hardship, even death, among his fellow peasants, while maintaining the master's excessive luxury.

At the end of the sketch, the Lone Wolf catches a peasant stealing firewood. He subdues and ties him up in order to deliver him to the authorities on the following day. To the man's pleas to let him go, and to his description of the extreme poverty that caused the attempted theft, the forester only replies, "Can't be done, I'm telling you. I'll be called to account. And besides there's no need of pampering your kind" (S, IV, 173). The last sentence is in one sense superfluous, since the already stated claims of law and duty should suffice as an explanation; the additional comment shows, however, that the forester has embraced the values as well as the rules of the prevailing system. He acts not merely from a sense of duty, nor simply because he fears punishment if he is derelict, but also because he has come to believe in the merit of what he does: he is only a surrogate for his master, all individuality lost.

But "Lone Wolf" concludes with a surprise. Though for a long time the prisoner's pleas have not made the slightest impression, the forester does in the end suddenly decide to release the man. No reason is given for this abrupt change of heart—nor in fact could there be, given the logic that obtains in the world of *Notes of a Hunter*. The values of the political structure seem so all-encompassing that a rejection of them could only come about abruptly and inexplicably, like grace descending. For the Lone Wolf to act as he does involves nothing less than a transcendence of all the elements that seemingly constitute his personality, a leap toward a basic humanity that is nowhere visible beforehand. In general, the peasants have been persuaded to view the injustice of the world less as a problem than as a fact of life, its corrosive effects to be accommodated as well as possible.

Turgenev's description of serfdom invites the reader to view *Notes of a Hunter* as a plea for the underdog. We are presented with a picture of terrible suffering; quite naturally, our sympathies go out to the victims. Although that response *is* part of the experience of reading *Notes of a Hunter*, it should not be the whole of it. The work is far from the spirit of Stowe's *Uncle Tom's Cabin*. Turgenev does more than elicit compassion for the peasantry. Indeed, the character who is most present, appearing on every page, is a nobleman. That, of course, is the narrator, and his predicament is finally the most compelling aspect of Turgenev's design. On the face of it, the narrator's life seems without problems, especially in comparison to the peasants'. He is materially well off, free to move around the countryside, capable, because of his education, of enjoying refined pleasures. These, however, are secondary characteristics. What defines the narrator, what makes him memorable, is his remarkable reticence about himself. It is a highly ambiguous quality. If it often appears as a becoming modesty, a means for the narrator to confer all value on his material, it must also, in a world where individual assertion is so difficult to attain, suggest powerlessness.

Since reticence is the form that the narrator's problem assumes, he can never fully express his unhappiness. There are only tremors of unease. One such tremor occurs at the end of the sketch "The Tryst." After the supercilious valet and his serf-girl lover Akulina have departed, the narrator emerges from his hiding place to retrieve the bouquet that Akulina has offered as a gift and which had been carelessly discarded. The sketch closes with these words: "I came home; but for a long time the image of poor Akulina would not leave my mind, and her cornflowers, withered long since, are treasured by me" (S, IV, 269). In one perspective, the narrator's rapt attention to the cornflowers points beyond them to the pathetic circumstances of peasant life. But if the focus is shifted slightly from background to foreground, it is the narrator himself who dominates the scene. His attention to the peasants, his sympathy and concern, turn out to be elements in the personality he is desperately constructing for himself. Nothing *seems* to block the narrator from asserting himself except his own disposition; on the other hand, the status quo in mid-nineteenth-century Russia often managed to shape the constraints on the individual into the form of a personal choice.

In fact the narrator enjoys only one moment of great and unrestrained feeling in the course of the book, one moment when his whole being comes into play. It is a moment of exuberant pleasure; but significantly it is also the single moment in *Notes of a Hunter* when we can best begin to identify the cause of his pervasive discontent. It occurs in the sketch "Kas'ian of the Beautiful Lands," when the narrator stops to rest in a forest clearing:

I lay down flat on my back and begin admiring the peaceful play of the tangled leaves against the far-off radiant sky. An amazingly pleasant occupation, this lying on your back in a forest and gazing upward. It seems to you that you are looking into a bottomless sea which is spreading wide beneath you, that the trees are rising not out of the earth but just as if they were the roots of enormous plants, and going down, are plunging straight into those glassily limpid waters. . . . You do not move—you gaze; and there is no expressing in words how joyous and gentle and delectable is the mood that enters your heart. You gaze: and that profound pure azure brings to your lips a smile as innocent as [the azure] itself, as innocent as the cloud against the sky . . . and all the time your gaze is receding farther and farther into the tranquil shining abyss, and is drawing you after it, and it is impossible to tear yourself away from that height, from that depth.
[S, IV, 124]

The narrator experiences the world in terms of a visuality so powerful that it "draws" the rest of the man behind it. The normal agencies of consciousness relax; only in the absence of any mediating or interpretive reflex can the visual sense exert its effect fully. At this most intense moment, contemplation becomes equivalent to identification. The seductive attraction of the "abyss" absorbs the narrator in a way that eradicates the line between the external world and himself, a feeling that Turgenev captures in a turn of phrase that unreservedly equates the qualities of the narrator's smile with the qualities adhering in the sky. The physical activity of lying down is thus a prelude for a more radical change in attitude, an abdication of self-control so total that the self virtually dissipates. At the end of the passage "depth" and "height" are one, because it is no longer clear if the narrator is outside the natural world looking in, or inside looking out.

Though the emotion accompanying the activity appears to be pleasure, it must be a most ambiguous pleasure for someone who put as much stock in the ego as Turgenev. If the result in this case is satisfying, the experience suggests grave risk: once the individual loses his sense of himself as an independent agent, capable of maintaining the borders of his personality, what will happen should the enticing world prove evil instead of good, as it appears to be in "Kas'ian of the Beautiful Lands"? Identification with the world, allowing it fully to penetrate one's being, would be a truly terrible event. In fact, the moment in the forest clearing is less an ideal than a warning. It reveals Turgenev's persistent belief that man must confront the world; but it also shows his fear that without a confident and ready understanding of one's own prerogatives that confrontation can prove disasterous.

Though "Kas'ian of the Beautiful Lands" is the most graphic evidence, Turgenev also implies the narrator's potential weakness in the face of the world's power in many other passages of *Notes of a Hunter*. He places one piece of information so directly on the surface of the narrative that it almost escapes attention, but it is crucial. Virtually every sketch begins with the narrator departing from his estate and many end with his mentioning his eagerness to return there. But beyond the fact that the estate is located in Orel province, no information about it is given. We do not learn the shape or color of the house, nor the dimensions of the grounds surrounding it, nor the variety of the furniture within. Where there might have been a symbol of stability and tradition, there is a vacuum. Though the narrator could locate his residence on a map, in effect he is homeless.

The concept of home always played a major role in Turgenev's thoughts. Partly, home implied domesticity. As an expatriate and bachelor, he often wished for a place to settle, and his letters are filled with references to his desire to build a "nest." But "home" also had political meaning. Upon hearing in Rome that emancipation was nearing, Turgenev wrote, "Now every man should be at home in his nest" (*P*, III, 195). He meant his estate in Orel, in order to oversee the new arrangements with the peasants; he also meant Russia generally, and the chance to participate in the momentous social transformation. The emancipation promised not only liberation of the serfs but an end to the political dispossession of men like Turgenev.[2]

The absence of a true home in *Notes of a Hunter* is presented as a palpable psychological lack. Because he has no home to which to withdraw, the narrator must live out his life in a sphere dominated by Russia's public values. Aside from one or two small havens of personal pleasure, the landscape of *Notes of a Hunter* contains only one element: the system promoted by the central government. One sees only the homogeneity of the status quo, a stretch of terrain whose distinguishing features never change, whose moral and political problems never get solved, because there is no place where moral or political challenge could originate.

The one structure that would seem most likely to break up this depressing desolation is explicitly denied an existence: Turgenev is scathing in rejecting the nobility as a consequential political force. The sketches in the book that deal with the nobility depict it as a collection of fatuous and vague men—the presiding attitudes are

2. "Homelessness" as a metaphor for political dispossession was an established tradition in Russia, going back at least to Chaadaev's *Philosophical Letters* (1834): "We all resemble travelers. Nobody has a definite sphere of existence, we have no proper habits, there is no domestic life, there is nothing we could be attached to, nothing that could awaken our sympathy or affection—nothing durable, nothing lasting, everything passes, leaving no traces, either outside or within. In our homes we seem to be guests, in our families we look like strangers, in our cities we look like nomads—even more than nomads who drive their heads on our steppes, for they are more attached to their desert than we are to our country." Chaadaev's remark is cited by Andrzey Walicki, *The Slavophile Controversy* (Oxford, 1975), who discusses the "homelessness" metaphor at some length, pp. 337 ff.

neatly indicated in the description of the party at the opening of "Prince Hamlet of Shchrigrov Province," a remarkable gathering in that the only energy of the evening comes alternately from men posturing and men fearing that they will be caught out posturing. Nothing more substantial engages them. But the most dismaying fact about the nobility, Turgenev shows, is that its shortcomings are less a matter of personal insufficiency than of the prevailing political organization, hence less amenable to change. As the title character of "Ovsianko the Freeholder" remarks, complaining of the present condition of the nobility, "Those with smaller estates have all spent time working for the government or else can't stay put in one place. As for the bigger sort, there's no recognizing them" (S, IV, 68). Ovsianko believes that the nobility was once a significant political force, which has now degenerated. His belief in the golden age of the nobility is mostly wishful thinking, but his remarks accurately describe the factors that retarded the nobility's contemporary influence: enticement into government service, no continuity of landholding, the economic heterogeneity of the estate. Ironically, Ovsianko himself symbolizes the dilapidated condition of the nobility: a "freeholder" was a category halfway between the nobility and the peasantry, with some of the obligations and privileges of each estate—the freeholder status had to remind the Russian noblemen that the estate they belonged to was open and fluctuating, and finally regulated not by themselves but by the government. It follows that the nobleman-narrator feels himself homeless and lacks and confident vision that might come from commanding at least a small part of the world.

As depicted by Turgenev, the nineteenth-century nobility derives as little psychological satisfaction from Russian life as the peasantry. Material advantages do not guarantee a purposeful existence; political dispossession saps the spirit of individuals in drawing rooms as fully as it does the spirit of individuals in thatched huts. The surprising convergence of rich and poor is perhaps the most ominous element in Turgenev's design. The peasantry and the nobility are searching for happiness on the same narrow ground, and the moves of one jostle and unnerve the other. Throughout *Notes of a Hunter*, Turgenev makes the reader consider this question: can two groups exist in harmony when they are equally dispossessed politically but one has great social power over the other? The question, indeed, informs the way each word gets on the page. The nobleman-narrator always has great potential power over the peasants, who are only the material that fill his narrative. The narrator is sympathetic to peasant life, but his role must tempt him to exploit the thoughts and acts of others for his own ends. Can a nobleman in the mid-nineteenth-century Russia, however well intentioned, forbear using any means at his disposal to bolster his self-esteem?

"Bezhin Meadow" explores the ambiguity of the narrator's position. In this sketch the peasants make their greatest effort to resist the oppression of Russian life and to express their human potential. With the peasants engaged in a task that so clearly touches his most vital concerns, can the narrator stand coolly by? Would he not also try to assert his personality if he knew a way? Indeed, the sketch opens not by focusing on the peasants but by describing the narrator, at much greater length than is usual in the cycle. He appears in the precarious state of mind that was first described in "Kas'ian of the Beautiful Land": the external world has insinuated itself so fully that the outlines of his individuality seem about to give way—and this time the external world appears not beautiful but sinister. True, as the sketch begins, the narrator is lost, and that partly accounts for the unease he feels; but Turgenev by his style emphasizes a disorientation that is psychological as well as physical, and that turns unease into existential anxiety. The narrator is in a world where structure has disappeared, where all angles and purchase that might have been used to establish a sense of stability are lacking. The sky "drains" of color, the air "congeals," the night "sprawls out," darkness "pours down." The atmosphere oppresses and envelops, and the narrator's discriminating power flags. When in the course of his erratic wanderings he almost falls into an unseen ravine, it is symbolic not only of the nearness of physical extinction but of the deadly absorbing power of a world not properly kept at a distance.

Yet by the end of the sketch the narrator has managed to attain a remarkable mastery over his surroundings. The change is partly the result of impenetrable night passing into bright day, but again it would be wrong to give too much weight to mere circumstance. The narrator has somehow acquired a capacity to order and shape the world. There is a confidence and jauntiness to the last paragraph, a sense of achieved control, which a simple sunrise fails to explain:

> I had hardly gone a little over a mile when torrents of young hot light came pouring down all around me—over the far-spreading wet meadow and ahead of me, over the now newly green knolls, from forest to forest, and behind me over the long dusty road, over the sparkling, crimsoned bushes, and over the river, diffidently showing its blue from under the thinning mist—torrents of light, at first ruby-red, then red, then golden. [S, IV, 112-113]

The substance of the sketch is designed to explain the narrator's changed attitude, from his initial confusion to his final robust confidence. The process of change, however, is very subtle; for most of the sketch the narrator hardly pays any attention to himself. Instead, he gives himself over to considering the behavior of five peasant boys he encounters in Bezhin Meadow, where they are guarding a herd of horses. To pass the time before they sleep, the boys take turns relating wonderous stories, and each reveals an imagination in full play. Occasionally, the story-teller constructs such miraculous horrors that he is as terrified as his listeners. Despite the atmosphere of foreboding, when a strange sound is heard one of the boys plunges into the dark thickets to see if a wolf is threatening the herd. The narrator is filled with admiration and respect. Indeed, all the boys appear remarkably self-assertive: the stories they have told, myths about water nymphs and hobgoblins, seem to have given them a measure of control over the world. The peasant boys have managed to transcend their environment, which is the rarest of events in *Notes of a Hunter*.

Turgenev makes clear that the boys' achievement requires very special conditions. The peasant boys exist apart from the more insidious influences of Russian reality. Chronologically, they are, as boys, free from some of the pressures adults must face; geographically, as the narrator's disorientating experience at the beginning of the sketch emphasizes, it is hard to find the way to Bezhin Meadow from the workaday world. The light from the bonfire around which the boys sit marks off a piece of ground that is a realm of its own. "When one sits where it is light," the narrator remarks, "it is hard to make out what is going on in the dark, and therefore everything even near at hand seemed to have black curtains drawn over it" (*S*, IV, 96). In this circumscribed area, in this "ring of light," as the narrator twice calls it, the boys manage to act out their best creative impulses. Here they can assert their individuality. But, Turgenev shows, it is difficult to sustain the magical power of that "ring of light." In the last lines of the sketch, which constitute a postscript to the main action, we are told that one of the boys was killed in an accident shortly after the narrator's encounter with him. The evil and chaos of the world at large sooner or later make themselves felt.

The boys' attempts to impose order on the world must have a special interest for the narrator. Their attitude of bafflement and fear precisely parallels his own at the beginning of the sketch. Turgenev sets up that elegant symmetry of concerns to expose a welter of moral confusion. The narrator, instead of working through his own uncertainty, has simply positioned himself at a point of maximum self-interest, a spectator to others' work and risk-taking that proves happily relevant to his own life. Watching the peasant boys' effort to comprehend the world is inspiring, as watching manual labor can be inspiring. The very inadequacy of the boys' effort is bracing—if the boys manage as well as they do with such meager tools, the narrator with his greater capacities should have nothing to fear. By the end of the sketch, though he has done nothing and exerted little mental effort, he feels infinitely more in control than he did at the beginning. "Bezhin Meadow" presents a neat division of labor, the difficulties that the narrator experiences are resolved for him by the example of the peasant boys. But as with any division of labor, there is a threat of moral dissipation. The narrator is continually on the verge of exploiting the peasant boys, not for material gain but in order to bolster his sense of his own identity.

That may seem an extreme conclusion to draw from the commonplaces of literary method: the narrator's presence at the scene of the peasant boys' adventure is, after all, the best certification of the truth of his story. But it is Turgenev's great talent to let the reader see that seemingly dispassionate methodological choices may have moral implications. The action at Bezhin Meadow reveals the dubious nature of the narrator's position throughout *Notes of a Hunter:* a use of others in the hope of finding vicarious satisfaction, and a repression of the knowledge of one's own weakness through the contemplation of those who are weaker still.

In fact, Turgenev, in making visible the moral ambiguities of his narrative procedure, calls into question one of the dominant attitudes among Russian progressives in the 1840s and early 1850s. Wishing the peasantry well, Turgenev shows, can be a desire with complex implications; its authenticity may depend not only on the good intentions of the individual but also on social circumstances. The complicity of the narrator in the peasants' unhappy lot is a complicity not in the sense of reprehensible motive but in the sense of an entanglement in pernicious social bonds. The same ill effects of mere *location* were experienced by many progressive noblemen of the time. Caught between an oppressive and unresponsive government on the one hand, and an oppressed and largely docile peasantry on the other, they could reasonably feel that small acts of charity were all that political conditions allowed. Unfortunately, though their political analysis was correct, though their inactivity was forced on them, progressive nobelemen still ended as agents of corruption—by virtue of the social role they filled.

The government exploited the nobility's mediate position in society to create a buffer between itself and the peasantry. It was the local nobility that monitored and controlled the peasantry, collecting taxes, administering army recruitments, policing disturbances. Some noblemen undertook these tasks readily, happy to acquire any bit of social status that they could. Others, like Turgenev, filled their roles reluctantly and only intermittently. Very few, however, abdicated their responsibilities altogether. To have done so would have meant repudiating their connection with Russian society. There are examples in Russian history of individuals who adopted a stance of almost metaphysical rebellion, driven by a moral revulsion so passionate that they refused to participate in any way in the existing order; but, necessarily, those examples are rare.

Turgenev's treatment of the narrator in *Notes of a Hunter* reflects the more typical reaction of a Russian progressive in the middle of the nineteenth century: a genuine altruism that creeps ineluctably toward self-servingness. The narrator-nobleman exploits his peasant characters not from malice but simply because they are near at hand. Indeed, at that moment in Russian history, it was virtually impossible for a writer who belonged to the nobility to have portrayed the peasantry with unambiguous sympathy. *Notes of a Hunter* thus emphasizes a general rule of literature that is often denied or glossed over: a writer's choice of a subject is never innocent. In a letter to Annenkov in May, 1853, Turgenev wrote: "The peasants have completely overwhelmed us in literature. That in itself would be nothing; but I am beginning to suspect that we, no matter how much we may fuss with them, still don't understand anything about them. . . . It is time to send the muzhiks into retirement" (*P*, II, 160). The military image in the first sentence indicates Turgenev's realization that the peasantry is equivalent to a foreign force. A literary work dealing with the peasantry therefore can easily become distorted. Even if the theme is fully incorporated into the narrative, the result would be like a country that defeats an occupying army by absorbing it into the native population. Tactically effective, the effort entails a tremendous sacrifice of moral integrity.

No peasant character plays a major role in the novels that Turgenev began to publish in 1856. In fact, there are few references to the peasantry in these works. Increasingly, he came to realize that if an author were to comprehend the fullness of Russian reality, he had to begin by exploring the terrain he himself occupied. The muzhiks had to be sent into retirement not because they had become a trivial subject—they would never be that in Russian history—but because a prior step was necessary before the topic could be confronted in a thoroughly honest and thoroughly effective manner.[3]

Though *Notes of a Hunter* can be read in isolation from Turgenev's other works, and with great pleasure, it is as a stage in his career that it appears most powerful and sympathetic. It has the

3. The momentous decision of the Tver Assembly of the Nobility in 1861 may be said to constitute the political equivalent of Turgenev's literary attitude toward the peasantry. The Assembly's effort to sever all relations with the peasantry, those which were potentially profitable as well as those which were burdensome, was the result of the realization that *any* connection between the two estates would have unfortunate effects, which the central government would exploit. On the Tver Assembly see Terence Emmons, *The Russian Landed Gentry and the Emancipation of 1861* (Cambridge, 1968), pp. 313ff.

aspect of a question that urgently requires an answer. Most of the
sketches show Turgenev's great willingness to engage the world
around him, but the unfortunate result is that he is drawn into
complicity with prevailing evil: Was there any way for a writer to
describe mid-nineteenth century Russia while successfully projecting his own values, his own voice?

Turgenev's intention of surpassing the style of *Notes of a Hunter*
was announced most emphatically in a letter from October, 1852 to
Annenkov, who had for some time been urging him to take a new
literary tack. He wrote:

> All that you say I feel as clearly as you—it is irrefutable—and I sign
> my name under every word. It is necessary to go along a different
> path—and to say good-bye to the old manner.... But here is the
> question: am I capable of something big, serene? Can I achieve clear,
> simple lines?... This I do not know and cannot know until I try—but
> believe me, you will hear something new from me or you will hear
> nothing. [*P*, II, 77]

The letter, though full of personal doubt and complaint, suggests
the beginnings of an aesthetic. Turgenev's uncertainty about achieving "clear, simple lines" was partly the result of his belief that he
lacked a novelist's skills. In fact, he never learned to construct intricate plots or to delineate complex mental states. The technical problems, however, signaled more profound problems of sensibility. The
"old manner" exerted a tenacious attraction. He had become very
proficient at it—so proficient that it had begun to appear less a
chosen manner than his natural means of expression. At the same
time, however, he had to admit that *Notes of a Hunter* was not a
success; he had spoken in his natural voice, but he felt he had not
been heard. The ambiguous attraction of the novel was precisely
that it was an alien genre. Writing "something big, serene" meant a
leap into unknown territory; it would require giving a wrench to
habit and intuition. Turgenev could hope that the strain of writing in
a new form would impart distinctiveness to his authorial voice, as
muscles under strain acquire tone.[4]

---

4. The shift in Turgenev's style of writing has often been discussed by critics.
Perhaps the best treatment of this development is K. K. Istomin's "Staraia manera
Turgeneva (1844–1855)," in *Izvestiia otdeleniia russkogo iazyka i slovesnosti
Akademii nauk*, kn. 2–3 (1913).

The clearest sign of his move away from naturalness in the elimination of the first person type of narration. This was more than a formal adjustment; it involved his views of personality. In *Notes of a Hunter* Turgenev tried for an unapologetic presentation of his pleasures, sympathies, and concerns, but he refused to cast these aspects of himself in an insistently political or social light. As a result, the narration is often silent at points where we expect comment. The narrator's social pedigree and political allegiances are usually only hinted at. When they are mentioned, they are treated as unproblematical facts, demanding no attention. The narrator never meets anyone who asks him about his daily occupation, his opinion of the government, his view of serfdom, and he does not think of questioning himself. Thus, for all his directness, the narrator occasionally slips from view.

In the novels Turgenev shifts to a third-person type of narration. He expresses himself less directly, but nevertheless his personality stands out more clearly. Though none of the characters is a perfect copy of the author, the questions they raise about the connection between public and private roles defines a field of concerns that we recognize as uniquely Turgenev's. In *Notes of a Hunter* he had refused to worry about this connection; his career can thus be taken as a commentary on both his personality and the society in which he lived. The extreme oppressiveness of the Russian autocratic system drove even those with little taste for politics to assume a political stance: it was the only way to make oneself heard.

Turgenev did not suddenly become a fierce ideologue. The novels are neither scathing criticisms of Russian society nor passionate programs showing how to achieve utopia. In his review of *Faust* (1845), he had shown as little sympathy for Byron's all-out rejection of existing conditions as for Goethe's pose of wise detachment. Turgenev avoids both extremes. He does not deny that the autocratic system is a fact of life, something with which every Russian must come to terms; but he also scrutinizes the actions of characters whose social pedigree resembles his own, examining their choices, exposing their failures of nerve. That is, though he accepts the world as he finds it, he places himself directly within it. The novels are political because they are self-conscious about his position in mid-nineteenth century Russia.

Writing to Annenkov, Turgenev said, "No one more than I admits the fatal connection between life and literature of which you speak—but the connection is not made by us alone—that's the joke" (*P*, II, 123). Though he was most at home with the view that life was shaped by eternal forces and that Russia was only an example of the universal human condition, he came to see that a writer cannot always remain with the view he prefers. Russian history thrust itself upon him; with remarkable resilience, he accepted the challenge, and set about exploring the period in which he lived. In a letter to S. T. Aksakov in November 1856, he wrote: "I am one of the writers of the interregnum—that epoch between Gogol and a great future leader; we all dissipate and fragment that which a great talent would compress into a whole, extracted from the depth" (*P*, III, 32).

The unexpected use of the political term "interregnum" (*mezhdutsarstvie*, literally a period between tsars) is revealing. As the evocative phrasing shows, the diminution Turgenev feels, his sense of fragmentation, is very personal; but the causes are more than personal, they are connected with his historical situation. In his moments of greatest strength—which is to say, in the novels—he fights history on its own ground.[5] He was a nobleman in a period when the nobility's sense of purpose was questionable; a serf-owner in a period of emancipation; a man of amiable and conciliatory temperament in a period of ideological passion—indeed, almost all his political traits were of a sort to inspire unease. But in accepting politics as an important constitutent of his personality, he also began to find relief; for it meant that in questioning who he was, he was simultaneously questioning the political order of his day. Russia turned out to be not the eternal fact it presented itself as, but rather a contingent and alterable human construction.

---

5. It should be pointed out that not *all* contemporaries would have agreed with this positive assessment of Turgenev's novels. See, e.g., the following letter of Botkin, who was a friend of Turgenev, to the poet Fet: "Which one of his works did Turgenev read to you? If the previous one [*Rudin*], then it is one that has not at all succeeded as a whole, and indeed I believe he has succeeded in none of his novels. . . . His strength is in his sketches and details." Quoted in A. A. Shenshin, *Moi vospominaniia* (Moscow, 1890), p. 273.

Part Two

5.

The Novelistic Imagination

The decade of the 1850s was marked by a growing awareness of political possibilities. The turning point was 1855, when Russia's defeat in the Crimean War signaled an unexpected weakness in the autocracy and opened up the prospect of domestic reform: the complex process of emancipating the serfs, which involved overhauling the social order, began shortly thereafter and culminated in 1861 with the publication of the Emancipation Act. But even at the beginning of the decade, when governmental repression was in full force, pressures for change were building. Significantly, Turgenev's view of his literary tasks also began to change at the same time.

In 1852 Turgenev began the work that in manuscript had the title *Two Generations*. His notes concerning the project indicate that he intended to include more characters and to have a greater complexity of plot than in anything he had written previously.[1] In a word, *Two Generations* was to be a novel. Turgenev had proven himself a master of shorter forms; only a novel, however, could fully accommodate his vision. But two years after he began the project, he abandoned it. The episode can stand as a two-sided symbol of the difficulty of writing a novel at that point in Russian history and the pressure to make the effort, difficulties notwithstanding.

The success of the European novel was a main factor in the demand by Russians for similar home-grown products. The great European realists seemed to comprehend and illuminate the issues

1. Turgenev's work on *Two Generations* is discussed in S, VI, 377–388.

troubling their countries; Russians, with their growing social aware-ness, needed Russian novels for the same purpose. Unfortunately, even as late as the 1850s, there was no Russian tradition on which to build. Although great Russian novels were written in the first half of the nineteenth century—by Gogol, Pushkin, and Lermontov—they were too idiosyncratic to serve as models. They were monuments to be contemplated with awe, but which did not reveal the secrets of their construction.

The very definition of the genre was in doubt. There was no philosophical theory, such as existed in Germany in the writings of Hegel and Schlegel, nor more informal explorations of the novel's meaning, such as existed in England in the writings of Walter Scott. Russian critics urged Russian authors to produce novels without themselves understanding what they had in mind. In a very influen-tial essay, "A glance at Russian Literature in the Year 1847," Be-linsky trumpeted the enormous potential of the genre, then lumped it with the *povest'* (a long story).[2] Many journals, in an obvious effort to skirt the thorny issue, increasingly forced all prose into a section labeled "belle lettres." Turgenev's own "Khor' and Kalinych," first appeared in the "Miscellany" section of *The Contemporary*.[3]

At times it seemed that the only criterion used to define a novel was length. Any prose work of fiction covering a large number of pages qualified. Many works appeared at the beginning of the 1850s which were based on the principle of accretion. In them event followed event with startling rapidity, and the plot was designed to expand infinitely, in any direction, like a marvelously elastic saus-age. The poet Nekraskov, who produced one such monstrosity, ad-mitted that it was so much literary fodder, intended to fill the pages of a journal that was desperate for a work that at least approximated a novel.[4] His judgment applies as well to a host of similar efforts

2. V. G. Belinsky, "Vzgliad no russkiu literaturu 1847 goda," *Polnoe sobranie sochinenii* (Moscow, 1956), X, 279–369.

3. See B. M. Eikhenbaum, *Lev Tolstoy, kniga pervaia, 50-ie gody* (Leningrad, 1928), esp. pp. 33–85, for an excellent discussion of the situation of literature at the beginning of the 1850s.

4. Of his work, Nekrasov wrote to Turgenev, "If you see my novel, do not judge it too harshly: It is written haphazardly, and just so that there would be something to put into [*The Contemporary*]." Quoted in the appendix to N. N. Nekrasov, *Mertvoe ozero* (Moscow, 1959), p. 677.

churned out by hacks. Most significantly, however, not only second-raters but men of talent were seduced by the idea of length. Goncharov complained that there was no logic to keep him from adding scenes and chapters to his works *ad infinitum:* "There is no overriding necessity that determines how an entire novel is created, that permeates it and ties it together. . . . It is easy to portray, but how difficult it is to bring the portrayal to a center, to a goal."[5]

Early in his career, Turgenev sensed the need to distinguish a novel in other than quantitative terms. "A novel," he wrote in 1847, "is not simply a stretched out *povest'*, as some people think" (*P*, II, 159). However, since his critical writings were occasional, meant to illuminate the work at hand, Turgenev never elaborated a theory to support his intuition. Even his most extensive commentary on the state of the novel in Russia, which occurs in the course of a review of Evgeniia Tur's *The Niece*, is hardly a programmatic statement: Turgenev spends most of his energy trying to find a way to criticize a friend's feeble effort without giving offense. The opening paragraphs, however, in which he directly addresses Belinsky's "A Glance at Russian Literature in the Year 1847," signal a more serious purpose.[6] Here is the most suggestive passage; Turgenev has just finished dismissing the contemporary relevance of the Russian historical novel, and proceeds to evaluate other types of novels:

> Novels à la Dumas, with their quantities of volumes *ad libitum*, do exist with us, to be sure; but the reader will allow us to pass them by in silence. They are, if you please, a fact, but not all facts signify something. There remain two other types of novels more similar to ouoh othor than might uppour ut firot glunoo, novolo that wo will oall by the names of their chief representatives: Sand and Dickens novels. These novels are possible in Russia and, it seems, will take hold; but at the moment, it may be asked, have the elements of our social life manifested themselves to the degree that a four-volume work which

5. I. A. Goncharov, *Sobranie sochinenii* (Moscow, 1952–55), VIII, 336.

6. Belinsky built his argument arount an elaborate distinction between writers of genius and writers of talent. Turgenev virtually parodies Belinsky: "There was a time—a few years back—when our native literary criticism produced its own particular table of ranks—the subdivision of writers who, according to their capabilities, had achieved various levels: the simple belle-lettrist, the daguerreotype depictor of mores, the simple talent, and finally even the genius. There was even the level of world genius, but this level was attained by few. That time is now gone, and, by the way, we can see the short-livedness of many talents and geniuses; it has passed and we will not laugh at it" (*S*, v, 368).

sought to depict [these elements] should be in demand? The recent success of various notes (*otryvki*) and sketches proves, it seems, the opposite. For the time being we hear in Russian life separate sounds, to which literature responds with similarly brief echoes. [*S*, v, 373]

The reference to Sand and Dickens is regularly cited by critics as a prefiguring of Turgenev's own development: the works of the two European writers were widely acclaimed in Russia for their capacity to render contemporary social issues vividly, and Turgenev's novels would shortly receive similar acclamation. Sand's and Dickens' novels, however, are related to Turgenev's as an object is to its image in a distorted mirror. Dickens especially could have been only a most ambiguous influence. His works are crowded with the paraphernalia of the legitimized political structure. The actions of judges, policemen, lawyers, and businessmen of the City drive his plots along, and it is often a will, a neat symbol of established law, that serves as the instrument of his narrative climaxes. Dickens continually makes his characters measure themselves against the economic, social, and legal constraints of the world they inhabit.

Turgenev's novels lack these features, conspicuously. In *Rudin* (1856), *Nest of the Nobility* (1858), *On the Eve* (1860), and *Fathers and Sons* (1862), there are only a handful of characters who engage in any activity other than the management of provincial estates. Though this was a period of unprecedented discussion of Russia's social issues, his novels often seem to breathe an air of innocence about contemporary events. To the extent that he mentions political or economic factors, they are peripheral, insidious rather than overt influences on the main action. Thus, for example, the estate that is the setting for *Fathers and Sons* is troubled by peasant unrest, but all acts of rebellion are kept off stage and reported only by hints and brief allusions; and the Bulgarian revolution against the Turks that inspires the hero of *On the Eve* is never more than distant thunder. Also, the law informing the events of a Turgenev novel is not that of the statute books, as it is in Dickens, but the conventions of a small group of individuals gathered on their isolated estates. In comparison to Dickens, and to Sand also, Turgenev's novels represent a curious form of social commentary: criticism whirling in a void, unwilling or unable fully to engage its implied target.

Nevertheless, Turgenev's novels do embody a specifically social vision. They resemble their European counterparts only obliquely because Russian political life resembled that of European countries only obliquely. The great European realists are part of a tradition of resistance to the established order, which gives them the confidence to engage social injustice directly; but in Russia the idea of organized opposition to the autocracy was only beginning to acquire currency—indeed, Turgenev's novels were themselves instrumental in its inception. In the Tur review, Turgenev remarks that it is very uncertain if "the elements of our social [*obshchestvennyi*] life have manifested themselves." Where there is no "social life," there is nothing to offset the values of the status quo; literature is necessarily reduced to "notes and sketches" that only "echo" what already exists. His own *Notes of a Hunter* had shown him how easily a Russian author's outrage could be subverted, his disgust with existing evil changed into a form of complicity. His novels are attempts to provide more than an echo; they are not yet, however, aggressive social criticism.[7] They present a view of Russia that would make criticism possible.

Turgenev's novels revolve around very personal matters. The key events in the four he wrote between 1856 and 1861 are a man's refusal to elope, a young woman's decision to enter a convent, another young woman's decision to go unescorted to a young man's apartment, a beautiful widow's discussion of art with a radical medical student; and much time is devoted to exploring subtle emotions. Nevertheless, the novels possess expansive scope—not because they cover much terrain or span many years, but because Turgenev links even the seemingly most personal matters to the national situation. Even love may turn out to depend on the health of the body politic. The strategy of a double focus, simultaneously on the small part of the world and on the whole, is most evident in the physical setting that he develops for these works. It represents the "center" that Goncharov felt was so crucial to a Russian writer's design.

In *Notes of a Hunter* each sketch begins with the narrator setting

7. It is worth noting that the radicals, presumably more eager to attack existing institutions than Turgenev, also consistently criticized a literature of confrontation, so-called "accusatory literature" (*oblichitel'naia literatura*). See, e.g., N. A. Dobroliubov, "Blagonamerennost' i deiatel'nost'," *Sobranie sochinenii* (Moscow and Leningrad, 1961), VI, 190–210.

off in a different direction, open to any adventure he might chance to find. His encounters with peasants and other noblemen and with nature always have an element of surprise, the wonder of discovering something new. But the wonder is bought at the cost of tolerating a high level of randomness; the narrator accepts Russia as it is, refusing to impose his own attitudes and beliefs. In the novels the action is always centered by the presence of a provincial manor house. The house represents a specific set of values. The characters, as they move from room to room and out into the gardens, are always aware that they are in a space set apart from the worst aspects of contemporary life. Some of the characters accept their privileged position smugly, others rebel; but in all cases the manor house remains a constant reference point. Arrivals and departures have the flavor of return to the safety of a haven or of exile into chaos.

The manor house is distanced from the great world, yet is never fully separate. It is a part of the whole. The first work in which Turgenev used this structural device was *Rudin*. He begins with the topographical gesture, a marking out of boundaries. In the opening scene Alexandra Pavlovna Lipina, a young noblewoman, visits the hut of a dying peasant woman. Lipina's motive is charitable. She offers to move the peasant from the hut to a hospital, but is told that it is better to die in one's own bed. She offers a supply of tea and sugar, which is accepted but without thanks and with the comment that it will be necessary to borrow a samovar. Throughout the encounter, Lipina's good intentions are skewed by social circumstances. The difference in class and levels of culture which permeates every spoken word turns Lipina's charity into condescension, her concern into curiosity.

Immediately after the visit, Lipina returns to her manor house and apparently never gives the dying peasant woman another thought. Significantly, however, Turgenev suggests no persisting taint of immorality; Lipina proves to be a character who does much good, and her role marks a very important departure in Turgenev's thought. In *Notes of a Hunter* there seemed to be no escape from the fatuity, sometimes even the perniciousness, that underlay the nobility's altruism toward the peasantry. In *Rudin* the nobility's manor houses form an enclave providing Lipina with a refuge that is psychological as well as physical. In her home she has the chance to put her morally dubious charity behind her and to redirect her energy. She cannot alter the unfortunate relationship that exists between the nobility and the peasantry, but she can distance herself from its more corrosive effects, in a way that the homeless narrator of *Notes of a Hunter* could not. Turgenev's novels give nobleman and noblewomen the time and opportunity to show their best qualities.

Thus, though Turgenev's treatment of the dying peasant woman seems abrupt, almost cruel, it has a point. The issue of sympathy for Russia's downtrodden masses is raised only to be unceremoniously dropped, but the terrain that the downtrodden and the sympathizers inhabit is vividly demarked. Russia, Turgenev makes clear in a flash, is not a blank and homogeneous space: it consists of spheres, each requiring a different set of actions and attitudes. In *Rudin*, Turgenev does more than casually place a collection of nobleman and noblewomen on their estates: he suggests a community strategically distanced from the fullness of Russian reality.

To a degree, indeed, topography stands in for explanation. Residence in the nobility enclave, whatever the minor drawbacks, is its own reward; and improper behavior is sufficiently punished by banishment from this favored realm. Thus when the hero, Dmitri Rudin, is exposed as a poseur, his penalty is that he must leave the estate. Two scenes in chapter 12, which takes place several years after Rudin's forced departure, serve to map out the emotional landscape of the novel. The first is a gathering on the veranda of Rudin's old friend Lezhnev. The movements of those present, Lezhnev and Lipina (now his wife) and their guests, is languorous, the weather sunny and pleasant, the conversation correct and responsive. The talk turns to Rudin, as to some exotic creature who momentarily claimed their attention, and the company recapitulate their opinions. Although these range from scorn to praise, there is no real conflict. The characters are moved and sustained by a common feeling that precludes disagreement, a feeling of satisfaction, even complacency, which they derive from the pleasure of the setting: they are *here* while Rudin is *there*. They all intuitively know that they understand one another better than they understand, or care to understand, Rudin. The sentence closing this episode—"Anna Pavlovna [Lipina] smiled and pressed [Lezhnev's] hand" (S, VI, 351)—

thus has meaning other than its sentimentality: it connotes an atmosphere where communication requires only the most minimal gestures, because there exists a commonality of beliefs.

In the scene immediately following the veranda episode, Turgenev shows us Rudin, disheveled and tired, making his way along a dusty provincial road to a poststation, where he must enter into a petty argument with the stationmaster about the availability of horses to get him to his destination. The contrast between the two scenes is not only in degrees of physical comfort. What moves the second episode along, what gives it a pathetic quality, is the way all the characters—Rudin, stationmaster, driver— pay attention only to their own concerns. Rudin, whose outstanding feature is his eloquence, suddenly finds it impossible to obtain the interest of his audience, let alone their imagination. A sense of randomness and selfishness presides which seems to rule out any human contact. When Rudin finally agrees wearily to change his destination in order to get somewhere more centrally located—"All right," he says, weakly, "it's all the same to me. I'll go to Tambov" (S, VI, 353), though he meant to go to Penza—he is not only seeking to bring an unpleasant argument to an end; he is also acquiescing in the disorder of the world as it exists beyond the enclave of the nobles.

Turgenev never suggests that the retreat to a safe enclave is a perfect strategy. Many of its inhabitants only exploit their privileged position for selfish ends. In *On the Eve*, Turgenev seems to have taken pains to make those who reside in or near the Stakhov manor appear singularly unattractive. The group includes an adulterous husband, his weak-willed wife, an elderly relative who has turned into a hanger-on, a boring pedant, and a preening sculptor with no real talent. Their way of life excludes any test that would make them see themselves for what they are; but the location of the manor, set apart from the fullness of Russian society, also may have a beneficial effect on someone in whom a moral sense is latent. Elena, the heroine, becomes a force for good in a way that would have been impossible had she been exposed to prevailing corruption. When she is ten, she befriends a young beggar called Katia, who must live with a sadistic aunt and who longs to run away and "live in 'God's free world'" (S, VIII, 34). Elena realizes at once that she is in a better position than Katia; she also realizes that compared to Katia's

88

plight, the concerns of her mother and father are vacuous, their attitudes smug. She keeps the details of her friendship with Katia from her family, feeling that she "would sooner allow herself to be torn to pieces than to reveal her secret" (S, VIII, 34), and in that moment of secrecy she learns the true structure of Russian life. Only the enclave offers an escape from the evil of the world—Katia's abrupt death from a fever symbolizes its rapaciousness—but only beyond the enclave can one find purpose. Turgenev says of Elena's life at home, "She struggled like a bird in a cage, though there was no cage" (S, VIII, 35). She must accept self-imposed limits to her activities, even as she sees that her ultimate role will take her beyond those limits. Though Turgenev portrays her fate mainly in erotic terms, it depends as much on coping with Russia's political topography as on the maturation of her emotions.

Making the enclave appear articulated with the surrounding world yet distinct from it required a fine calibration of the imagination. There were, however, historical circumstances that made Turgenev's job easier. Russian intellectuals of his generation had lived through a period when the only alternative to directly confronting the general corruption (a risky step, as *Notes of a Hunter* shows) was retreating to absolutely private concerns. The philosophy that was most studied was the most abstract; literature was largely reduced to a compendium of witticisms and, sometimes, pornography; the most cultivated emotion was that between two individuals, whether love or friendship. Turgenev's exposure to these intellectual tendencies made him sensitive to their faults. Even when he is most disdainful of the public realm, he recognizes the most important battles must ultimately be fought there. The tension in his vision is particularly evident in a passage from *Nest of the Nobility*, the novel in which he presents the enclave of the nobility in its most insular aspect. The hero, Lavretsky, is contemplating his estate:

> Lavretsky sat near the window, not moving, listening to the current of the tranquil life which surrounded him, the intermittent sounds of rural isolation. Over these somewhere behind the nettles, someone is singing in a thin, thin voice; a mosquito echoes him precisely. . . . "It is as if I were at the bottom of a river," Lavretsky thought. And always, at all times, life here is tranquil and unhurried. He thought,

"He who enters this circle needs restraint: here there is no need to rush, here only he is successful who sets his path unhurriedly, as a ploughman who sets a furrow with his path. And what strength there is around, what health in this inactive quiet. . . . Let boredom sober me, let it calm me, prepare me so that I will be able to go unhurriedly about my business." [S, VII, 189-190]

Turgenev seems to have painted a picture of the easy pleasures of rural life: the "circle" induces a state of pleasant lethargy in Lavretsky. In fact, the passage, and the novel in general, shows a hero who has temporarily retreated to gather his forces for a future ordeal. Lavretsky has come to his estate after several years spent frequenting glittering balls and sumptuous dinners, a period that has exhausted his energies and dulled his powers of moral discrimination; he has even unthinkingly promoted his wife's infidelity. Now he intends a fresh start, a new role for himself that will simultaneously reveal the nation's latent spiritual strengths. This passage represents the start of his training. Though he sits motionless, his senses are active. His eyes pick out minute details, his ears hear the smallest sounds. The passage, indeed, is less a celebration of the beauty of the country than of its constitutive influence: Lavretsky is building a new personality, which he will use to confront the world. (It is worth comparing this episode with the narrator's epiphanic confrontation with nature in "Kas'ian of the Beautiful Lands": there is a similarity in the tone and imagery of the two descriptions, but in the sketch the viewer's personality seems to dissipate, while in the novel it grows stronger.) The metaphor of the ploughman encapsulates Turgenev's meaning: Energy must be husbanded, the rewards of effort are in the future; the "circle" is a source of values not to be found elsewhere.

Turgenev did not stress the innovative nature of his work. His novels do not have striking effects underscoring the originality of their conception; in some of their aspects they appear very conventional. Perhaps the best example of his apparent traditionalism is his rendering of male characters, several of whom seem to have much in common with that recurrent figure in the Russian cultural imagination, the Superfluous Man. Upon finding that Russian society does not permit him to make use of his talents, the Superfluous Man either sinks into inertia or vents his anger fruitlessly. Turgenev's male characters often endure a similar fate; but there are important differences also.

It could not have been otherwise. Turgenev wrote his novels at a time when the tradition of the Superfluous Man, which extended back to Pushkin's Onegin and Lermontov's Pechorin, had taken a decisive turn. It was manifestly impossible to think of the world after the Crimean War in the same way as before it. Alexander II's remark, to a convocation of the Moscow gentry in 1856—"It is better to abolish serfdom from above than to await the day when it will begin to abolish itself from below"—only crystallized and confirmed the obvious: Russian society stood on the brink of wide-scale change. Even if no radical transformation took place (and the extent and quality of change is still argued by historians), a hope for true reform emerged, and that altered the way individuals lived. The Superfluous Man, who justified his inactivity by pointing to the bleakness of Russian political life, was now an anachronism.

Turgenev does not naively repeat the famous literary figure; instead, his novels depict the Superfluous Man mainly to interrogate his pedigree and his assumptions. The larger outlines of the representation are preserved, but key details are altered. Turgenev's great cultural sensitivity inclined him to reshape old values rather than to innovate; but it is a radical reshaping. Though his heroes fit into an established tradition, they are mutants, not direct descendants of earlier literary types.

In the epilogue to *Rudin*, Turgenev neatly defines the singular status of his hero. Rudin undertakes to tell his old friend Lezhnev how he has spent the time since they last met. After describing how he worked for two years helping a rich and eccentric landowner carry out extensive experiments in "agronomy," he says:

> "There you have the first episode of my adventures." Rudin resumed after a pause. "Should I continue?"
> "Continue, please."
> "Eh! I don't feel like talking. I'm tired of talking, my friend—but all the same, so be it. Having trudged about some more to various places—by the way, I could tell you how I almost became secretary to a well intentioned important dignitary and what came of that; but this would take us too far afield. Having trudged about to various places, I decided finally to become—don't laugh, please—a man of business, a

practical man. This is what happened. I fell in with one—perhaps you have heard of him—one Kurbeiev. No?"
"No I haven't heard of him. But how, Rudin, how could you with your intelligence not see that your business does not consist—excuse the pun—in being a businessman." [S, VI, 359]

Rudin's language defines the worth of his labors. Though he has so much to relate that his syntax breaks down, event flowing over event, none of his activities merits extended exposition, for none has been fruitful. And by the same token, Lezhnev can dismiss four years of varied efforts with a pun. But that pun also fixes an important implicit attitude. For if Lezhnev scorns the activity of being a businessman, he does so by suggesting that another activity may have gained his respect. Rudin has only made a wrong choice. He has tried to fit his large and extravagant spirit to a cramped form. In all, the scene tends to place exacting standards around the idea of work; but such a focus is very different from the one usually associated with the Superfluous Man, who could not even take the first step along the path to practical activity.

Because Turgenev proceeded by adjusting an existing tradition, by a provocative reorientation instead of by innovation, not all contemporaries immediately perceived what was at stake. One who did was Nikolai Chernyshevsky. From one point of view that is surprising, since Chernyshevsky was a radical, a "man of the sixties," whereas Turgenev was a liberal, a "man of the forties." But, as we shall see, the opposition between liberals and radicals in this period, while intense, was often less important than the antagonism both groups felt toward the central government.

Indeed, Chernyshevsky made his most telling remarks concerning *Rudin* in the course of a polemic with Stepan Dudyshkin, who though a liberal failed to understand the devious way by which the status quo was perpetuated. In a review of recent fiction, Dudyshkin claimed that Turgenev endorsed the concept of the Superfluous Man. Turgenev's characters, Dudyshkin says, "fastidiously withdraw from the world, from the virulence of the vulgar [poshlost']."[8] Because they fear the "infection of the vulgar, they do nothing, and scorn those who do engage in concrete activity."

8. S. S. Dudyshkin "Povesti i razzkazy I. S. Turgeneva," *Otechestvennye zapiski*, CX (1857), p. 5.

Chernyshevsky argues, however, that Dudyshkin's insistence that the individual engage in practical work is equivalent to a demand that man must place himself "in harmony with his surroundings." As he explains, "to work" in Russia in 1856 can only mean being a "good bureaucrat" or an "efficient landowner" (which is code for "serf-owner"). *Only* those roles seem available that the status quo sanctions. Though Chernyshevsky yielded to no one in his scorn of the Superfluous Man's idleness, he also saw that activity might promote nothing except the existing order.[9]

To make his position precise, Chernyshevsky examines Rudin in an historical perspective. He compares Rudin with other prominent examples of the Superfluous Man, and especially with Beltov (the hero of Herzen's *Who Is to Blame?*), who represents the historical stage immediately prior to Rudin's. "You see the difference between Rudin and Beltov. One [Beltov] is contemplative by nature, ineffective, perhaps because the time has not yet come for men to act. The other [Rudin] works, works ceaselessly, but almost fruitlessly."[10] Beltov altogether lacked a field of activity; for Rudin one exists, but he does not utilize it effectively. To be sure, Rudin fails in part because of his purposeless flamboyance, but Chernyshevsky makes clear in his essay (as Turgenev did in the novel) that the crucial factor is the bewildering nature of the society in which Rudin lives. The prospect for meaningful change exists, a large number of occupations are open to the man of talent; but if "work" now seems eminently possible, it is work that may bind men to the prevailing corruption. The best intentions and energies become tainted by the status quo; men who engage in practical activity risk becoming infected by the invidious practices of the world.

A metaphor of disease governs the writing of both Chernyshevsky and Dudyshkin, although they employ it for different ends. In fact, because the metaphor began to define an historical situation that was often experienced as shifting and uncertain, its use was wide-

9. N. G. Chernyshevsky, "Zametki o zhurnalakh. Ianvar, 1857," *Polnoe sobranie sochinenii* (Moscow, 1950), IV, 697. In suggesting that Turgenev and the radicals shared certain assumptions, I do not wish to deny their disagreements. These were real and bitter. G. A. Bialyi, *Turgenev i russkii realizm* (Moscow, 1962) traces the ongoing dispute lucidly and judiciously.
10. Ibid., IV, 702.

spread. Turgenev's novels, with their central image of a haven set apart from a rapacious world, are themselves striking elaborations of the metaphor of disease. It is, therefore, worth digressing a bit on the implications of the metaphor.

Mostly, of course, disease suggests debilitation. When society resembles a disease, evil is pervasive. Improvement is difficult to imagine, since remedies must be applied everywhere at once. At a limit, when the disease is conceived as extremely virulent, it appears that not even the first step to improvement is possible: since anyone who lives in the diseased world must suffer from its effects, who will have the energy to act in the interests of health? Chernyshevsky developed this aspect of the disease metaphor in another essay in which he commented on *Rudin*—the famous "The Russian Man at the Rendezvous" (which was printed, incidentally, in the liberal journal *Athene*). Again Chernyshevsky does not overlook the personal flaws of the Turgenev hero, but his governing image makes clear that failure of will follows directly from the diseased condition of the world. Discussing the obstacles facing the well intentioned man confronting Russian society, Chernyshevsky states: "He who lives in a tavern cannot help smelling like a drunk, even though he does not drink himself. He who lives in a society that has no interests except petty day to day concerns cannot help being imbued with a pettiness of mind."[11] And again, to explain the social dynamic of evil: "The infectiousness of yawning is not an exceptional phenomenon. Social infectiousness is found in all phenomena that exist among large groups."[12]

Even if some individuals escape the general malaise and undertake to alter existing conditions, change is not likely to occur. Disease symbolizes not only that the world is corrupt but also that it is corrupting. Those who actively try to ameliorate Russian life will only make themselves most directly subject to contamination, like a doctor entering a sick room. The perspective had an almost religious quality: in a world run by the devil, all works, even works that start from benign intentions, become works for the devil. In such a world, to act for change, as indeed to engage in any practical activ-

11. Chernyshevsky, *Polnoe sobranie sochinenii*, v, 171.
12. Ibid., p. 170.

ity, is most problematical, for each action only brings one closer to the infection it is imperative to avoid. Chernyshevsky's friend and colleague Dobroliubov put it succinctly in his essay "The Provincial Sketches of M. E. Saltykov-Shchedrin."

> We will be asked: why will the environment not manifest its influence on others, Why will it act so fatally on talented natures? The answer is simple. These natures, thanks to their perceptions, run ahead further than others, grasp more than they can carry, and thus often encounter obstacles that they have not the strength to oppose.[13]

The comments of Chernyshevsky and Dobroliubov must be read in the context of their world views. They were anxious to convince their contemporaries of the urgent need for social changes, so they pictured society in the darkest colors. Moreover, their deterministic bias, which led them to infer that men were no more than the sum of environmental influences, made it natural for them to adopt the disease metaphor. But it was not necessary to endorse the politics and philosophy of these two—which were respectively more extreme and more utilitarian than many Russians of the period could accept—in order to agree with their picture of society as an infectious evil.

In fact, it is likely that the most influential propagator of the disease metaphor was a liberal and a devout Christian. He was Nikolai Pirogov, a surgeon who first became famous when he supervised the mission of the Sisters of Mercy during the Crimean War. In December 1856 he published an essay entitled "The Questions of Life" that causes a sensation and propelled Pirogov into a major role in the history of Russian education and in the history of Russian women's rights.[14] The main thrust of the essay, however, pointed at

13. Dobroliubov, "Gubernskie ocherki M. E. Saltykova-Shchedrina," *Sobranie sochinenii*, II, 126-127.

14. N. I. Pirogov, "Voprosy zhizni," *Izbrannye pedagogicheskie sochineniia* (Moscow, 1952), pp. 55-84. E. D. Likhacheva, *Materialy dlia istorii zhenskogo obrazovaniia v Rossii* (St. Petersburg, 1899-1901) cites the following contemporary response to Pirogov's essay: "The essay caused a complete transformation of our views of upbringing and education.... It was read at the court as well as in poor apartments, by women in society and by average mothers in family circles" (II, 17). Significantly both Dobroliubov and Chernyshevsky were among those who acclaimed "The Questions of Life." See, e.g., Chernyshevsky, "Zametki o Zhurnalakh. Iiun 1856," *Polnoe sobranie sochinenii*, III, 686.

nothing so specific. Written with more passion than precision, it was first of all a moral outcry against what Pirogov saw as a prevailing insincerity and weakness of will. The source of moral corruption is society, which Pirogov compares to a "festering sore." His attitude is very pessimistic. Society cannot be changed, since its values have acquired a momentum of their own. Individuals who come into contact with society are swept along by its force. "Our society is organized so that the large majority of people act unconsciously from the force of inertia, which sets them off in some direction or other."[15]

Nevertheless, the picture Pirogov paints is not hopeless. Indeed, "The Questions of Life" shows that a possibility for diminishing society's corrosive effects is built into the seemingly gloomy metaphor of disease. For all its deleterious implications, the metaphor suggests that evil has a logic, an etiology that explains the existence of disease and predicts its progress. For perhaps the first time in Russian history, rampant corruption seemed a phenomenon capable of being understood, instead of a blank, ineluctable force. If Russians of the period rarely dreamed of eradicating the disease of social evil, they did at least begin to imagine a strategy for avoiding its worst influences.

In describing the individual's perilous situation, Pirogov says, "We must be prepared by education for the unavoidable and fatal battle" with society.[16] Society will almost certainly triumph in that confrontation; significantly, however, Pirogov's description indicates that individuals are not immediately *in* society, they only come eventually to confront it. "The Questions of Life" is built on the idea that life is like a passage from a relatively safe sphere (the school), where individuals may live in touch with their virtues, to a sphere of high danger (the world at large), where many pressures insidiously subvert the individual's best efforts. Pirogov writes as if the passage is unavoidable. Indeed, from the point of view of individual development (it is impossible to stay in school forever) and of Russian history (the private values that individuals cultivated in the 1840s do not meet the demands of the 1850s), a confrontation with the world in inevitable. As a result, the tone of the essay is that of a

15. Pirogov, *Izbrannye pedagogicheskie sochinenia*, p. 82.
16. Ibid., p. 63.

cautionary tale, predicting the likelihood of an awful fate. Nevertheless, in construing Russian reality as not of a piece, in defining a quarantined space where individuals have the time and opportunity to develop their inherent strengths, Pirogov—and other writers who used the metaphor of disease—made an important political advance.

A later essay by Pirogov indicates the extreme precariousness of that achievement. It was very difficult even to imagine a safe space apart from the corrupt and corrupting whole, let alone to devise a practical equivalent. Every potential haven is embattled and threatened from without, always on the point of losing its privileged status:

> I compare these institutions [Russian schools] with hospitals. No matter what has been done to improve hospitals, nothing helps against "hospital disease" (*gospital'naia bolezn'*), neither larger quarters, nor ventilation, nor hygiene.
> Life, which arises independently of the school, affects the school incomparably more than the school does life. And this powerful influence that surrounds schools can penetrate through the walls of any closed institute.[17]

Pirogov believes that evil will prevail, penetrating every corner of the country; nevertheless, even as he delivers that most gloomy prognosis, he manages to suggest a path to success. The country is not a flat and homogeneous landscape that permits evil to flow unimpeded. There exist areas that are isolated from the general corruption. The task is to improve the defensive capacities of these areas, and while that may be difficult, it is not impossible. Pirogov's view gives Russians a precise focus for their aspirations for change.

It is important to be precise about the efficacy of the disease metaphor. The increased sense of control Russians felt at this time was partly the result of changed historical circumstances, an alteration in the concrete facts of political and social life after the Crimean War; but political and social realities must be given an apprehendable shape. They are too broad and intricately interwoven to be experienced directly. The disease metaphor allowed Russians to understand events after the Crimean War. In its complex connota-

17. N. I. Pirogov, "Ob ustave novoi gimnazii," *Izbrannye pedagogicheskie sochinenia*, p. 303.

tion of an encompassing evil that might be comprehended, the metaphor fixed in mind a concept that might otherwise have slipped away. But even more important than the metaphor's capacity to organize one's view of existing reality was its capacity to promote thinking about ways to alter that reality.[18] Individuals increasingly elaborated the meanings, functions, and location of the "circle" which would be safe from the corruption of Russian life. By the end of the period I am discussing, the issue was no longer whether such a removed and distanced entity could exist, but what its ultimate purpose should be. Was it to be a place permanently quarantined, where some men would be able to live out a profitable existence—in which case it would serve as a symbol of a moral community? Or was it to be a place where men could build up such strength as would immunize them when they ventured forth to confront social evil—in which case it would serve as a training ground for political action?

The different interpretations would lead to acrimonious debate, but for a time the image of a sanitized place apart from the general corruption was able to sustain a most significant political alliance. That was *obshchestvo*. Literally the word means "society," which would imply the values associated with the concept of civil society; but the situation in Russia required the word to have an idiosyncratic twist. There was virtually no Russian civil society. Sometimes usage, Turgenev's included, suggests that *obshchestvo* was synonymous with "the educated classes," but then it would have included many government functionaries. If that interpretation is too broad, one limited to authors, publicists, and journalists (and Turgenev sometimes uses the word in this meaning) is obviously too narrow. If nothing else, allowance has to be made for readers who responded with sympathy to what those people wrote.

Subsequent commentators have not had notably better luck in explaining the term. *Obshchestvo* is often equated with the Russian intelligentsia, or is made a forerunner of the intelligentsia. That is misleading in a crucial respect. The intelligentsia consisted of men with little or no stake in the prevailing order and were therefore

18. The idea that tropes and metaphors condition, rather than merely ornament or simplify, modes of thought has been powerfully expressed by Kenneth Burke, *A Grammar of Motives* (Berkeley, 1969), in the chapter "Four Master Tropes," pp. 403–517.

open to new ideas, whereas most members of *obshchestvo* were very much a part of the system they scorned.[19] The task of *obshchestvo* was specifically a transcendence of what existed, a confrontation with the prevailing order, not an abrupt and innovative beginning. Finally, *obshchestvo* defies easy definition; and that perhaps is the point. Although there was a consensus regarding its goal—to provide a moral alternative to the government—there was little understanding of how to translate that goal into concrete social action. Contemporaries ardently believed in the existence of *obshchestvo*, but it was less a real entity than a symbol of desperate hope.[20]

Though the term is used in discussing earlier periods, it is only after the Crimean War that it connotes a political entity, for it was not till then that *obshchestvo* evolved even the beginnings of a political strategy. *Obshchestvo* was not a party, since it had no defined program. Even a word like "group" suggests a stricter organization than existed. To call it "a collection of like-minded men" is closer to the mark but a bit misleading, since the members of *obshchestvo* were like-minded on only one point. *Obshchestvo* was a loose alliance of men with various political aims and engaged in

19. Definitions based the role of the intelligentsia are further complicated by the notorious difficulty of establishing that group's composition and origin. Two excellent attempts, which are also relevant to the present discussion, are Martin Malia, "What Is the Intelligentsia?" in *The Russian Intelligentsia*, ed. Richard Pipes (New York, 1961), pp. 1–18; and Michael Confino, "Intellectuals and Intellectual Traditions in Eighteenth and Nineteenth Century Russia," *Daedalus*, CI (Spring 1972), 117–144.

20. One of the few historians who has studied the phenomenon in detail puts it this way: "To begin to understand late Tsarist Russia we must restore the concept of *obshchestvo*. Until the revolution this term was ubiquitous in Russia, the shibboleth of scholarly works on modern Russian history. The society of educated men, in which the intelligentsia *per se* were at most ministers, became one of the principal groupings in the nation. For the salient feature of educated Russia in the nineteenth century was the cleavage between *pravitel'stvo* [the government] and *obshchestvo*, a rift as deep and irreparable as between 'court' and 'country' in Stuart England." Anthony Netting, "Russian Liberalism: Years of Promise, 1842–1855," unpublished diss. (Columbia, 1970), p. 20. Nicholas Riasanovsky, *A Parting of the Ways: Government and the Educated Public in Russia: 1801–1855* (Oxford, 1976), and A. A. Kornilov, *Obshchestvennoe dvizhenie pri Alekksandre II* (Moscow, 1909), also contain valuable information about *obshchestvo*.

In this book I shall use the word "*obshchestvo*" instead of trying to translate it into English; when I use "society," which is the literal translation, I am referring not to *obshchestvo* but to the existing order, which was largely controlled by the central government.

various pursuits who were bound together by the wish to introduce alternate values into the dominant culture. In writing novels that symbolically projected that wish onto a map of Russian life, Turgenev became one of its chief spokesmen.

Turgenev's imaginative division of Russia into spheres suggests a cultural perspective of long standing: his picture of an enclave distanced from a rapacious reality seems a form of pastoralism, which in fact enjoyed a resurgence of popularity in the nineteenth century. There are important differences in emphasis, however. The modern pastoral ideal flourished in countries suffering through the first stages of capitalism; the dream of a natural paradise was an antidote to the reality of the machine. As a student of the phenomenon in America has noted, "Since Jefferson's time, the forces of industrialization have been the chief threat to the bucolic image of America."[21] To Turgenev the threat seemed to come from a different direction. At the time he wrote his novels, industrialization was still in the future for Russia. More important, economic forces of any sort had to appear of secondary importance compared to the constant and intrusive displays of political power. As in no other nineteenth-century nation where the dominant public values were perceived as threatening, in Russia the government was viewed as the agency of corruption. Not technology but an ever-encroaching bureaucracy was the enemy.

In the four novels that Turgenev wrote between 1856 and 1861, he rarely acknowledges the enemy explicitly. His averted glance, which he focuses instead on the representatives of his own camp, indicates anxiety about the overwhelming odds, not ignorance that a battle rages. He depicts only three characters who actively serve in the government, though that was a main occupation among noblemen of the period; and two of these characters are granted only very brief appearances, as if Turgenev did not want to monumentalize their noxious power. In *On the Eve* he employs a stylistic device that further mutes any appearance of strength in a governmental functionary: the movements of Kurnatovsky, a Secretary of the Senate, are reported only in a letter written by Elena, thus passing

21. Leo Marx, *The Machine in the Garden* (New York and London, 1967), p. 26.

them through the prism of her critical judgment. In fact, though she seeks to dismiss Kurnatovsky as cold and prosaic, Elena must admit that he is also capable, intelligent, determined. In *Fathers and Sons* Turgenev devotes a short chapter to Koliazin, a bureaucrat sent by the central government to investigate a local political dispute. Koliazin is an ambitious fraud, his officious manner does not disguise his selfishness; but significantly, there is no hint that he will pay for his flaws or even be forced to acknowledge them. Koliazin can even condescend to the hero Bazarov, whose talent everyone else is forced to admit. When the two encounter one another at a ball, their eyes meet momentarily, but Koliazin's self-confidence does not waver. It is as if Turgenev could conceive of no realistic way of diminishing the government's aura of omnipotence.

The epilogue to *Rudin* is the single instance when Turgenev allows himself to explore the nature of the government's power. Rudin and Lezhnev meet accidentally in a small provincial town several years after the main events of the plot. Lezhnev is on his way to fulfill his obligation to administer an army recruitment, while Rudin is traveling to an enforced confinement at his home, the penalty for allegedly subversive activity. Both men, that is, are beyond the benign influence of the manor house; and both have become subject to bureaucratic restraints. We are made to recognize the government's encompassing sway in the world at large: it effects compliance not only through outright punishment but through insidious administrative demands. Significantly, as Rudin and Lezhnev sit and talk over their wine, they comport themselves as perfect equals. That Rudin has briefly rebelled against the prevailing order and Lezhnev routinely accepted it is a distinction they do not consider. In the sphere of the world that is controlled by the government, all actions appear to have equivalently little purpose.

A resistance to such a weakening of the capacity to make moral discriminations is, indeed, one of the main characteristics of life around Turgenev's manor houses. Most of the individuals who live in that enclave are ineffectual; but not equally. Turgenev always implies shades of difference that allow their actions to be arranged along an ethical spectrum. Turgenev's talent for making fine distinctions is exemplified in a scene in *Rudin* in which he depicts Lezhnev visiting his neighbor Lasunskaia to discuss the boundary of their

DOUGLAS COLLEGE LIBRARY

abutting lands. When Lezhnev arrives, Lasunskaia immediately begins to scold him for his unsociability. By way of clinching her argument, she declares, "Vous êtes des nôtres" (S, VI, 277), and indeed she is correct. Lezhnev's manner during this encounter, his sense of decorum and his polite ironies, not to mention his easy understanding of the French in which the observation is made, confirm Lasunskaia's claim. The very purpose of the visit—since landowning in Russia was limited to a certain few individuals—establishes a commonality of values. Their similarities do not give Lezhnev and Lasunskaia an identical perspective on contemporary Russia; they only denote a common foundation, upon which each builds in a different way. In fact, Lezhnev scorns Lasunskaia's intellectual pretensions and believes she only pays lip service to humanitarian principles. He meets her frivolous comments with a stony silence and departs abruptly. In all, the scene is a remarkable depiction of contrary moods and conflicting goals constrained by social convention, of disagreement held in check by overriding agreement.

An awareness of the fact that differences need not lead to a severing of all bonds was crucial to the existence of *obshchestvo*. Because *obshchestvo* consisted of various factions, arguments occurred with regularity and alarming intensity. But bitter as these often were, they did not destroy the alliance. A polemical opponent was treated not as an alien but as an uncomprehending deviate from an obvious truth, to which he might still be persuaded to return.

Historians have tended to emphasize the disagreements within *obshchestvo*, and for good reason: they contain the seeds of much subsequent Russian history, particularly the disputes between liberals and radicals which burst forth with new ferocity at the beginning of the twentieth century. Though correct, that interpretation of Russian history distorts the daily attitudes of men living in the post-Crimean War period. The government's centuries-long dominance of the political arena made it a natural target of liberals and radicals alike. Strife among the different factions constituting the opposition would develop in time; first the very idea of opposition had to be solidified.[22]

22. The following comment by Chernyshevsky is worth noting. It simultaneously suggests the broad range of the composition of *obshchestvo* and its predominating

Though the composition of *obshchestvo* made it an unstable phenomenon, always on the verge of exploding into its diverse elements, it was rather its relation to the rest of the world which determined its existence. When *obshchestvo* fell apart—historians date the event variously—it was because its strategy via-à-vis the government failed.[23] That released the spirit of antagonism within *obshchestvo* which its members previously had worked to contain.

Conceived as an adversary entity, *obshchestvo* had continually to assert itself, had continually to counter the influence of the government; but because *obshchestvo* almost altogether lacked strong political power, it had to proceed tentatively, finding a position that would neither inspire governmental repression nor entail a retreat to the merely abstract complaining that had characterized Russian intellectual life before the Crimean War. Turgenev's response, while in Rome, to the news that some *obshchestvo* members were celebrating the coming of emancipation, typifies *obshchestvo's* general position. "I liked the idea of the luncheon. But now is not the time to make noise" (*P*, III, 192).

The strategy of *obshchestvo* was like that of a boxer who knows he cannot win but who is determined to extend the match for as long as possible in the hope of exposing the failings of his opponent. The

---

mentality: "The incompatibility between the convictions of the Slavophiles, whose organ *Russian Talk* wishes to be, and the convictions of people against whom they argue touches on many important questions. But in still more essential aspirations the opponents coincide; of this we are convinced. We wish for light and truth—so also does *Russian Talk;* we resist the mean, the base—so also does *Russian Talk;* we consider our complete enemy at the moment to be ignorant apathy, deadly weakness of soul, false meretriciousness—*Russian Talk* does also. Our agreement in our essential aims is so strong that argument is possible only about abstract and therefore foggy questions. As soon as the talk turns to the firm soil of reality . . . there is no real disagreement." N. G. Chernyshevsky, "Zametki o zhurnalakh," Mai 1856 goda," *Polnoe sobranie sochinenii,* III, 651. Chernyshevsky's tone is both despairing and rallying. Precisely because Russian life represents a catalogue of fatal flaws, it is urgent that all individuals seeking to resist evil should join together, whether they be radical like Chernyshevsky, conservatives like the Slavophiles, or liberals like Turgenev.

23. Franco Venturi, in his magisterial work *Roots of Revolution* (New York, 1966), suggests that the critical date was 1859, when the terms of the Emancipation Act were becoming clear and opposition to the government was splitting along lines of economic self-interest. See pp. 156 ff. I shall argue that the ideal of *obshchestvo* continued to be important until 1861, when the Emancipation Act was published.

For an interesting survey of events leading to the *creation* of *obshchestvo*, see Riasanovsky, *A Parting of the Ways.*

following statement by Herzen reveals this mixture of belligerence and weakness:

> It is time to stop playing at being soldiers. Let us leave the government to govern, and we will keep busy with our own affairs. For this we will retire from the service; the economy must be rebuilt, children educated, laborers made out of landowner's children.
> We will weaken the government with out nonparticipation. . . . From a sense of obligation, they [the bureaucrats] must stay with the government, like rats with a sinking ship.
> But we will be off by ourselves (*sami soboi*).[24]

Herzen's statement reveals the essence of *obshchestvo*. It was less an established political entity with a specific program than a spirit of dismay struggling to give itself form—whose existence in itself would constitute a sufficient political program. For as Herzen suggests, Russian political life after the Crimean War was designed to deny even a degree of power to those who were outside the central government. The government, precisely because its omnipotence had been put into doubt by the military fiasco, was all the more sensitive to anything resembling political independence.

A long historiographic tradition, including both prerevolutionary and Soviet historians, argues that the Emancipation Act was proof that the government had to bend to meet the demands of nongovernmental forces. Prerevolutionary historians generally claim that individuals who were repelled by serfdom exerted sufficient moral weight to cause the government to abolish the institution, while Soviet historians are more apt to insist that the Emancipation Act was the government's cunning way of forestalling rebellion by an increasingly discontented peasantry. Recently, however, several American historians have argued persuasively that the Emancipation was not at all a concession by the government but a step to tighten its hegemony.[25] The system binding all Russians to the centralized apparatus, which over the years had developed some slackness, was streamlined and rationalized. If the government of

---

24. A Gertsen, "Za piat' let," *Kolokol*, No. 72 (June, 1860).
25. The most extensive presentation of this view is in Helj Aulik Bennett, "The *Chin* System and the Raznochintsy in the Government of Alexander III, 1881–1894," unpublished diss. (University of California, Berkeley, 1973). A portion has appeared in *California Slavic Studies*, X (1977), 1–44.

Alexander II showed fewer signs of the overt repression that characterized the reign of Nicholas I, it made up for that with its greater bureaucratic efficiency.

Government policy was not the only obstacle to the purpose of *obshchestvo*. Many Russians, though progressive in outlook, found that opposing the government required a considerable psychological wrench. "Playing at soldiers," as Herzen called it, exerted a tenacious attraction. Given Russia's history, cooperation with the government seemed natural, especially for members of the nobility. The nobility was beholden to the government for economic benefits, in the form of commercial privileges and loans from the state treasury, and for political safeguards, including the maintenance of order in a countryside that sometimes seemed on the brink of chaos. The government was the banker and policeman of the nobility, which implied that it should be supported, not resisted.[26] But even the radical *raznochintsy*, who did not have a vested interest in the existing order, often yielded to the government's insidious influence.[27] The belief of Chernyshevsky, acknowledged spokesman of the radicals, that he could publish in the official organ *The Military Journal* without compromising himself symbolizes the uncertain situation. The government was the enemy, corrupt and corrupting; but because it was ubiquitous, there appeared to be no choice but to accept its auspices.[28]

The ultimate dilemma of *obshchestvo* was that it possessed a principle—the need for a moral alternative to the government—but

26. The nature and extent of the nobility's ties to the government are detailed in M. Aleksandrov, *Gosudarstvo, biurokratiia i absoliutizm* (St. Petersburg, 1910).

27. "*Raznochintsy*" literally means "men between the ranks," connoting Russians who by accident of birth or of bureaucratic inefficiency fit into none of the established social categories. Though "radical" is a somewhat misleading epithet (they were radical only by the standards of the time), I shall nevertheless use that term hereafter, since the *raznochintsy* were often joined by men who shared their political outlook but not their social background.

28. Even *The Contemporary*, supposedly the most outspoken outlet for radical opinion, seemed occasionally to fall within the sphere of government influence. B. P. Koz'min, "Vystuplenie Gertsena protiv Sovremennika v 1859 godu," in *Iz istorii revoliutsionnoi mysli y Rossii* (Moscow, 1961), argues that Herzen's essay was in part inspired by the belief that *The Contemporary* was cooperative with the recently established paragovernmental committee to oversee all publications. The purpose of the committee was to advise, but the real aim was censorship, helped along by the journals themselves, as had happened recently in Berlin and Vienna.

lacked the institutional framework to express it. Only an institution could keep *obshchestvo* away from the government's fatal embrace; but it seemed that all Russia's institutions had been preempted by the government. The Church groveled like a penitent. The Military was traditionally the Emperor's toy (the attempt, at the beginning of the 1860s, to make the Navy partially autonomous only proved the strength of centralization). Commerce could not serve as the basis of an independent social force, since the government was by far the country's biggest buyer and seller and in effect held a lease on the major industries. The existence of chartered private clubs, like those which thrived in eighteenth- and nineteenth-century Europe, might have alleviated the frustration of *obshchestvo* by providing a forum for nonofficial ideas, whether scientific, economic, or from some other field; but all private clubs had been outlawed in 1822, except for a few charitable organizations. Russia's professions also provided no outlet, since they were either underdeveloped or in the service of the government. Indeed, the legal profession, the grand path to public influence for many Englishmen and Frenchmen, was in Russia a tool of government policy, helping to shape the Emancipation Act to meet the government's needs.[29] Given the bleakness of the social picture, it becomes evident that the famous vitality of the "thick journals" during this period was, to a considerable degree, a merit they acquired by default: *obshchestvo* could find no sturdier place than their flimsy pages to express its energy.[30]

Turgenev's proposal in 1859 to establish a journal devoted to the question of emancipation reveals in the space of a few pages the uncertainty constraining men like him. The proposal is dispassionate,

29. See Richard Wortman, *The Development of a Russian Legal Consciousness* (Chicago and London, 1976).

30. One of the strongest recent claims for the power of the forces opposing the government is by Terence Emmons, *The Russian Landed Gentry and the Emancipation of 1861* (Cambridge, 1968). He remarks, "By the reign of Alexander II it had become clear—abundantly clear in the years 1857–62—that there had come into existence a 'public opinion' ultimately the product of the expansion of education and the means of communication, and that the autocracy, if it were to undertake significant change, would henceforth be constrained by this public opinion in one way or another" (p. 416). This is true, but at the same time, "public opinion" was always threatening to disappear in the face of government encroachment; what is more, contemporaries acutely felt this threat. Thus, e.g., Dobroliubov in "Sbornik, izdavaemyi studentami S. Peterburskogo Universiteta," *Sobranie Sochinenii*, II, 93–100, could complain bitterly that university journals, purportedly giving voice to independent opinion, were actually controlled by the government.

almost official, as befits the occasion; but underlying it is anxiety and uncertainty. That is not surprising, given Turgenev's view of his task: *The Economic Journal*, which would appear at the moment of greatest controversy over the impending emancipation, was to be a vehicle for defining the relationship between the nobility and the government. They key paragraph is:

> The point is that, acknowledging the inarguable fact of the weak feeling of sympathy among the nobility for the views of the government, one must put the following alternatives: whether [the nobility ought] to yield to the government alone [the right]—by its measures and action, and by its interference and influence—to defeat the resistance of the nobility, to force it to make concessions, to override its fears; or for [the nobility] to offer to the government that independent but active and honest cooperation of thought and work without which the most limitless power cannot establish anything enduring or sturdy. [*S*, xv, 236]

Turgenev wants to establish the government and the nobility as equal partners in a joint venture; but the project is tainted before it begins by his knowledge that the government holds all the advantages. His threat in the last words of the quoted passage—vague, and referring to an unspecified time—only emphasizes the government's present strength. Indeed, four pages after the passage quoted, Turgenev exhibits the very flaw he has been cautioning against. He says, "In a word, the journal will be, despite all its independence and dispassionate editorship, despite the various opinions that will be allowed in it—a government journal in its very essence" (*S*, xv, 240). His concession is all the more striking because journalism was considered sacrosanct, supposedly most resistant to government influence. Lacking a solid institutional base, progressives like Turgenev found it difficult to set out a program: every move toward autonomy threatened to collapse into an acceptance of political servitude.[31]

31. Writing of a slightly later period, Leopold Haimson pinpoints the cause of the psychological problem of those opposing Russian autocracy: "The ultimate absence, in their confrontation with the redoubtable and omnipresent state power, of the sense—so pervasive among English country gentlemen in the eighteenth century House of Commons and among deputies of the French Third Estate in 1789—that they constituted in their own right the adequate representatives of country and nation." See "The Parties and the State: The Evolution of Political attitudes," in Michael Cherniavsky, ed., *The Structure of Russian History* (New York, 1970), p. 317.

The structure of Turgenev's novels reflects the precarious position of *obshchestvo*. He seems unsure of the exact location of the "circle," that space set apart from prevailing corruption; it is less a particular Russian institution than the symbol of a hope. In *Fathers and Sons*, as we shall see, he associated the "circle" with the Russian family (he had been moving gradually in that direction: *On the Eve* was in manuscript entitled *A Moscow Family*), but the Kirsanovs represent a blueprint for an ideal, not an empirical fact. In the other novels from this period, Turgenev pitched his argument still more fully on a symbolic level. The depiction in non-Russian nineteenth-century fiction of escapes from social influence provides a measure of Turgenev's inability to deal in historically specifiable entities. In *Wilhelm Meister*, a secret society; in *Hard Times*, a circus troupe; in *Moby Dick*, a whaling ship; in *The Bethrothed*, the church: these avenues of escape provide success in varying degrees, but the capacity of Goethe, Dickens, Melville, Manzoni, and many other contemporary authors, to conceive of such concrete possibilities stands in sharp contrast to Turgenev's procedures.

Turgenev had to project the idea of a haven where a haven did not in actuality exist. As a result, his novels often appear to be permeated by an air of great nervousness. He can appear remarkably lucid in describing even the most turbulent emotions, but it is the lucidity of a man struggling to hold back an always threatening chaos. His endings are invariably sad, as if resistance were possible only for a limited time. In *Fathers and Sons* Bazarov dies alone, his soul swept up into the incomprehensible expanse of the universe. In *On the Eve*, Elena is left widowed and in a foreign land, cut off from all familiar ties. In *Nest of the Nobility*, Lavretsky is a broken man, his sole hope being that the succeeding generation will do better than he did. In these works Turgenev implies that despair will overtake those who fail to exploit the capacities of a haven, and in the epilogue to *Rudin* he makes that belief explicit. Rudin says to Lezhnev, "I never knew how to build. And it is quite a trick my friend, to build when you have no ground under you, when it is necessary to build with you yourself as your own foundation" (*S*, VI, 359). Rudin has just recounted how he has successively served as a manager of a large estate, introducing new principles of agronomy (which in the context of the times implies tampering with serfdom), attempted to construct a navigational canal, and, finally, taught at a provincial *gymnazium*, instilling hope of a university education in students usually resigned to much less. The list of Rudin's occupations is impressive by any standard; compared to what the other characters in the book do, it assumes a Herculean dimension. But Lezhnev nonetheless dismisses all Rudin's efforts as irrelevant, and Rudin agrees with the judgment. Evidently, successful action requires more than energy and diligence. As Rudin's evocative and troubling image suggests, to achieve his purpose a Russian progressive must proceed from some firmer ground than an individual by himself can command. He must find some foundation, some source of alternative values, from which to propel himself against a recalcitrant world.

The episode closes with a passage that is unlike anything else in the book. As Rudin parts from Lezhnev for the last time, Turgenev writes:

> And in the yard the wind picked up and sounded a sinister howl as it beat forcefully and angrily against the rattling windows. The long autumn night set in. Lucky is he who on such nights sits alone in the shelter of his house, he who has a warm corner.... And may the Lord help all homeless wanderers. [S, VI, 368]

The outburst is almost out of control. Turgenev's style, so decorous throughout the book, suddenly seems to have exploded in a whine, a cry of helplessness in the face of the unremitting threat of homelessness. The passage makes clear what is elsewhere only implied—that maintaining the privileged circle, that place apart from the savagely corrupting world, is no easy task, however smugly or knowingly the inhabitants behave. It is an imaginative action of the most uncertain sort.

In 1860 Turgenev and Annenkov conceived an elaborate project for raising the level of literacy. They named their proposed organization The Society for the Dissemination of Literacy and Elementary Education, and Turgenev wrote to a number of people trying to enlist their support. The plan never got off the ground; but the incident shows Turgenev's awareness of contemporary pedagogical concerns.[32] As we shall see, pedagogical issues play vital roles in his

---

32. See "Proekt programmy Obschestva dlia rasprostraneniia gramotnosti i pervonachal'nogo obrazovaniia" (S, XV, 245–252).

novels. He stresses that the hero of *Fathers and Sons* has learned his politics in the medical faculty of St. Petersburg University, the most radical division of Russia's university system, that the hero of *Rudin* has acquired his intellectual style while studying Hegel in Moscow, and that the heroines in all the novels are who they are because of a domestic upbringing that has permitted them great freedom. In *Nest of the Nobility* the education of Lavretsky is such a prominent theme that the book was reviewed in the *Journal of the Ministry of National Education*.[33]

Given the task Turgenev set himself, his interest in pedagogy is not surprising. Education was the area in which *obshchestvo* made its greatest effort to acquire an institutional base. The vigorous pedagogical debate that existed in the years 1856–1861 was also a debate about the introduction of alternate values into the dominant culture. In pursuit of its goal, *obshchestvo* was able to obtain such new regulations as the one (in 1860) that permitted private individuals instead of government departments to finance and manage grade schools.[34] But even when the schools remained nominally under government control, they appeared as uniquely suitable places for *obshchestvo* to gain a foothold. Schools were set somewhat apart from the world at large, in two ways: they involved individuals still too young to be fully implicated in the prevailing order, and they were often physically removed from the ongoing social life, by a tradition of extraterritoriality in the case of universities and by location in the countryside in the case of many other institutes. The school seemed to represent a breathing space where individuals might gather their strength before confronting the world. As such, it fit neatly into the central strategy of *obshchestvo*.

One indication of the great interest that pedagogy evoked during the period is that the subject engaged many writers whose main concerns lay elsewhere. Among others, Dobroliubov, Cher-

33. A Piatkovsky, "Dvorianskoe gnezdo Turgeneva," *Zhurnal ministerstva narodnogo prosveshcheniia*, CII (1859), 95–111.

34. The most extensive treatment of *obshchestvo* activity in education during this period is by V. Z. Smirnov in *Reforma nachal' noi i srednei shkoly v 60-kh godakh XIX v.* (Moscow, 1954). Smirnov reports not only on the various committees who were charged with considering educational reform but also on the significant writings concerning the question that appeared in official and nonofficial journals.

nyshevsky, Pisarev, and Tolstoi, as well as Turgenev, addressed themselves to educational questions. Sometimes these writers discussed particular cases, such as the opening of a new school or an innovative teaching method, but more often education served as a springboard to other issues. It provided an opportunity to focus on a comprehensible part of society and yet imply a view of the whole. As *The Contemporary* put it, in a burst of eloquence: "The school question passes over into more general questions—about human individuality, about the laws of social existence, about economic life, about the laws of civilization and social education.[35] *The Contemporary* began to devote considerable space to pedagogical questions, but what is even more important is that several new specialized journals came into existence.[36] They were private journals, not government publications, and they were designed expressly to voice the opinions of *obshchestvo* without having recourse to the official *Journal of the Ministry of National Education*. True, the level of debate in these unofficial journals was generally not elevated. A typical issue of one featured such articles as "What Is Upbringing?," "A Doctor's Advice to Mothers," and "The Significance of Morally Defective Children," as well as a discussion of the proposal to eliminate backs on classroom benches.[37] The style was most often a passionate assertion of commonplaces. But beneath the bland exterior was a striking consistency of assumptions. Virtually all the writers in the nonofficial pedagogical journals insisted that the school must be an autonomous institution and that it should foster the student's inherent strengths instead of inculcating society's norms. Even the inane discussion about eliminating the backs of schoolroom benches was to the point, since its author argued that such a manner of instilling proper deportment was mechanical, and promoted unthinking servility.

35. Quoted in Eikhenbaum, *Lev Tolstoi*, p. 102.
36. These included *Russkoi pedagogicheskii vestnik* (*The Russian Pedagogical Herald*) and *Russkii uchitel'* (*The Russian Teacher*); and the already existing *Journal for Upbringing* (*Zhurnal dlia Vospitaniia*) became much more active and adopted a new editorial policy. Also, *The Contemporary* began to devote considerably more space to pedagogical questions, and its chief writer on this topic, F. Tol', was among the most outspoken critics of government educational policy.
37. All these articles appeared in *Zhurnal dlia vospitaniia*, 1, No. 1 (1857).

To a certain extent, of course, *obshchestvo* was interested in reforming the substance of education. Such matters as curriculum, teacher training, and theories of classroom procedure were discussed with remarkable vehemence, and for the first time Russians began to pay serous attention to Western philosophers of education, such as Pestalozzi and Locke (whose "Some Thoughts Concerning Education" was translated in *The Contemporary*). Nevertheless, the overriding concern was structural rather than substantive. Educational questions were an aspect of the political aim of *obshchestvo*: to be close enough to Russian life to influence it but not so close as to collapse into the general perniciousness. Once that topographical problem was solved, it was felt, other matters would prove more tractable.

Maintaining education at a carefully calibrated distance from the world proved immensely difficult. Schools *seemed* good ground for *obshchestvo* to exercise its strategy, education *seemed* potentially an autonomous institution, but suspicion persisted that government control was actually total, merely temporarily disguised to meet the changed political situation. Long-standing tradition was hard to dismiss. Education in Russia had alternately been relegated to the extreme periphery of society, set to exploring obscure or otherworldly matters, or indentured fully to the service of the state.[38] In 1856, it was the latter danger that appeared more urgent. Under Nicholas I, Russian schools after 1848 had been largely transformed into training grounds for future bureaucrats. A policy that one historian has aptly named "state utilitarianism" was strictly enforced: by the end of Nicholas' reign there were more schools under the jurisdiction of the various government departments, all seeking to stock their bureaucracies, than under the jurisdiction of the Ministry of Education.[39] For a time there was talk that the universities should

38. The best general history of Russian education is by N. A. Konstantinov and V. Z. Smirnov in *Istoriia pedagogiki* (Moscow, 1955). In English, consult Nicholas Hans, *History of Russian Education* (London, 1934). It is perhaps worth noting the recent contention by John Talbot, "The History of Education," *Daedalus*, C (Winter, 1971), 133–150, that the history of education is in general still an underdeveloped field; this view is particularly applicable to the field of Russian education.

39. P. N. Miliukov, "Universitety v Rossii," in *Entsiklopedicheskii slovar'* (St. Petersburg, 1890), LXIII, 791.

The Novelistic Imagination

close, because, notwithstanding drastic changes in their curriculum, they did not yield immediate resources to the state.[40] After 1855 the government's stated policy was less self-serving; but that was hard to accept on face value.

In fact, the attempt of *obshchestvo* to gain control of education after it had been so long under government domination created considerable anxiety. The markings of the previous occupant were everywhere. Who would vouch for the teachers? Could the school administrators forget their traditional allegiances? The very buildings and rooms, property of the state, breathed an air of homage to the government. Various proposals were made to shift the balance of influence, such as opening the annual oral examinations to the community. A more extreme idea, one that particularly attracted *obshchestvo*, was to remove education from the schools altogether and locate it in the home. Pirogov wrote: "The better part of our society is not without reason becoming more favorably inclined to the uses of a home education. Sooner or later, all become convinced that it is harmful to tear a young person from the circle of his family, or even from a [family] circle not his own."[41] Even someone as wary of the retrograde quality of Russian family life as Chernyshevsky endorsed domestic education.[42]

The proposal for an "open university," which circulated at the end of the 1850s, shows the delicate effort of *obshchestvo* to promote its alternate values. Although the model was taken from progressive France and had many democratic features (lectures free and open to the general public, elimination of student uniforms, abolishment of the tradition of extraterritoriality), it seemed to many that the result in Russia would only be an exposure of the university to the general

40. For a contemporary account of this episode, see A. V. Nikitenko, *Dnevnik* (Leningrad, 1955–56), pp. 320 ff.
41. Pirogov, "Ob ustave novoi gimnazii," p. 306.
42. N. G. Chernyshevsky, "Sleduet li otdavat' predpochtenie shkolnomu vospitaniiu pered domashnim?" *Literaturnoe nasledstvo*, Nos. 25–26 (1936), 124–131. Cf. Dobroliubov's comment in "Mysli ob uchrezdenii otkrytykh zhenskikh shkol," *Sobranie sochinenii*, II, 364: "Thinking on the subject calmly and rationally they [the supporters of institutional education] will themselves see that throwing children, and especially girls, out of the family . . . can only be justified by extreme material or moral necessity."

113

corruption. As one professor who was opposed to the proposal commented, "The public in the lecture halls would have been directly under the jurisdiction of the city police."[43] Professor Chicherin's speech during the "open university" debate is worth quoting because its enflamed language shows clearly that the specific question was actually part of the general flight from a besetting evil:

> The noise of passions that worry society at large should not penetrate the walls of this institution. Here we must, by going deep within ourselves, prepare ourselves in peace for the business of life or for useful edification. For you [students] the time of activity, passionate involvement in social questions, will come in its time. . . . The man who is called to life and activity must guard those rare moments when he can gather himself up internally and direct his glance at the idea that is close to his soul.[44]

In a nicely ambiguous phrase, Pirogov referred to the universities as "the barometers of society,"[45] which could suggest that the university was the indicator of values which society at large would shortly adopt; or it could suggest that the university was merely an instrument that passively recorded the values that already existed. In fact, the university—and education generally—hovered between these possibilities.

The continually shifting balance of forces did not, however, make members of *obshchestvo* more willing to excuse any apparent deviations from the alliance's principles; rather the uncertain situation seemed only to heighten anxiety in a way that made criticism quick and extreme. It is worth pausing over one such incident, because it shows clearly what was at stake for *obshchestvo*. Though Pirogov's "The Questions of Life" had been welcomed as an innovation, many of its points had been anticipated in an article published several months before, also in *The Naval Almanac*. A. Bem had also argued that education must promote the harmonious development of all strengths inherent in the individual, that contemporary society was seriously flawed, and that the schools were not doing their jobs properly. What finally accounts for the significance attributed to "The Questions of Life" is Pirogov's insistence that the educative process might be

43. Quoted in V. D. Spasovich, *Sochineniia* (St. Petersburg, 1889–1902), II, 63.
44. Quoted in N. Barsukov, *Zhizn' i trudi M. P. Pogodina* (St. Petersburg, 1904), XVIII, 260–261.
45. N. I. Piorgov, *Izbrannye pedagogicheskie sochineniia*, p. 99.

The Novelistic Imagination

meaningfully separated from society. The form of Pirogov's essay, built on the device of a supposed passage between separate spheres of activity, implies a distinctly segmented world. Bem, on the other hand, tied school and life inextricably together. "The bad tendencies and shortcomings of people's upbringings," he said, "are always linked with bad tendencies of society in general and cannot be otherwise improved than with the improvement of the society."[46]

That contemporaries perceived in Pirogov's essay a special view of the social structure is confirmed by the reaction of Dobroliubov, who first hailed Pirogov and happily concurred in what he took as Pirogov's basic idea, "that the ideals of education are hopelessly out of harmony with society."[47] But beginning with his essay "Literary Trifles," Dobroliubov began to attack the man he had recently hailed as the hope of Russian education.[48] The immediate issue was Pirogov's endorsement, in his capacity as curator of the Odessa school system, of a set of rules permitting corporal punishment in the schools. Previously, Pirogov had passionately condemned such punishment, and Dobroliubov's attack was aimed first of all at the hypocrisy involved, a hypocrisy that Dobroliubov claimed was spreading among the liberals; they were all poseurs, and Pirogov's action was a perfect example of their behavior. One rule to which Pirogov subscribed angered Dobroliubov in particular. He quotes it in full:

> But it is impossible suddenly to eliminate the practice of whipping. As long as children who have been whipped at home continue to come to our educational institutes, it is difficult to think of another form of punishment (at least at first) in those instances where no delay is possible. For the time being there is nothing left to do but to assert the following rule: use this method with the utmost care, and only when disgraceful guilt requires speedy, strong, and instantaneous action.[49]

46. A. Bem, "O vospitanii," *Morskoi sbornik*, No. 1 (1856), p. 68.
47. N. A. Dobroliubov, "O znachenii avtoriteta v vospitanii," *Sobranie sochinenii*, I, 494.
48. N. A. Dobroliubov, "Literaturnye melochi proshlogo goda," *Sobranie sochinenii*, IV, 48-112. For an account of Dobroliubov's changing attitude toward Pirogov, see G. Berliner, "Literaturnye protivniki Dobroliubova," *Literaturnoe nasledstvo*, Nos. 25-26 (1936), 34-35.
49. Quoted in N. A. Dobroliubov, "Vserossiiskie illiuzii, razrushaemye rozgami," *Sobranie sochinenii*, VI, 15.

Whipping had to be allowed in the schools, since the practice existed in society in general; the schools had to accept the prevailing morality. In other words, the school had collapsed into life, its potential as an autonomous area nullified. It was Pirogov's disavowal of his original map of reality that accounts for Dobroliubov's change of opinion toward him. Pirogov had not only endorsed the morally despicable action of whipping students, but he had subverted a whole social strategy as well.

In defense of Pirogov it might be said that the immediate demands of his job forced his hand; and, more generally and more to the point of the present discussion, that fixing the proper distance between school and the world was a most delicate procedure. Neither too far removed nor too close to the general perniciousness—institutions are not easily manipulated to such a fine degree.

Turgenev's novels, though they address the same issues as were addressed in the discussions and writings of other progressives of the period, present the *obshchestvo* ideal with singular flexibility. In projecting a map of society onto the plane of literature, Turgenev endorsed a system of values and simultaneously tested it. His characters do not merely act but question their acts, or at least have them questioned by others. The novels, that is, do more than reflect contemporary Russian life: they construe it as a set of possibilities.

On the one hand, it seems ironic that the *obshchestvo* ideal, which was conceived with such great difficulty, should have been criticized almost as soon as it came into existence. On the other hand, it is clear that a part-whole vision of the world, such as *obshchestvo* promoted, has inherent flaws, which Turgenev had to acknowledge as he worked through the intricacies of his novels. A refusal to face up to the fullness of social life leads to constraints on all aspects of experience, even the most private. The next three chapters examine how Turgenev exposed the ill effects of *obshchestvo* politics on the capacity of Russians to make judgments, to enjoy work, and to fall in love—which were all intensely important matters to Turgenev himself. The *obshchestvo* ideal was both a great historical achievement and a means for Turgenev to escape the flaws of his personality; but the ideal produced distortions of its own. Turgenev, the eternal skeptic and scrutinizer of extravagant claims, was just the man to explore its ambiguities.

6.
Judgment: *Rudin*

〰〰

The daily life in *obshchestvo* circles is suggested by the following story told by Chernyshevsky:

> I assumed that [relations between Dobroliubov and Turgenev] were the same as between me and Turgenev: no fervent sympathy, but the considerable mutual regard of acquaintances, who having no desire to become more intimate are lacking also any desire to break relations . . . .
>
> Nekrasov [told me], "Could it be that you have not seen till now? Turgenev hates Dobroliubov." . . . Apparently, Dobroliubov had once said to Turgenev, who was boring him with alternately witty and amiable remarks, "Ivan Sergeevich, it bores me to talk with you, so let us stop this conversation,"—and he got up and crossed over to the other side of the room.[1]

According to Chernyshevsky, though the exasperated Turgenev several times subsequently tried to engage Dobroliubov in conversation, "Dobroliubov invariably walked away from him, either to the other side of the room, or into another room."

The most striking element in this anecdote is Dobroliubov's abruptness. He suddenly disavows the rules of social discourse. He does not argue with Turgenev or mock or insult him, all of which would have expressed hostility but would still have maintained a social connection. He simply walks away. Turgenev is not allowed to remonstrate or explain, because nothing that Turgenev could say would alter Dobroliubov's judgment. Indeed, Chernyshevsky

1. N. G. Chernyshevsky in *Turgenev v vospominaniiakh sovremennikov*, ed. V. V. Grigorenko (Moscow, 1969), I, 354–355.

makes clear that Turgenev's behavior even before the moment of rupture has been similarly discounted. Though Turgenev has been "witty and amiable," that does not count at all with Dobroliubov, who invokes more profound standards to measure Turgenev's character.

That Dobroliubov is the hero of this episode, Chernyshevsky its approving narrator, and Turgenev its villain has a political point. Differences between the liberal and radical members of *obshchestvo* inform the confrontation. But the episode also measures the extent of such differences. These are men who still meet in the same room with the hope of finding ideas in common. In 1859, when this incident took place, all of *obshchestvo* was still more concerned with its positions vis-à-vis the government than with its internal disagreements.

Chernyshevsky's anecdote is most interesting for what it says about a particular mode of judgment, rather than about political ideology. Indeed Turgenev provoked similar types of condemnation from men with whom he was in fairly close political agreement. His behavior invited suspicion of his deeper motivations; actions that contradicted the suspicion were swept aside as irrelevant. In his memoirs, Fet recounts an argument between Tolstoi and Turgenev that is remarkable for the singular melodrama that only these two mismatched friends could achieve, and yet resembles the encounter recounted by Chernyshevsky:

> "You can't imagine what scenes there were. My God! Turgenev starts to croak, squeezing his throat with his hand and making his eyes seem like those of a dying gazelle. 'I can't stand anymore, I have bronchitis,' and with tremendous strides he begins to walk back and forth through the three rooms.... Tolstoi lies on a Morocco sofa in the middle, intervening room and sulks, while Turgenev pulling open his short jacket, with his hands in his pockets, continues to walk back and forth through all three rooms....
>
> "'I will not permit him,' Tolstoi says, with flaring nostrils, 'to do anything to me out of spite. Look how he now is intentionally walking back and forth in front of me waggling his democratic haunches.' "[2]

Again it is Turgenev who is most active and remonstrative, seeking to maintain some degree of social communication; and again it is Turgenev who is declared devious, his apparent excitement dis-

2. A. A. Fet in *Turgenev v vospominaniiakh sovremennikov*, I, 185–186.

missed as a trick. There is no need for all such extravagant behavior, Tolstoi says, for Turgenev's basic insincerity is established.

Describing Turgenev in a letter, Tolstoi remarked that his habitual manner was only the "conceit of luxuriating in sincere or insincere self-chastisement."[3] The phrasing is revealing. Tolstoi is convinced that he can comprehend Turgenev fully and adequately; but in the eagerness to discount all obfuscatory gestures, to guard against the most subtle insincerity, the norms of language break down, as do the norms of conventional judgment. Sincere and insincere acts are crowded into an indiscriminate heap. Tolstoi's swaggering style does not altogether hide an irritable confusion about just what it is that is wrong with Turgenev.

That says something about Turgenev; it says as much about Tolstoi; but the most telling implication, far more encompassing, is the difficulty that *obshchestvo* in general had in finding a proper mode of judgment. A good indication of the dilemma is Dobroliubov's "Nikolai Vladimirovich Stankevich." The article was a reply to a review in the *Library for Reading* of Annenkov's recently published *Stankevich: His Correspondence and Biography*. The author of that review, V. Lkhovsky, had not discussed the merits of Annenkov's book at any length; instead he questioned why it should even exist. Stankevich, Lkhovsky held, was a man of no historical significance and therefore not worth commemorating. In general the influence of writers and intellectuals will "quickly disappear and fade; they do not have those enduring qualities that things carried over into life and activity possess."[4] And that applied all the more to Stankevich, who had written practically nothing but letters to friends.

Dobroliubov, even more than Chernyshevsky, his predecessor as the literary critic of *The Contemporary*, questioned the political energy and sincerity of the liberal members of *obshchestvo*. Lkhovsky's review seems, on the face of it, to conform closely to Dobroliubov's opinion that the men of the 1840s indulged in philosophical posturing at the expense of concrete activity. As the center of one of the most important intellectual circles of the 1830s

3. Quoted by B. M. Eikhenbaum, "Artistizm Turgeneva," *Moi vremennik* (Leningrad, 1929), p. 95.
4. V. Lkhovsky, "Nikolai Vladimirovich Stankevich. Perepiska i biografiia, napisannaia P. V. Annenkovym," *Biblioteka dlia chteniia*, CXLVIII (1858), 4.

and early 1840s, Stankevich symbolized all that Dobroliubov usually derided. But Dobroliubov defends both Annenkov's book and Stankevich himself. He enthusiastically seconds the view widely held among liberals that Stankevich "had a wonderful character, was a man of very brilliant intellect, lively awareness, and attractive nature."[5] These epithets describe habits of mind, and, in fact, Dobroliubov declares that Stankevich's practical inactivity is no cause for condemnation. In words that sound strange coming from a committed social activist, Dobroliubov announces the importance of private and contemplative values: "An individual who is highly honest and moral in his life deserves the respect of society, just for his honesty and moral worth."[6]

Appearances to the contrary, Dobroliubov is not making an exception in his usual score for the Superfluous Man. Dobroliubov never wavered in his demand for social action. In describing Stankevich, however, he focuses on the psychology of social action, which carries him beyond mere propaganda to more ambiguous ground.

Lkhovsky attacked Stankevich not only because Stankovich concerned himself with the life of the mind, but also because he had achieved his renowned intellectual harmony too easily. "In that battle that we witness in the development of many great men, there is great interest and edification, and the more difficult the battle and the greater the contradictions, the greater the edification."[7] The belief that only a struggle guarantees a true and passionate commitment to ideals was common among Russian intellectuals in the middle of the nineteenth century. The source of that belief, all but mentioned by Lkhovsky, was Belinsky, whose personal and intellectual tribulations were already legendary. Dobroliubov's own allegiance to Belinsky's memory was very strong, but he nonetheless refused to accede to Lkhovsky's argument. On the contrary, he proclaims Stankevich's natural and easy attainment of spiritual balance a great virtue. That Stankevich was "someone who never forced himself, and did not bother with that for which he did not experience a heartfelt attraction, did not load himself down with the chains

5. N. A. Dobroliubov, "Nikolai Vladimirovich Stankevich," *Sobranie sochinenii* (Moscow and Leningrad, 1961), II, 386.

6. Ibid., p. 396.

7. Lkhovsky, "*Stankevich. Perepiska i biographiia*," p. 6.

of moral penance, did not sacrifice himself for the uses of society"[8]—which some held against him—seems to Dobroliubov altogether praiseworthy. Stankevich's strength, in other words, was that his acts were always in perfect accord with his feelings; his visible gestures always matched who he was.

Dobroliubov's definition of Stankevich's character demands much of human behavior. It also entails a rationale for successful social action—more purposeful, in fact, than Lkhovsky's. It is only the extremity of Dobroliubov's desire to ensure the absolute authenticity of action that allows him to acquiesce in no action at all. In his scheme concrete actions, though necessary, are redundant: they are the overflow of who one is. Since Stankevich's nature was admirable, Dobroliubov as much as says, his behavior would necessarily have been good also: had he acted, it would have been with inner and outer states of being perfectly welded, with no chance of discrepancy. Lkhovsky's demand that individuals exert themselves in pursuit of social justice implies that they must wrench their characters in order to do good, and thereby guarantees that their actions will be insincere.

Though Dobroliubov could be a narrow-minded writer, shifting ideas about in order to prove limited ideological points, in his "Stankevich" article he reflects a widely held view. It was not simply that his laudatory estimate was confirmed by general opinion (including Turgenev's, who wrote an article recalling his friendship with Stankevich); more important is that Dobroliubov presents a picture of human nature in general that fits the demands of *obshchestvo*.[9] The claim that individuals should be judged by their inner qualities was elaborated repeatedly, in various contexts. Perhaps the treatment cited most often by contemporaries was the most compact. That was Pirogov's nine-line epigraph to his famous essay "The Questions of Life":

> "For what are you preparing your son?" someone asked me.
> "To be a man," I answered.
> "Don't you know," replied my interlocutor, "that men as such do

8. Dobroliubov, *Sobranie sochinenii*, II, 384.
9. Cf. Turgenev's description of Stankevich, "Vospominaniia o N. V. Stankeviche" (S, VI, 394): "In his whole being, in all his movements, there was a kind of graciousness, an unconscious distinction—as though he were the scion of a kingly stock but unaware of his origin.

not exist in the world? That "men" is merely an abstraction, completely unnecessary for society. We require businessmen, soldiers, mechanics, sailors, doctors, jurists, and not men."
    Is this true or not?[10]

"Man as such" is set against the various occupations of the world. A core of inner qualities, not visible behavior, is the primary standard of judgment. In fact, Pirogov does not altogether discount practical activity—the careful enumeration of occupations signals his awareness of that side of existence, and in the body of the essay (and in his other writings), Pirogov directly states that the economic and social facts of Russian life require that men work. His acknowledgement of the workaday world does not, however, alter his basic assumption. The inner self is paramount: when a man works, he is simply endowing that self with a visible form. The result of Pirogov's concession to the pressures of Russia's modernization is a very unstable view of human behavior. When action is conceived as an afterthought, a supplement to a persistent and underlying self, the possibility arises that the individual may, in choosing the wrong sort of activity, slip out of gear with who he really is. In effect, Pirogov's scheme simultaneously sanctions practical activity and demands that it be regarded with deep suspicion. He admits that Russia in 1856 is a world that is seemingly waiting to be remade politically and economically, but adds that even the slightest step in that direction may carry individuals away from their best qualities.

    Pirogov's writings are a direct outgrowth of the belief by *obshchestvo* that Russia was like a disease. "Man as such" must remain in touch with his true nature because the world is always ready to exploit him for its own corrupt ends. Only when there is not the slightest disharmony between inner and outer states of being will it be impossible for the world to intrude its own values. In a later essay, significantly entitled "Being and Seeming," Pirogov made his argument explicit. The immediate issue he was discussing was students' participation in amateur theatricals. To him that was hardly an innocuous topic, since it immediately raised the question of the consistency between the inner and outer man.

    It may be asked: Generally does correct moral pedagogy permit children and youth to appear before the public in a form more or less

10. N. I. Pirogov, "Voprosy zhizni," *Izbrannye pedagogicheskie sochineniia* (Moscow, 1952), p. 55.

distorted and, consequently, hypocritical for them? Are not true teachers obliged to look on the spiritual side of youth as a holy temple?... Does not the parent who permits the appearance of a youth in a distorted form at a public spectacle inculcate the principle of lies and hypocrisy in a receptive soul? In playing a role well, in assuming a studied pose, knowing how to make a gesture and how to adopt with alacrity a facial expression that shows false feeling, is not this, I say, a school for lies and deceit?[11]

Pirogov goes on to say that oral explanation and classroom reading should replace public performances, thus emphasizing that his complaint is not against dramatic literature as such. The issue is the development of a proper man. He insists that the core of inner qualities which constitutes a man's truest self is the final standard of judgment; action is good or bad to the extent that it conforms with that core. Since dramatic performances require the student to act in manner different from his natural one, they are necessarily bad. Of course, the idea that the theater promotes dissemblance, and thus damages morality, is a recurrent one in Christian cultures. But there was relatively little official distrust of the theater in Russia, where the Church had been instrumental in establishing the theatrical tradition, and there was certainly little criticism of dramatic readings in the schools. Pirogov's remarks must be understood as an attempt to meet *obshchestvo's* conflicting views of action in the post-Crimean War period.

The privileging of the inner self, making it a bastion of virtue in the midst of corruption, was a scheme that required careful elaboration. If placing virtue exclusively within each individual made it appear more resistant to prevailing evil, the result was also to make virtue very difficult to measure or to nourish. How does one deal with qualities locked away in individual consciousness? One area that seemed to offer tools for the task was education. Pedagogical issues like discipline (students who were obedient in the hope of reward as opposed to those who were truly good), curriculum (the teaching of skills, as opposed to the cultivation of humanistic impulses), and teaching method (inculcating facts by rote as opposed to

11. N. I. Pirogov, "Byt' i kazat'sia," *Izbrannye pedagogicheskie sochineniia* (Moscow, 1952), p. 112. It is an example of the radicals' enthusiasm for Pirogov's views that Dobroliubov endorsed his condemnation of theatrical readings. See N. A. Dobroliubov, "Rechi i otchet chitannye v torzhestvennom sobranii Moskovskoi prakticheskoi akademii," *Sobranie sochinenii*, IV, 303.

allowing the student to use his creative powers) closely paralleled the general concern about visible action as opposed to inherent character. Pedagogical writers during the post-Crimean War period almost invariably gave more weight to the side of the argument which endorsed "the inner man" or "a core nature" or some other term connoting an entity not visible to the untrained eye. A typical comment in a pedagogical journal was: "In general, upbringing must embrace the whole man as he is created by nature, and consequently upbringing must act on all his natural strengths and capabilities."[12] Another writer expressed the same idea more forcefully. "The fault," he wrote, "is often with the teachers. Wishing to see the quickest possible elimination of vices, they rush to the most efficacious and harshest means of discipline, which are often incompatible with the character of the boy and have a negative effect on him."[13]

Whatever concrete knowledge got imparted, the school was first of all an arena for the student's inner development, and teachers the cultivators of natural strengths. Even such professed exponents of scientific training as Dobroliubov and Pisarev argued for the priority of the inner man. It was a time when progressives of every stamp insisted that the authentic self had first to be nourished; meaningful practical activity would follow.

But the progressives' view of the individual's relationship to his world had unexpected implications. Though it arose as a way to resist oppression, from the need to husband one's personal strengths in a rapacious society, the privileging of the inner self promoted an evil of its own. To dwell insistently on the likelihood that manifest behavior does not coincide with real intentions is at once morally correct and morally dubious: the laudable desire to expose deceit coexists with the arrogant belief that one can penetrate another man's soul. Such a mode of judgment not only presupposes an unusual power of insight but also claims for itself a terrible finality—all rebuttals and remonstrances may be ignored as only another, more subtle variety of the insincerity that has already been

12. N. Redkin, "Chto takoe vospitanie?" *Zhurnal dlia vospitaniia*, I, No. 1 (1857), 272.

13. I. Fokht, "Ispravlenie nravstenno-izporchennykh detei," *Vospitanie*, I, No. 1 (1857), 601.

condemned. In fact, the more emphatically the inner man was privileged in this period, the more imperious did judgment become: as the relevant evidence was continually set at a more inaccessible level, correlatively greater self-confidence was needed to appraise it. As one pedagogical writer put it, "How rare in general are those teachers who are capable of appreciating in students that bright ray of inner development which is more valuable than all the shimmer of superficial knowledge!"[14] It follows that teachers who were capable of such discernment, as well as those who only thought they were, would brook no argument about their assessment.

The attempt to deal with such subliminal qualities as "inner development" often led writers into logical difficulties, though not often of the sort that they felt constrained to resolve. The stress on an essential nature was sufficiently an article of faith to require no explanation, and certainly no apology. Thus in the very first widely noted pedagogical article of the postwar period, A. Bem insisted that identical transgressions by different students deserved varying punishments, according to the relative "moral development" of each.[15] Bem did not offer a means for measuring this quality; nor was he in the least troubled by what seems a most disturbing possibility, that action in his scheme tends progressively to lose any moral content of its own. Indeed, pushed far enough, the argument suggests that action is not merely irrelevant but obfuscatory, since it distracts attention from that essential nature which alone is the basis of true judgment. As it happens, not everyone shied away from the last step. In an article entitled "Dull Students," Dobroliubov claimed that acting in accordance with school rules was proof of spiritual corruption.[16] In another article, Dobroliubov restated the reasons for his extreme judgment:

> Is it necessary to speak of that pernicious influence which the habit of unconditional obedience produces in the development of the mind? It would seem completely superfluous, and we would willingly pass by the point in silence if we did not have before our eyes the strange suggestion of Zelgerholm [a contemporary pedagogue], asserting that

14. "O shkolnoi ditsipline," unsigned article, *Vospitanie*, VII (1860), 18.
15. A. Bem, "O vospitanii," *Morskoi sbornik*, No. 1 (1856), 56.
16. N. A. Dobroliubov, "Tupye uchenki. Iz zapisok uchitelia," published without signature in *Zhurnal dlia vospitaniia*, I, No. 1 (1857), 171–192.

effort made by children to conquer their own will and submit to another develops moral strength."[17]

To Dobroliubov, as to *obshchestvo* generally, the reverse is true. The greater the effort required to act in a particular way, the more reason to regard the action with suspicion. Those who demand some strenuous wrench in consequence of which an individual would do good had only allowed for a chance of discrepancy between inner and outer self.

Dobroliubov's larger aim in this article, as elsewhere, was to foster active resistance to any form of prevailing authority, whether embodied by teachers, bureaucrats, or policemen. Not all members of *obshchestvo* were willing to follow him that far. Also, when Dobroliubov and other radicals argued that the ultimate standard was an individual's inherent nature, they had in mind an entity structured quite differently from the individual as conceived by most liberals. To men like Dobroliubov and Chernyshevsky, the individual was a totally biological phenomenon; even desires and ideals were reducible to physiological laws. The radicals scorned the liberals for yielding to romantic dreaminess in assuming that some human aspirations could not be explained by science. The liberals, for their part, criticized the radicals for their mechanistic and sterile view. But both groups agreed that between man's inherent nature, however construed, and his manifest actions there could be no discrepancy. If there were, action would be weak and unfocused, like a spasmodic limb the brain can no longer control. Prevailing authority could easily exploit such action for its own ends.

Turgenev's necrology written for his friend the historian Granovsky is a vivid application of *obshchestvo* standard of judgment:

All are unanimously agreed that Granovsky was a wonderful professor; regardless of his somewhat halting speech, he possessed the gift of true oratory. Nonetheless, others, judging him by his literary efforts and also aware that he could have no pretension to the designa-

17. Dobroliubov, "O znachenii avtoriteta v vospitanii," *Sobranie sochinenii*, I, 503.

tion of scholar in the true sense of the word—they wonder at the seemingly inexplicable, miraculous strength and general effect of his influence on people. [*S*, VI, 374]

Explaining Granovsky's paradoxical ability to appear intelligent without resorting to visible forms of expression, Turgenev uses a striking image. Granovsky, Turgenev says, could be compared to a "bright light, which passing through transparent crystal does not change its essence as it plays its bright colors" (*S* VI, 374). That truly is a perfect representation of the ideal: the majestic self inclines itself to meet the demands of the obdurate world, but without any diminishment or distortion of its inherent qualities. The image is striking, but also disconcerting: can any man really live up to the standard it invokes?

In *Rudin*, which he wrote one year after the necrology, Turgenev in effect takes the image he applied to Granovsky and elaborates it over the course of one hundred and fifty pages, and in the process calls into question many of the period's assumptions about the need for congruity between inner and outer states of being. Dmitri Rudin is introduced in terms that evoke Granovsky. He also is an accomplished orator, yet has a poor ear for language. If on the one hand, he is captivating in his speech, on the other hand, he is often imprecise and at times stutters. In the necrology, the combination of oratorical strengths and weaknesses appears merely unusual; in the novel, it becomes a source of anxiety, and the other characters strive implacably to comprehend Rudin's manner. Turgenev's observation that Rudin is not a "phrasemaker" but rather someone whose expressive ability is stifled by overly great inspiration is not so much an explanation as the outline of the problem: it is necessary to account for both Rudin's beautiful and ingenious words and the mind that forms them.

The conceptual complexity that results more than makes up for the simplicity of the plot, which consists essentially of one event, with a preamble and an epilogue. Dmitri Rudin is an impoverished nobleman and a passionate exponent of German Romantic philosophy. When he finds himself unexpectedly at the manor house of Daria Lasunskaia, he immediately gives vent to enthusiastic, if vague, pronouncements about the need for social change. Especially impressed is Lasunskaia's daughter Natalia. Indeed, during Rudin's stay at the manor house, Natalia becomes progressively more infatuated by his intellectual energy, finally reaching the point of suggesting elopement. But at the critical moment, Rudin hesitates, citing the need to observe proprieties. Rudin's inability to match his grand pronouncements with action turns the plot to its conclusion. Rudin leaves the manor house in disgrace, Natalia marries the uninteresting but good man who has been courting her, life resumes the placid course that Rudin's arrival had interrupted.

Turgenev prepares us for the denouement by introducing in the opening chapters several characters who resist Rudin's enthusiasm: Pigasov, the cynical hanger-on who disbelieves all extravagant statements; Volyntsev, Natalia's rather simple-minded suitor, who relies exclusively on common sense and his aristocratic intuitions; and, most important of all, Lezhnev, who in various ways is the conscience of the book. Lezhnev knows Rudin from their student days in Moscow, when both were members of the same intellectual circle (which Turgenev bases on the famous Stankevich Circle); and as a result of that acquaintance, Lezhnev as much as predicts Rudin's failure of nerve. He is quite sure he can see Rudin's moral failings, the reprehensible inability to translate thought to action.

Rudin, therefore, repeats one of the most vexing questions of Russian intellectual life: what is the connection between abstract ideals and purposeful activity? But Turgenev has very significantly altered the usual perspective on this question. He forces us to consider those who ask it as well as the object of their curiosity. Thus, although by the end of the book Rudin stands condemned, his guilt is not absolute. He is no simple poseur; he has at least groped toward an ideal. Those who condemn him, on the other hand, only sit smugly by. Much of the time, *Rudin* breathes a sanctimonious air. In a world of fools and idlers, the man who most energetically tries to integrate value and action is most harshly judged. That is to call into doubt the concept of judgment. Indeed, the movement of the book, from Rudin's first public success when he arrives unexpectedly at Lasunskaia's to his public exile into the world beyond the manor house, emphasizes the theme of collective judgment. Once it becomes clear that Rudin is not exactly the man he claims to be, all the other characters pursue the secret of his personality so fervently that all other concerns virtually vanish. The book's title is doubly appropriate: it names both the hero and the main preoccupation of all the other characters.

There are two major pieces of evidence to support Rudin's eventual condemnation, and both reveal as much about the mode of judgment that is invoked as about Rudin. The first is Rudin's interview with Natalia by Avdiukhin Pond. Rudin is much to blame for what passes here; his lack of will, his invidious ability to absorb all events into a bewildering system of his own interpretations, makes disaster almost a foregone conclusion. But only "almost," for Natalia also must bear some responsibility. Though Natalia comes to Avdiukhin Pond intent on proclaiming her readiness to unite her future to Rudin's—indeed she passionately offers herself to him—her actions during the interview work to narrow drastically the acceptable basis for cooperation.

Throughout the first part of the rendezvous Natalia remains remarkably and purposefully noncommittal, dryly reporting the awful news that her mother has learned of their love, but not indicating her own reactions to this new obstacle. Natalia in effect tests Rudin, and the test is explicitly twofold: Will Rudin unequivocally reassert his love in the face of difficulty and, correlatively, will he comprehend that Natalia is the sort of person who will welcome such a declaration despite the certain hardships the lovers will have to face? In other words, will Rudin instantaneously reveal who he is and recognize who she is? Rudin fails on both counts. As Natalia says, "Yes, you did expect this, you did not know me" (S, vi, 325). As a result, they must part, at once and forever. Since Natalia has invoked standards that measure individuals for what they are in their essence, there is no discussion of any mitigating circumstances in the past, nor any contemplation of adjustments for the future.

Natalia's abruptness appears fully justified. Rudin has worked, aggressively and cunningly, to make Natalia believe he possesses a capacity for action that he only wishes for. Moreover, Natalia's proposal to elope is one that no genuinely feeling man would decline. Rudin is a phrasemonger, who makes enthusiastic gestures but lacks the will to bring any project to fruition. When Rudin hesitates while answering her offer, it is reasonable that Natalia's love should turn to scorn; but it is also true that she has herself set obstacles to their mutual happiness. By withholding any expression of her feelings and by narrowing to an instant the time when Rudin could express his, she has manipulated the rendezvous so that it becomes a test of personality instead of an occasion for mutual declarations of love.

It is a test, moreover, that is based on a rigorous conception of what personality implies. To Natalia, character is fixed. What a man does once, what he expresses in an unguarded instant, is a sign of what he always is. She sees no need for a discussion that would permit Rudin to modify his ideas and propensities to meet her expectations. Instead, Natalia forces the rendezvous into a form of revelation. Her abrupt termination of the conversation and withdrawal to her mother's house, leaving Rudin to shout his justifications to the empty air, is a fitting conclusion to the episode: it gives dramatic shape to her belief that an essentially unchanging self is the standard of value, and if an encounter does not instantaneously produce a sympathetic connection between individuals, nothing can narrow the gap.

Natalia represents an extreme position, which seems to foreclose the possibilities of understanding even before they have a chance to develop. But Turgenev insists on the point. He introduces another episode that projects the same standards as those invoked by Natalia. The central character in this episode is Lezhnev. For much of the beginning of the book, he has remained in the background, hinting darkly at special knowledge he possesses about Rudin's character. Only in chapter 6 does he finally tell his tale about Rudin, after much hesitation and only at Lipina's insistence, not only because it is against his code to gossip but because he is sure of the dreadful condemnatory power of what he will relate.

In fact, his charge proves highly ambiguous. While studying in Moscow years before, Lezhnev had fallen in love, and had told his secret to his older friend, Rudin, who had responded by going into raptures—a response that Lezhnev found proper. Beyond that, however, Rudin took it upon himself to explain to the lovers the importance of what they had hit upon. Such interference certainly shows poor taste; but on the other hand, Lezhnev remarks that he had "practically insisted" on introducing Rudin to his love. Considering how directly the affair proceeded under the auspices of Romantic philosophy, Rudin's behavior appears justifiable: in a period when true love was construed as a means of achieving unity with the cosmos, interest in specific instances of the emotion indicated not idle curiosity but metaphysical concern. Lezhnev makes clear that he had fully accepted Romanticism, having gone so far as to write a play modeled on Byron's *Manfred*. He has now recanted, but can he blame Rudin merely for believing in what he himself once did?

Though the charge against Rudin goes on for several more pages, listing several more putative transgressions, much of what Lezhnev reports is contradictory and unfocused, an indictment so full of charges that there is no room for proofs. Lezhnev's only unambiguous complaint is that in the emotional turmoil at the end of the love affair, Rudin stayed calm. While Lezhnev fell into a condition where "lies seemed truth," Rudin was "like a swallow flying above a pond," aware but not passionately involved (*S*, VII, 302). Rudin's reprehensible fastidiousness could have had little to do with correct action—indeed, Lezhnev had been arguing that Rudin too often interfered in matters that did not concern him. Lezhnev apparently guessed Rudin's thoughts, and did not like what he perceived. Lezhnev breaks off his story with melodramatic abruptness, not permitting Lipina to question him: "But enough of him. Perhaps all will end well" (*S*, VII, 303). His manner underscores his inability to show Rudin's guilt in terms of concrete infractions, and also insinuates his belief that he does not have to.[18]

At first glance, Lezhnev's role appears redundant. He repeats the condemnation of Rudin which Natalia makes more forcefully, and he uses the same standards of judgment that she does. But he puts the case against Rudin in an especially chilling form. Natalia exposes the flaws she intuitively believed were in him, she makes his inner weakness manifest. Lezhnev needs not a shred of evidence to confirm him in his opinion of Rudin. His confused and intricate tale blurs all lines of causality; he presents a picture that has no moment

---

18. Not many critics have paused to consider the substance of Lezhnev's account; but see K. K. Istomin, "Roman *Rudin*. Iz istorii turgenevskogo stilia," *Tvorcheskii put' Turgeneva*, ed. N. L. Brodsky (Petrograd, 1923): "In what does Rudin's guilt consist? Do not look for an answer in [Lezhnev's] self-serving, cowardly, and intentionally disjointed tale. Only between the lines can one see that the anger of Lezhnev is unjustified" (p. 89).

when Rudin could have done something to swing judgment in his favor. Most remarkably, Lezhnev goes on to comment that his lengthy diatribe does not even include the real reason for his animosity, that his break with Rudin actually "occurred later, when we met abroad." It is as if the critical event in the relationship between Lezhnev and Rudin has been made to regress ever further until it slips from sight altogether, and judgment comes to rest entirely on intuition.

The mode of judgment employed against Rudin is not only extreme but final. Stung by his failure at Avdiukhin Pond, he writes letters to Natalia and to Natalia's suitor Volyntsev, trying to explain his motives. The letters are a departure from Rudin's usual style: he admits his errors and seeks only a measure of understanding from those he has hurt. But everyone who learns of the letters dismisses them as the strategy of an insincere man who is trying to salvage his pride. The mode of judgment that prevails in the community constituted by Lasunskaia's and Lezhnev's manor houses permits no explanations or qualifications; explanations and qualifications are aspects of the manifest behavior it is wiser to ignore when evaluating a man's essential being.

Turgenev seems to endorse the way that the community judges Rudin, but he also questions it. He shows that the same standards that are invoked in condemning Rudin can be turned back upon the judges. In the very first chapter, Turgenev begins to prepare us for a picture of a community where judgment is out of control, where intuition runs rampant. The encounter between Lipina and Lezhnev seems a nonchalant flirtation, but the implicit attitudes of the two signal a moral crisis. Lezhnev says:

"I am happy to meet you."
"And why?"
"What a question! As if it is not always pleasant to meet you. Today you are as fresh and nice as the morning."
Alexandra Pavlovna laughed again.
"Why are you laughing?"
"What do you mean, why?" If you could see with what an apathetic and cold expression you uttered your compliment. I am surprised you did not yawn at the last word." [S, VI, 240]

Lezhnev's words are treated suspiciously and then discounted altogether, even as he will deal with Rudin; and his remonstrances, like Rudin's, are rejected out of hand. The tone of the scene is light and playful, but it marks an unbridgeable distance that separates all the characters. Life in the enclave proves to be full of barbed and brittle encounters, and the larger gatherings suggest not real community but a precarious equilibrium of diverse tendencies. The characters are shown rubbing up against one another, occasionally flaring up from the friction, and then withdrawing unchanged into themselves.

Even the most positive moment in the book is made problematical by the way that members of the community habitually regard each other. Lezhnev and Lipina, now married, sit on their veranda, luxuriating in the comfort of pleasant surroundings and a company of acquaintances. Though happy, however, they lack intensity or passion. During their courtship they were never more than affectionate, and the marriage seems only a declared willingness to accept the other for what he or she is without trying to effect great change or make intimate contact. Lezhnev says to his wife, "Here we love each other and are happy, aren't we?" His polite and quizzical tone, his sense that love requires confirmation, measures the distance separating the characters in *Rudin* even when they are happiest. The decorous setting on the veranda, it becomes clear, is not so much a sign of harmony as a symbol of the care and restraint that is necessary to forestall an always threatening discord.

Altogether, the prevailing mixture of uncertain emotions, petty malice, and abrupt anger in *Rudin* makes for a noisome brew, and it is not a pleasant book to read. It is, however, for the same reason, immensely informative about the state of *obshchestvo* in the 1850s. It begins to explain why, even beyond the obvious disagreements over political stands, the grouping was so highly unstable. The salient point about *obshchestvo* is that all disagreements were continually aggravated by irritable and erratic personal judgments.

Historicans have often remarked that relations between the nobility of *obshchestvo* and its more radical members were exacerbated by the inclination of both groups to reduce ideological differences to questions of personal style.[19] The nobles scorned the bad manners

19. E.g., Joseph Frank, "Dostoevsky and Russian Nihilism: A Context for *Notes from the Underground*," unpublished diss. (Chicago, 1960).

and rudeness of the radicals; the radicals mocked the noble's fastidiousness. The more pressing danger, however, lay in another direction. Ideological differences were not reduced to personal ones but raised to an abstract level: a polemical opponent was finally judged neither on the merit of his ideas nor on his manner of delivering them, but simply and irrefutably as a man of inadequate character. The most striking contemporary accounts describe social gatherings at which men would be called upon to express their "convictions" (a word of wide currency) and then would have these dismissed as mere posturing.[20] The standard was "sincerity" (another word in vogue): the qualities of the inner man were all that counted.[21]

From one point of view the way *obshchestvo* judged made sense. In the lull between the political relaxation following the Crimean War and the confrontation with the government which everyone was sure would come, it was easy for an individual to claim a decisiveness he actually lacked, to delude his audience with grand gestures he did not yet have to back up "[Criminals] act despicably," Chernyshevsky complained, "but at least one can recognize them as despicable people."[22] Poseurs were infinitely worse, morally and politically. Men like Rudin, with their shifting commitment to action, had to be exposed; but the process of exposure, Turgenev's novel shows, could have its own debilitating effects.

Indeed, *obshchestvo's* form of judgment subverted precisely what it was meant to safeguard, a unified opposition to the government. Using as the only standard what man *is* rather than what he *does* makes unity either instantaneously achievable or hardly achievable at all. If a negative judgment is rendered, there is no way to appeal it, since no act is acceptable evidence. Even in the rare instances when the original judgment is changed voluntarily, the result is of dubious value. Lezhnev does finally excuse Rudin his flaws, but significantly, his change of heart occurs in the same scene in which he discounts all Rudin's practical efforts in the interval since they last met. Rudin's work on a canal, as an agronomist, and

20. See Eikhenbaum, *Lev Tolstoi, kniga pervaia, 50-ie gody,* pp. 216 ff.
21. See A. A. Grigor'ev, "O pravde i iskrennosti v iskusstve," *Sobranie sochinenii* (Moscow, 1915), I, 1–28.
22. Chernyshevsky, "Russkii chelovek na rendezvous," *Polnoe sobranie sochinenii* (Moscow, 1950), V, 156.

as a teacher mean nothing to Lezhnev. He changes his opinion not because of anything Rudin has done, but because he feels a surge of sympathy. His benign judgment is like a bestowal of grace, and as such is something to be thankful for but not something that can lead to real understanding. The scene ends with Rudin declining Lezhnev's invitation to visit his estate and going off to a solitary destiny. The novel thus endorses the culture's form of judgment and also questions it: in making the inner self the standard of value, men like Lezhnev help to establish a purity of motive among the members of a community, but they also put the very idea of community into jeopardy.

In "Hamlet and Don Quixote," an essay published five years after *Rudin*, Turgenev offered an image that vividly underscored the threat of chaos that is implied in the novel. Though the essay is first of all a typology of literary heroes, Turgenev insists that it is also a typology of human psychologies. There are two types and they are immutable: either Hamlet or Don Quixote, and one cannot change his own type. The world necessarily takes on the aspect of atoms in flux, some of which rebound off each other, some of which blend into a union:

> . . . this whole life is nothing else than the eternal accommodation and eternal warring of two unceasingly dividing and unceasingly uniting principles. If we were not afraid of troubling your ears with philosophical terminology, we would bring ourselves to say that Hamlet is the expression of the radical centrifugal force, according to which all that lives considers itself the center of creation. . . . Without this centrifugal force (the force of egoism) nature could not exist, just as it could not exist without the opposite, a centripetal force, according to which all that lives, lives only for another. [*S*, VIII, 184]

Once man's nature is defined as unchanging, harmony between men becomes a fortuitous event—and that is true whether the definition of man derives from Bentham and Fourier, as it did for the radicals, or from a pessimistic interpretation of German Romanticism, as it did for Turgenev.[23] In either case, *obshchestvo*, an un-

---

23. Elie Halévy, *The Growth of Philosophical Radicalism* (Boston, 1966), notes that once man's nature is defined as fixed, there are only three ways to imagine a harmonious community. One: harmony can be imposed by legislation that forces individuals to restrain their desires in the interests of the common good. Two: though all individuals are allowed to pursue their own interests, these fortuitously prove to be

certain endeavor to begin with, becomes even more problematical. Progressives in the post-Crimean War period had to struggle not only against an oppressive government but also against their own theory of personality.

---

mutually sustaining and helpful instead of in conflict. Three: altruism is a component of all individuals' essential nature, so as they satisfy their own impulses they promote general harmony (pp. 13–18). Since the Russian government could not be relied on for unbiased legislation, *obshchestvo* ruled out the first possibility. The radicals in *obshchestvo* often spoke as if they believed the second possibility would come true, but only at some unspecified future date. Turgenev, along with other liberals, hoped the third possibility was true, but, as the passage from "Hamlet and Don Quixote" indicates, he knew that altruism did not explain all of life.

7.

Work: *Nest of the Nobility*

Turgenev was notoriously lazy. Though he enjoyed being a land-owner, bragging of his gardens and making plans to overhaul relations with his serfs, he turned over day-to-day management of the estate at Spasskoe to an uncle almost as soon as he inherited it. Sometimes he justified his inactivity by claiming ill health, but most of his friends were skeptical. There is no doubt he exaggerated: several of his letters incongruously juxtapose descriptions of supposedly immobilizing ailments with references to hunting expeditions.

He was also a lazy writer. He continually proclaimed his most recent creation as his last, behaving as if writing extracted an unbearable physical toll. When he contracted to deliver a manuscript, he invariably missed the deadline, sometimes by several years. He exasperated all the editors with whom he worked, or drove them to despair. After agreeing to Nekrasov's proposal that he and three other leading writers enter into a contractual arrangement obligating them to contribute exclusively to *The Contemporary*, he submitted even less material than before the agreement.[1] Certainly composition did not come easily; one of his letters describes his method:

> I am now occupied with the composition of the plan, *etc.*, for a new story: this work is quite exhausting—especially as it leaves no *visible*

---

1. N. V. Ismailov's introductory essay to *Turgenev i krug "Sovremennika"* (Moscow and Leningrad, 1930) traces Turgenev's complex dealing with *The Contemporary*.

traces: you lie on a sofa or pace the room, while in your mind you ruminate on some character or situation. You glance up—three, four hours have passed—and it seems that not much has moved forward. [*P*, III, 280; italics in original]

This suggests a classic case of writer's block, but that can be only a description, not an explanation. Nekrasov believed that Turgenev did not produce more easily because of his "lordly" (*barstvennoe*) attitude toward the hard work that writing required. That is probably more to the point, but it fails to convey any sense that Turgenev was in a predicament he did not enjoy.

In fact, Turgenev's view of work was considerably complicated by historical circumstances as well as by personal predispositions. When the government revealed its intention to emancipate the serfs, it became clear that the occupations of most Russians would change. Turgenev was so well off that the emancipation, though decreasing his wealth, would not cause hardship. But the *idea* of work, the political and social implications of daily occupations— whether writing or farming or something else—impressed itself on his sensibility. A letter from November 1857 in which he tries to dissuade Tolstoi from giving up literature, suggests the form of his concern:

You write that you are happy you did not heed my advice and become only a littérateur (*literator*). I will not argue, perhaps you are right, only I, poor sinner, no matter how I rack my brain cannot imagine what you might be if you are not a littérateur: Officer? Estate owner (*pomeshchik*)? The founder of a new religious teaching? Bureaucrat? Businessman? Please resolve my difficulties and tell me which hypothesis is correct. [*P*, III, 170]

There is an uncharacteristic nervousness in the style of this letter. The listing of occupations is so free of grammatical subordination or qualifying terms that it appears capable of infinite expansion. In fact, though Tolstoi did try his hand at *some* of these occupations (and did so with a morose intensity that was designed to irritate men like Turgenev), he never came close to becoming a businessman or a bureaucrat, and his attempt to found a new form of religious teaching took place years after Turgenev's letter. The serial listing of occupations in itself seems to bewitch Turgenev: he believes that even to consider diversity is to risk an unending proliferation of roles.[2]

Two days after the letter cited, Turgenev made the following observations about Tolstoi in a letter to Annenkov:

> Here's a fine fellow. Possessed of a wonderful pair of legs, he insists on walking about on his head. He recently wrote a letter to Botkin in which he said, "I am very happy I did not listen to Turgenev and become only a littérateur." In answer to that I asked him, what is he, an officer, estate owner, etc.? It seems that he is a forester (*lesovod*). I am only afraid that with such little jumps he will dislocate the spine of his talent. [*P*, III, 175]

Turgenev's use of "etc." in the letter is a curious stylistic gesture. Apparently, Tolstoi's potential occupations need not be listed; not Tolstoi's particular vagaries upset Turgenev, but diversity in general, and that can be evoked with the slightest of rhetorical devices. The letter also indicates that Turgenev distrusts diversity for more than its suggestion of purposeless activity. He also believes that men in their frenzy may distort who they really are—they will "dislocate the spine" that connects to their inner nature.

Tolstoi's behavior was particularly galling to Turgenev because it reminded him of his own misuse of talent. He always feared he was squandering his gift for writing, but he was most anxious just at the time that Tolstoi's example loomed in front of him. Thus his feelings about reaching the landmark age of forty (in 1858), which made the death he always dreaded appear imminent, were cast in the form of a wish to overcome dilettantism:

> I will soon be forty. Not only my first youth but my second is past and it is time to become if not a man of accomplishment, then at least a man who knows where he is going and what he wants to do. I can be

2. It is worth noting that a serial listing of occupations has a long and meaningful history in Western culture. See Elizabeth Wilkinson and L. A. Willoughby, " 'The Whole Man' in Schiller's Theory of Culture and Society: On the Virtue of a Plurality of Models," *Essays in German Language, Culture and Society*, ed. S. Prawer (London, 1969); the authors trace what they call "this serial formula—an enumeration of classes, ranks and occupations" (p. 185) from Schiller through Herder and Hölderlin to Rousseau. Ultimately, they suggest, the distrust of occupations that is at the heart of this view of man should be contrasted with the Renaissance ideal of *l'uomo universale*, in other words, "the Whole Man" as opposed to the man of fine parts.

nothing except a littérateur—but till now I have been more of a dilettante. In the future that will change. [*P*, III, 173]

In another letter, to Countess Lambert, he again resorted to the device of a serial listing of occupations, this time applying it to himself. His purpose was to prove his dedication to a correspondent who had questioned it: "But you will agree that I must serve my fatherland not as a soldier, nor as a bureaucrat, nor an agronomist, nor a manufacturer. I can make a real contribution only as a writer, an artist" (*P*, v, 279).

Neither before nor after the period immediately following the Crimean War was Turgenev so concerned with the issue of dilettantism. Certainly he himself believed that the question was an aspect of Russia's historical situation. The letter to Countess Lambert assumes a shared awareness of the general movement of events; and in another letter to Tolstoi he made even more explicit his belief that history and dilettantism were intimately connected:

> You were right if I, in suggesting to you that you are exclusively a littérateur, had limited the meaning of literature to a lyrical twirping. But our times are not suitable for birds singing away in the branches. I only wanted to say that every man, while not stopping to be a man, should be a specialist; specialism excludes dilettantism (excuse the "isms") and to be a dilettante means to be powerless. [*P*, III, 187–188]

The fear of powerlessness—so acutely felt at this point in Russian history because for the first time it seemingly was not an inevitable condition—engenders a particular psychology of work. Man must be a specialist, for only in this way can he effectively marshal his strengths. By specialism, Turgenev usually had in mind the job of writing; but the particular job was less important than the opportunity that specializing offered to focus one's endeavors, concentrate one's energies.

The endorsement of specializing is emphatic, but its very stridency implies an exquisite sensitivity to the forms of dilettantism. The serial listing of occupations, designed to warn people of a danger, also inscribes a set of choices for the inspection of the curious. Turgenev's is not a confidentally held position; it represents the hope that the force of dilettantism will not prove overwhelming.

Turgenev's concern with the concept of work coincided with his visit to Rome in the winter of 1857–58. While there he was in close contact with the circle surrounding the Dowager Empress Elena Pavlovna, in which there were constant discussions about the impending emancipation of the serfs.[3] It is also while he was in Rome (in December 1857, to judge from a letter to Herzen, *P*, III, 181) that he learned of Alexander's crucial new order to the committee drafting the Emancipation Act, which made emancipation a foregone conclusion.[4] Shortly after he heard the dramatic news, he wrote to Countess Lambert: "In May I hope to arrive in my village, and I shall not leave until I have rearranged affairs with the peasants. Next winter, if God is willing, I will be a landowner (*zemlevladelets*), but no longer an estate owner (*pomeshchik*) or a master (*barin*)" (*P*, III, 163).

The prospect of a new society is welcome, since it will eliminate the onerous roles that Turgenev had to enact previously. But the role that he envisions for himself in a future where traditional designations have been abolished seems based on wishful thinking. His "landowner" is not a real occupation—indeed Turgenev would never be able to describe himself by that term—but rather a symbol for simplicity in a world that was becoming frighteningly complex.

Turgenev's view of work, in common with that of many of his contemporaries, was made uncertain by the influence of the country's economic history. Russia in the years 1856–1863 was in what economists call a "take-off" situation: all elements for thoroughgoing change were in place and waited only a final nudge for the process to begin.[5] The nudge would be the emancipation of the serfs. In fact, the expected modernization of the country did not develop with either the speed or the direction that had been anticipated—but that is another story. What is important for this discussion is that in the post-Crimean War period, the attitude of *obshchestvo* toward

3. For Turgenev's account of his stay in Rome, see *Russkaia starina*, No. 9 (1883), 6.

4. Daniel Field, *The End of Serfdom* (Cambridge and London 1976), presents a step-by-step account of how the Emancipation Act came into being. On the event I refer to, see pp. 265–323.

5. See Alexander Gershenkron, "The Problem of Economic Development in Russian Intellectual History of the 19th Century," *Continuity and Change in Russian and Soviet Thought*, ed. Ernest Simmons (Cambridge, 1955).

work was abstract: "work" was not something that could be defined merely by looking around at existing occupations, since these would shortly vanish or be radically altered, but rather had to be conceived in the imagination, in accordance with the new forms that Russian life would presumably assume.

From a country based on agricultural units, each relatively stable and self-sufficient, to an industrialized society with a large mobile labor force; from the traditional relationship of master and serf to a relationship based on financial and administrative obligations; from an essentially feudal economy to one based on money and contracts—all this suggested that the established roles of Russian society would vanish and men would have to invent new ones. From what was known, if often despised, to something unknown: it was natural that some caution should creep into Russians' view of the future. Change was necessary, but chaos had to be forestalled.

A recurrent literary symptom of Russia's concern with diversity was the one that appeared in Turgenev's letters. Whenever discussion turned to the idea of work, there seemed to exist something like a cultural reflex to invoke the serial listing of occupations. The most prominent example was doubtless Pirogov's famous epigraph to "The Questions of Life," noted above, where "man as such" is set in opposition to "businessmen, soldiers, mechanics, sailors, doctors and jurists," and by implication to all the activities the world might offer. But the listing was used by many writers, and always to make the same point: to illustrate the vertigo of excess and to announce the sorry fragmentation of man into aspects that no longer cohered.

The area where the fear of Russian man's fragmentation was most explicitly discussed was education. For if schools were the institutions that traditionally engendered those humanistic values that could provide men with a sense of wholeness, they were also institutions that would most directly have to meet the diverse technical demands of a new society. The literary critic Pisarev, an acute and sardonic observer of the situation in pedagogy, noted the dilemma:

> There has arisen a whole abyssful of various sorts of educations. This people say is juridical, and that technical and that *real*. By going along this path it is possible to arrive at a cuirassier [education] as opposed to a hussar [education], to an education particular to a bureaucrat of the financial chamber that is completely dissimilar from

an education of a senator or a postoffice bureaucrat; or to arrive at an education of a tanner that has nothing in common with the education of a soapmaker or a butcher.[6]

Very few writers—and certainly not Pisarev himself—opposed a new educational orientation, with more stress on practical and technical training. The new society required that absolutely. The problem, as Pisarev's comment begins to show, was not the practical bias as such but the way the bias seemed to lead to a disconnected profusion of occupations. It appeared that the revamped educational system would produce only empty-minded job holders rather than men who worked. What was needed, clearly, was some means that would give educational diversity an underlying unity, a persisting crux of value that could inform all particular tendencies—in a word, that would link with man's essential nature, in a way Turgenev endorsed in his letters.

Attempting to resolve their difficulties, pedagogical writers and theoreticians of the post-Crimean War period almost without exception resorted to the same conceptual framework. It had a bracing simplicity. It also raised new problems, as simplifications often do. Education was divided into two strains: on the one hand, the so-called *real* bias, the utilitarian side of education, which would prepare men for the demands of the modern world; on the other hand, a classical bias, which drew on universal values and instilled a broadly humanistic vision in students.[7] And then the two tendencies were yoked. The ideal was to be a *real* education heavily dosed with

6. D. I. Pisarev, "Nasha universitetskaia nauka," *Izbrannye pedagogicheskie sochineniia* (Moscow, 1951), pp. 130–131.

7. The term *real*, borrowed from the German, had wide currency, but it was not used with absolute precision. An attention to science seemed one defining element, but *nauka* (the usual word for rendering "science") was a very loose category, accommodating almost every type of intellectual activity. Wayne Vucinich, *Science in Russian Culture* (Stanford, 1963), studies the problem of science in Russia extensively. Loren Graham, *The Soviet Academy of Sciences and the Communist Party* (Princeton, 1967), includes a short account of the characteristics of science during the tsarist period; see pp. 7–12 for the distinction in Russia between practical and pure science.

E. Power, *Evolution of Educational Doctrine: Educational Theorist of the Western World* (New York, 1969), provides a historical view of the concept of *realism;* see esp. chapter 9, "Commenius: The Champion of Realism." To avoid confusion I shall italicize the terms *real* and *realism* when I have their educational meaning in mind.

classicism. In an essay entitled "What Do We Want?" Pirogov observed:

> But if we demand that a university education must be preserved in its elemental unity, this does not mean that it should be backward and uncontemporary; it does not mean that it must in no way be *real*. No! The basis of a true university education is science (*nauka*) in its broad meaning; and science cannot be unprogressive. We desire of our education only that it preserve *the humanistic principle in an unbreakable connection with the real,* and in no way lose sight of those innovations which have lately enriched the *real* side of our knowledge. [Italics in original.][8]

Pirogov's exasperated tone was to the point. Though contemporaries agreed that only a blending of the practical and humanistic principles could forestall the danger of dilettantism, all proposals to achieve the ideal provoked great controversy. Thus the most sustained pedagogical effort to meet the needs of a new society almost expired in a seemingly endless series of counterproposals and amendments: the question of how to merge the existing two-track system in the middle-level schools (one track having a predominantly practical bias, the other being more humanistic) engaged the attention of various committees and was discussed in pedagogical journals for years before a minor reformation was finally put into effect.[9] Some of the objections were substantive—it seemed that the material a student would have to cover in a combined program would be too vast for him to master.[10] But the more telling objections had broader implications: the attempt to forge an amalgam of the *real* and the classical tendencies violated certain rules of the cultural imagination. Pisarev again defined the issue succinctly:

> We apparently have lost the point of both the actual meeting of the *real* and the true goal of a general education. There begins to be a chase after two hares, who are running away from us by two separate roads. There begin to arise general-education schools with hints of a *real* bias. There appear *real* institutions with pretensions to general

8. N. I. Pirogov, "Chego my zhelaem?" *Izbrannye pedagogicheskie sochineniia* (Moscow, 1952), p. 186.

9. V. Z. Smirnov, *Reforma nachal'noi i srednei shkoly v 60-kh godakh XIX V.* (Moscow, 1954), considers these projects in detail.

10. D. I. Pisarev, "Shkola i zhizn'," *Izbrannye pedagogicheskie sochineniia*, pp. 246–260, details the hours of study a combined program would entail.

education. Finally, and most of all, the idea takes hold in society that it is possible at one and the same time, with one and the same lessons, to make a Varenka and Kolenka an educated individual and also, for example, a good sailor or an efficient jurist.[11]

The cultural situation was thus one in which the ideal was clearly perceived but perceived as unattainable. As Pisarev's comment implies, it hardly mattered how much the curriculum was tinkered with or how schools reorganized. Such efforts did not get to the root of the matter. There were elements in the very definition of the ideal that made it difficult to realize.

Most important among these elements were the political connotations that attached to a *real* bias. Though a *real* bias had never before been such a prominent concern in Russian education, it had at various points made itself felt. Usually it had been part of a generally progressive movement. When Peter the Great moved to modernize Russia, an emphasis on technological and scientific education had been an integral part of his policy; and Alexander I had similarly stressed a *real* bias in the schools during the early, reforming period of his reign (and in fact the educational statute of 1804 explicitly relied on pedagogical theory taken from revolutionary France).[12] But beginning in 1848, the connection of a *real* bias with progressive politics became problematical. *Realism* became an instrument of a policy that rendered politics largely irrelevant, by transforming Russia into a vast governmental preserve where the only question was the degree of acquiescence to the status quo. A *real* bias had often been at odds with the humanistic, classical impulse, but it had been so in the name of at least a theoretical commitment to the best of modern science. Under Nicholas I after 1848, such a commitment was systematically excluded. As Pogodin, who was usually not unsympathetic to the government, pointed out, "The reaction of 1848 undermined classical education, while the teaching of science did not make any headway."[13] Education was made to serve the bureaucracy almost exclusively (Turgenev noted

11. D. I. Pisarev, "Nasha universitetskaia nauka," *Izbrannye pedagogicheskie sochineniia*, p. 130.
12. Nicholas Hans, *History of Russian Educational Policy* (London, 1934), pp. 43–49, discusses the influence of French pedagogical thought.
13. Quoted in Vucinich, *Science in Russian Culture*, p. 255.

the trend when he has a character in *On the Eve* say, "There was, they say, a good time for Moscow University. But now it is an educational institute (uchilishche), not a university" [*S*, VIII, 50]). After 1856 the bureaucracy became less obviously agressive in the field of education, but history made many Russians suspect that an emphasis on utilitarian training would become an instrument of government policy.

The political pedigree of *realism* provoked unease especially within *obshchestvo*, which already regarded any nurturing of the practical impulse with suspicion. True, the modernization of the country required men trained in a new way, which meant that their education had to include a strain of *realism;* but if the result was workers who had been bred to accept the government's influence, modernization was hardly worth the effort. *Obshchestvo* was caught on the horns of a dilemma. Necessarily, its picture of the new ideal of work was highly confused. Often it seemed that *obshchestvo* writers simply presented the key concepts in a tidy opposition, hoping that would in itself constitute an explanation. Dilettantism as opposed to specialization, *real* as opposed to classical, *izuchenie remesla* (the learning of a craft) as opposed to *vospitanie* (upbringing in general)—it was left to the reader to comprehend a synthesis. At other times the terms appeared in clusters, as if that were the only way to capture the meaning of the elusive new ideal. Thus Pirogov could write, "Is there not some other means, some other way for a *real*-specialized type of training? Is there not some possibility of acquiring a specialized-practical education?"[14] The language signals a mind caught up fully in the play of abstract concepts; but the tone suggests anxiety, like that of an acrobat suddenly aware of his precarious predicament.

Another contemporary critic's comments on the issue of dilettantism are worth quoting at some length, since they exhibit such a proliferation of terms that meaning almost vanishes. Indeed, though the critic italicizes the key words in order that no one mistake his frame of reference, his point is not the usual one. Apparently

14. N. I. Pirogov, "Dokladnaia zapiska o khode prosveshcheniia v Novorossiskom krae i o vopiiushchei neobkhodimosti preobrazovaniia uchebnykh zavedenii," *Izbrannye pedagogicheskie sochineniia*, pp. 66–67.

the prevailing terminology was so loosely tied to concrete fact that
it could be easily shifted:

> It is not many-sidedness, not idealistic-moralistic strivings that we
> lack, but social morality and *specialization* . . . . To work for the com-
> mon good without denying one's personal interests requires *speciali-
> zation.*
>
> Among us can be found thousands of people with the most varied
> capabilities and moral aspirations, which, however, do not lead to the
> best results. That is beautiful content without a defined form, and
> consequently without a possibility of manifesting itself and applying
> itself in activity. In these people there is no center around which they
> could concentrate their strengths and through which they could ex-
> press themselves in some sort of specialized activity. These people
> are neither scholars nor artists nor factory workers nor bureaucrats
> nor missionaries. They are *dilettantes.*[15]

Some writers were aware that the discussion about dilettantism
had taken on an abstract air. Even they did not doubt, however, that
Russia had to produce a new type of worker, an amalgam of elements not usually found together. Pisarev, writing with his characteristic irony, mocked the crude efforts of his contemporaries to
yoke moral and practical instruction, but his own ideal, which he
designates *obrazovanie* (education) and which he hopes will "teach
the future man to live up to his own strengths," is vague. *Obrazovanie* has no definable content of its own; it is only an interpola-
tion from two flawed categories that magically makes a good:

> But false appearances . . . do not give peace and do not allow us to
> work through to a correct view of *obrazovanie*. And how is it possible
> to work through [to such a view] when we toss into one pile *vos-
> pitanie, obrazovanie,* and *izuchenie remesla*? We respect *vospitanie*
> very much because it makes our heart endlessly happy to see in
> children and youths good morals and humility. *Izuchenie remesla* we
> also respect in our own way, because a salary and a subsidized apart-
> ment finds a responsive place in the most stoic heart. And what is
> *obrazovanie*—this we do not know. There on the border between
> *vospitanie* and *izuchenie remesla* there is an indefinable amalgam, a
> kind of moving shadow we call *obrazovanie* . . . . Why should *ob-
> razovanie* be placed in the most inferior position and *vospitanie* and

15. V. Lkhovsky, "*Nikolai Vladimirovich Stankevich. Perepiska i biografiia,
napisannaia P. V. Annenkovym,*" *Biblioteka dlia chteniia,* CXLVIII (1858), 43–44.

specialization, which should have a secondary position, be moved forward.[16]

In *Nest of the Nobility*, Turgenev uses almost the same intellectual framework as Pisarev, except that Turgenev includes an emphasis on the political perspective of *obshchestvo* and thus exposes ambiguities about the idea of work which left Pisarev puzzled. The opening of *Nest of the Nobility* restates Turgenev's cherished hope: the individuals who live within the magic circle that symbolizes *obshchestvo* have the opportunity to escape the prevailing corruption. Their manor houses constitute a haven. Turgenev's smallest narrative gesture reinforces his claim that there is an impressive stability and continuity to this setting. Thus when he first mentions the heroine, he notes that her mother's father had brown hair. The mother plays only a small role in the novel, and the mother's father none at all, but Turgenev's reference is nonetheless purposeful: it signals a novelistic design in which the depicted events are part of a rich and vibrant history, knowable down to the smallest detail. Almost invariably, when Turgenev introduces a character, he pauses for an extended digression on the character's background; when the characters do act, the action appears logical and meaningful, for they move before our eyes trailing their histories behind them. When the hero Feodor Lavretsky comes on the scene, Turgenev's technique reaches its extreme. The story of Lavretsky's past fills thirty pages. It is introduced by a formal apology— "the reader must excuse me for breaking into events" (S, VII, 148)—and is summed up in a coda that calls attention to itself even as Turgenev prepares to resume the more natural tones of narrative: "... not staying in Moscow, [Lavretsky] arrived in the town of O—where we parted with him and where we now ask the good reader to return with us" (S, VIII, 175). In *Nest of Nobility*, the past is palpable and continually gives weight and purpose to the present.

In learning to deal with the past, the characters acquire a sense of who they are. To a considerable degree, in fact, *Nest of the Nobility* is the story of how Lavretsky tries to overcome his debilitating history. As a young man he had a most erratic upbringing imposed

16. D. I. Pisarev, "Nasha universitetskaia nauka," *Izbrannye pedagogicheskie sochineniia*, pp. 132–133.

on him by a willful father, who treated his son as material for the testing of educational theories. Totally unprepared for real life, Lavretsky marries a flighty and vacuous woman, who first induces him to waste his time amid European high society, then leaves him for a Parisian fop. Events have worked to make Lavretsky bitter and confused. Nonetheless, when we first see him, when he has returned to the town of O—, he is a man determined to apply himself to purposeful work. He will set the painful past behind him by drawing on the sustaining energy of his nobleman's nest, the privileged "circle" that confers power on those who know how to utilize it. When the news reaches him that his wife has died abroad, his triumph over the past seems complete. He falls even more fully in love with Liza, to whom he had been immediately attracted and who seems to possess just those qualities of simplicity and directness which had been previously lacking in his life, and he prepares to set out on a new path.

Lavretsky's resistance to hobbling influences marks a noteworthy quality in a Turgenev hero. Much more than Rudin, Lavretsky has an inner strength, a sense of his own potential. But if Lavretsky's power is inarguable, there remains the very real issue of where it is to be applied. From his first appearance, he is a character on the verge of action; but he cannot take the next step. When pressed about his plans, he announces, "I shall plough the field, as my grandfather did" (S, VII, 233). The ambition seems reasonable, but the novel portrays a host of unforeseen obstacles. Indeed, the very terseness of Lavretsky's proclamation, which at first suggests modesty, comes to signal the hauteur of a man who willfully ignores the complexity entailed in the concept of work. Lavretsky pursues a lofty ideal, though he dresses it up in homespun clothing. Like Turgenev's remark in his letter that after the emancipation he "will be a landowner," no more, no less, Lavretsky's claim that he "will plough the fields" is only a yearning for some still point in a world that seems to engender infinite roles, a hope that "specialism" can withstand the pressures of "dilettantism."

Turgenev makes the opposition between dilettantism and specialism concrete by his depiction of the antagonism between two characters, Vladimir Panshin and Christopher Lemm. Though Lemm's lowly status precludes any direct confrontation, each passing encounter between the two men resonates with the clash of opposing sensibilities. Even when they are physically apart, each man continues to define himself by a palpable disgust for his antagonist: any other character who meets Lemm or Panshin is made to choose between competing values. Liza, who is linked with both men—Lemm is her music teacher, Panshin her suitor—finds that any warm response to one is simultaneously a rejection of the other.

Panshin is socially charming and physically attractive. He is an excellent horseman, composes musical romances, and sketches. He also holds an important government position, in Turgenev's novels a telltale sign of moral failure. Panshin's first appearance befits a man of his varied but trivial accomplishments. "There was a sound of hooves and a well built horseman, on a beautiful grey horse, appeared on the road" (S, VII, 131). Such éclat symbolizes the insistently superficial nature of all his activities.[17]

Lemm is the son of poor German parents, and he has endured loneliness as well as deprivation in his devotion to his art. His post as a music teacher is poorly paid and requires him to put up with social snubs and expatriation. When at last he completes the composition that he has been working on for years, his exclamation of joy—"This I have done, for (*ibo*) I am a great musician" (S, VII, 238)—assumes the form of a syllogism that is meant to prove that the cultivation of the spirit can redeem a lifetime virtually void of visible accomplishment. Lemm at one point says of Panshin, "He is a dilettante, nothing more" (S, VII, 143), and by his scorn he argues for the superiority of his own specialized commitment.

Turgenev clearly prefers Lemm to Panshin. The one is sometimes ridiculous, the other always repellantly self-serving. Nevertheless, Turgenev does not endorse the concept of humanistic activity unquestioningly. Lemm's devotion to art entails a disregard of everyday concerns which proves disastrous. He always comes off badly in face-to-face encounters with Panshin, in part because of his lower social status but also because in staking so much on the spiritual life, he leaves himself unfit to deal with reality. Lemm's habitual attitude is wounded pride, a belief that his excellence goes unacknowledged,

---

17. Cf. D. I. Pisarev, "Dvorianskoe gnezdo. Roman I. S. Turgeneva," *Sochineniia* (Moscow, 1955), who says of Panshin: "He is a dilettante in his everyday life and in his professional activity, and especially in his art" (I, 21).

and his habitual action is to yield the field to his supposed inferiors—he does so with contempt, but he yields all the same. Even the moment of Lemm's highest achievement is recorded in words that cut two ways. "The sonata had a sweet passionate melody that gripped the heart immediately, shining and languishing with inspiration; it seemed to be everything valuable, mysterious and holy; it emanated an immortal sadness and retreated to die in the heavens" (*S*, VII, 238). Lemm's achievement leads into a realm beyond human rationality. His art leaves its mark "in the heavens," but its effect on the daily business of living is dubious. Turgenev's narrative manner reflects his attitude toward Lemm's cultivation of the spirit: in describing the sonata, Turgenev's language becomes highly charged, duplicating as well as describing the music's great emotionalism; but he soon gets back to the hard job of telling his story. Though he was intermittently attracted to irrationalism and transcendent feeling, he was never willing to lose control of his ego for very long.

In a letter to Pauline Viardot, Turgenev wrote, "À mon avis, les plus grand poètes contemporains sont les Américains, qui vont percer l'isthme de Panama et parlent d'établir un télégraphe éléctrique à travers l'Océan" (*P*, I, 282). The poetic sensibility must apply itself to concrete activity; industry becomes noble when informed by eternal spiritual values. These injunctions define the ideal that Turgenev sets for the hero of *Nest of the Nobility*. Lavretsky must avoid the shortcomings of Lemm and Panshin, while retaining the positive qualities of each. Practical activity is necessary, but it can be kept from splintering into dilettantism only by cultivating the inner life.[18]

Lavretsky's past endows him with an awareness of utilitarian ac-

18. In his next novel, *On the Eve*, Turgenev also defines his hero by juxtaposing him to two secondary characters who embody dilettantism and specialism. But in that case the dilettante is the artist, whereas the specialist is a scholar who writes articles so esoteric that no one reads them. In other words, Turgenev takes the framework of dilettantism/specialism and manipulates it very freely, which accurately reflects the uncertainty of *obshchestvo* regarding those concepts. The claim that the characters in Turgenev's novels fit a recurrent pattern has been made by many critics, most persuasively by V. V. Gippius, "O kompozitsii turgenevskikh romanov," in *Venok Turgenevu*, ed. A. A. Ivansenko (Odessa, 1918) pp. 42–97. But even Gippius ends up admitting there are many exceptions.

tivity. The education imposed on him by his father encompassed a broad range of the standard subjects of a *real* curriculum: "Music as a subject unworthy of man was set aside forever; natural science, international law, mathematics, the blacksmith trade—as Jean-Jacques Rousseau advised—and heraldry to nourish chivalric feeling: this is what had to be studied by the 'new' man" (S, VII, 162).

Though Lavretsky subsequently rebels against his upbringing, his anger is directed more against its form than its utilitarian bias. Entering the university after his father's death, he enrolls in the Department of Physics and Mathematics and holds himself aloof from intellectual circles, in which German Romanticism held sway. Indeed, Lavretsky's statement of purpose, "that he intends to plough the fields," constitutes a ringing endorsement of practical activity. Lavretsky clearly does not champion manual labor for its own sake; it is a means to a higher purpose. By ploughing the fields, he will be fulfilling a cultural destiny as well as turning over the soil. He wants to be a "poète contemporain," in the sense that Turgenev used the term in his letter.

But what in the letter was confidentially asserted, in the novel is skeptically scrutinized. Turgenev exposes the tremendous tension in the *obshchestvo* belief that the concept of work must comprise both *real* and humanistic tendencies. Lavretsky's hesitation in actually getting down to the work he proposes is a direct result of his effort to combine elements that do not easily mesh. He moves tentatively because he fears to upset a most precarious balance.

Turgenev casts Lavretsky's predicament in the form of an historical dilemma. Lavretsky wants to make himself into a type—a working *intelligent*—who never previously existed in Russian life; but he can imagine no other means than the readjustment of the inadequate forms he proposes to transcend. He intends no more than to combine practical and spiritual values, a new mixture of the standard ingredients instead of a fully innovative concept of work. For this failure of the imagination, Turgenev provides a perfect structural equivalent: Lavretsky moves through the novel less by fixing his own course than by alternately endorsing and rejecting the more explicit positions of Lemm and Panshin.

Thus his courtship of Liza, to take the central event of the action, proceeds by curious indirection. Lavretsky tried to prove his love mainly by contrasting himself with Panshin. Only by convincing Liza that Panshin is superficial and mean spirited, that his apparent talents disguise the fact that he "has no heart" (*S*, VII, 240), can Lavretsky prove his own spiritual strength. Panshin's flaws are the instrument by which Lavretsky defines himself to Liza—and, indeed, to himself. Lavretsky realizes the extent of his love for Liza only when he learns that Panshin has proposed marriage to her.

Lemm is similarly crucial to Lavretsky's understanding. Lavretsky looks on benignly, with a supervisory air, as Lemm instructs Liza in the humanizing value of music. Lavretsky knows that the lessons are to his advantage, for they will expose the meretriciousness of Panshin's taste. Music is Turgenev's symbol of deep feeling, and Lemm is the exponent of that side of human experience. Fittingly, Lavretsky feels his greatest surge of love not in Liza's presence, but in Lemm's. When he visits Lemm in his rooms and hears him play the composition that he had labored over for years, Lavretsky comprehends his own feelings most vividly.

Lavretsky's persistant need for others, his reliance on surrogates to fill out and give meaning to his life, determines the most perceptible aspect of the novel. *Nest of the Nobility* consists of many short chapters (some only a page or two), a series of nervous and unresolved encounters. Lavretsky meets other characters only to bounce off in a new direction, propelled by affection or scorn that is equally ineffable. As he proceeds, he senses that the characters he meets embody qualities that are vital to his understanding of himself. That Lemm and Panshin each represents an incomplete and flawed form of life makes Lavretsky's progress more anxious, but it does not halt it. Lavretsky careens from character to character like a man shopping among shoddy goods and somehow persuaded that he may accumulate enough usable ingredients to makes a glorious finished product.

In depicting Lavretsky, Turgenev is depicting a failure—not in terms of material standards, but one who is fatally unable to think himself into a coherent personality. That is a daunting task for an author, and indeed several critics were convinced that the vagueness surrounding Lavretsky was the author's failure, not the character's. Complaining of Turgenev's narrative method, the critic for *The Russian Word* remarked, "The Lavretsky of the sections concerning his family, the Lavretsky behind the scenes, so to speak, and the Lavretsky before the eyes of the reader are two characters having little to do with each other."[19]

But a scene early in the novel proves that Lavretsky's elusive personality is precisely the theme that Turgenev has set himself to explore. Shortly after Lavretsky returns to his familial estate, his school chum Mikhailevich arrives unexpectedly for a visit. The two friends launch into good-natured argument, "such as only Russians are capable of" (S, VII, 202). By that phrase Turgenev suggests a discussion about eternal and abstract questions, but what follows is very personal. The encounter consists almost entirely of Mikhailevich calling Lavretsky names. First Mikhailevich says that life's experiences have left Lavretsky "disenchanted," an obvious reference to the Superfluous Man tradition, which Lavretsky turns aside with a wry comment about how little his robust appearance fits the wan stereotype. Apparently persuaded, Mikhailevich offers three other epithets in quick succession: Lavretsky is "a skeptic," "an egotist," "a Voltaireist" (an allusion to his French-influenced education). None of the epithets truly describes Lavretsky, and the rapidity with which Mikhailevich keeps offering alternatives suggests he realizes his failure. He becomes desperate:

> "Now I have found what to call you," Mikhailevich cried out at three in the morning. "You are not a skeptic, not disenchanted, not a Voltaireist—you are a sluggard, and an evil sluggard at that, one with awareness, not an innocent sluggard." [S, VII, 203]

But Lavretsky, with his obsessive dream of work, is no sluggard. Apparently he fits no ready category, and on the following day Mikhailevich departs, his attempt to categorize Lavretsky still unsuccessful. He is not mentioned again until he is dismissed with a few words in the epilogue; his appearance has been similarly abrupt. The sole purpose of Mikhailevich's visit is to underscore the elusiveness of Lavretsky's character: a hero suffering from a malady that can be felt but not defined, neither by other characters nor by himself, because the ideal he tries to create of himself is unimaginable.

As is the case with all of Turgenev's novelistic heroes, Lavretsky's

19. See M. De-Pule, "*Dvorianskoe gnezdo* I. S. Turgeneva," *Russkoe slovo*, No. 11 (1859), 12.

life is critically altered by a great love. Indeed, *Nest of the Nobility* at points resembles a chivalric romance, employing the chief conventions of that genre: the suddenness of passion, the onerous demands of duty in the form of a loveless marriage, the renunciation of love, and the acceptance of society's rules. Love remains a subtheme, however; it illuminates the main topic of work. Lavretsky muses on his attraction to Liza and his hatred of his wife:

> "Can it be," he thought, "that at thirty-five years of age I have nothing better to do than once again to relinguish my soul to a woman? But Liza is not like *her:* she would not demand degrading sacrifices from me; she would not distract me from my occupations; rather she would inspire me to honest, dignified labor, and together we would go forward toward the beautiful ideal." [S, vii, 226; italics in original]

The substance of the passage indicates that the "beautiful ideal" is work, although the epithet itself indicates that work entails not mere labor but an activity ennobled by the proper spirit. To Lavretsky, the most obvious source of spiritual values is love. True love gives work a satisfying form as surely as bad love distorts it. When his love for Liza is in full bloom, Lavretsky believes his practical occupations acquire meaning and purpose—not because they are intrinsically different from what he engaged in at other times, but because work is now backed by proper feeling.

Lavretsky's view of work fits neatly into the *obshchestvo* vision: only activity that proceeds from an intensely felt purpose can withstand the corruption of the existing order. Absorbed fully by his personal predicament, he nevertheless represents a general political position. The broader implications of the novel are underscored by Turgenev in describing an argument between Lavretsky and Panshin. The argument takes place in the drawing room of Liza's home, where several guests have assembled for an evening's entertainment. The sounds of a nightingale can be heard from outside and "the first stars of evening were becoming visible in the rose-colored sky above the motionless crowns of the lime trees" (S, vii, 232). Panshin's presence disturbs the idyllic moment; more specifically, to Lavretsky Panshin appears as a representative of the existing order who intrudes into the nobility enclave: Turgenev takes the time to reemphasize Panshin's government connections, noting that he has "the title of *kammer junker* and a civil service career" and that he refers knowingly to "our business, the business . . . of civil servants" (S, VII, 232). Stung into uncharacteristic eloquence, Lavretsky informs Panshin that all activity must "recognize the national truth, and reconcile itself with it" (S, VII, 232). That truth includes Russia's "youth" and "independence." At first glance Lavretsky appears to be mouthing a narrow Slavophile nationalism; in fact, he cares less about Russia's position vis-à-vis other countries than about a native force capable of resisting government influence.[20] When Lavretsky tells Panshin that Russia's course cannot be shaped by policies imposed "from the heights of bureaucratic self-concern" (S, VII, 232), he pinpoints the object of his fear and of his animosity.

Though Turgenev clearly endorses Lavretsky's—and *obshchestvo's*—position, he also reveals its unforeseen pitfalls. Insisting that work be intimately informed by feeling may protect the individual from the evil influences of the world, but it also makes life precarious. Happiness becomes wholly dependent on quicksilver emotions, the vagaries of love. No work that a man does can be satisfying in itself—no work, indeed, can enrich his inner life and make him more capable of loving and being loved, for his inner life is primary, everything else a supplement. Thus the single most important reason why Lavretsky's work fails is that his erotic impulses go astray. When his wife returns unexpectedly from abroad—reports of her death were erroneous—and Liza enters a convent in contrition for loving a married man, *all* Lavretsky's activities suddenly seem sterile. Walking about his estate gloomily and aimlessly, he encounters a peasant on the way to work. "Look about you," he says to himself, "and see who is happy, who enjoys his fate. There's a peasant on the way to mowing; perhaps he's happy with his fate. . . . Do you want to change places with him?" (S, VII, 268). Lavretsky rejects the idea immediately. Though the peasant's physical movement in mowing may connote a pleasureable act, Lavretsky knows that the death of his love for Liza also kills his joy in farming. Work must be the overflow of what one feels, and he feels bereft and diminished.

20. Henri Granjard, *Ivan Tourguenev, La Comtesse Lambert et "Nid de seigneurs"* (Paris, 1960), argues that in general the novel presents the Slavophile point of view, but his evidence is mainly Turgenev's close relations with Countess Lambert, a Slavophile sympathizer, at the time of writing the novel.

The epilogue, describing events eight years after the main action, reasserts the folly of trying to work when one's soul is empty. "Lavretsky had a right to be satisfied: he had really made himself into an effective landowner, he had really learned how to *plough* the land" (S, VII, 293). But as Lavretsky wanders around the grounds where he and Liza discovered their love, it is clear that he is *not* satisfied. In fact, to the extent that his work appeared good, it only makes him feel a terrible disunity between his self and his activity. Describing Lavretsky's condition during the eight years since the climax of the novel, Turgenev says he has experienced "a dislocation in his life" (S, VII, 293). The phrase (which recalls Turgenev's observation that Tolstoi might "dislocate the spine of his talent" if he failed to express his natural capacities as a writer) suggests a moral impairment so complete that it assumes physical form. Indeed, the last comment that Lavretsky makes indicates his belief that his unhappiness is the result of having failed to keep constituent parts of his being in mesh: "We had to struggle to remain whole, and how many of us did not remain whole?" (S, VII, 293).

Lavretsky thinks he has failed because he has been unlucky, because fate has played him a nasty trick, but it is his own concept of happiness that is really at fault. *Nest of the Nobility* is the story of a man who stakes his life on the hope of finding satisfying practical activity and then rigorously closes off the best path to this goal. To Lavretsky, work is like a coat that becomes admirable only when a spiritually enlightened worker puts it on; he rejects the possibility that some forms of work may ennoble the worker, that an individual may move and grow to fit the contours of his occupation.

At the beginning of the epilogue, Turgenev writes, "Eight years passed. Once again the shining gaiety of spring flowed down from the sky, once again it smiled on the earth and on the people, once again" (S, VII, 287). The repeated phrase "once again" is a reference to the opening lines of the novel, which were similarly rhapsodic about spring. The world, Turgenev tells us, has retained its essential purity, its eternal rhythm. Indeed, the novel describes no real change—at the end, all the main characters are back in their original relationship, only more firmly locked in place. Turgenev does not disguise but rather emphasizes the lack of movement.

Turgenev's portrayal of a community that is built around the idea of work but which remains completely unchanged reflects the dilemma of *obshchestvo*. *Obshchestvo* believed that any new ideal of work had to be based on the individual's inherent strengths. Whatever form work took, practical activity had to conform to an abiding humanistic core of values. Only that way could the fragmentation of the individual's personality be forestalled, and only that way could the government be prevented from exploiting work for its own ends. No *obshchestvo* writer in this period considered the question from the other side, that work in a modernized society might permit human beings to acquire an ennobling mastery over their environment. There was no Russian counterpart to Melville's ecstatic itemization of whaling paraphanalia, by which he implied that technology increased man's confidence against nature, nor to George Eliot's homage to medicine in *Middlemarch*, nor to those moments in Balzac when a character realizes that the occupations of a modern city, though corrupt, may allow him to discover his best qualities. The value system of *obshchestvo* made a genuine understanding of work impossible; any appearance of intellectual flexibility was only a fine tuning of the system's constituent parts. *Real* versus classical, dilettantism versus specialization, practical versus humanistic—it was always the same coin, only spun so fast that no one noticed. In *Nest of the Nobility*, Turgenev stopped that spinning coin long enough for men to see its counterfeit design. His analysis of work was vital for *obshchestvo's* understanding of its political role; and it was also a way of coming to terms with his own laziness. What appeared at first as exclusively a flaw in his personality, a habit so ingrained that its source was forever hidden, now took on the aspect of a historical event. That was a first step toward a cure, and it does not argue against Turgenev's method that he was never able to take a second.

8.

Love: *On the Eve*

Turgenev's most important erotic relationship was so unusual that it implies neurosis, an inability to overcome the emotional damage caused by his domineering mother. His life-long love for the French opera singer Pauline Viardot, whom he met when she toured Russia in 1843, took the form of extravagant devotion. From the beginning he strove to proclaim his passion publicly. He attended all her performances in St. Petersburg's Bolshoi Theatre, applauding so loudly that other spectators complained. Since he had little money at the time, he had to force himself on friends with extra tickets, which he did shamelessly. Throughout Viardot's stay, he acted the role of the smitten swain, attending her constantly. Friends grew tired of his tales of spiritual ecstasy, his claims to have found perfect contentment when Viardot had rubbed his forehead with *eau de cologne* to relieve a headache.

Subsequently the relationship became less dramatic but more emotionally ambiguous. In 1845 Turgenev went abroad to be with Viardot, the first of many such sojourns. He lived for long periods in her house in Courtavenal, near Paris, staying on friendly terms with her husband; if that appears deceitfully self-serving, the other side of the coin is that Turgenev learned that his presence could not stop Pauline Viardot from being attracted to other men. Whether he was ever intimate with her is in doubt—some evidence suggests that they were lovers for a brief time in 1849—but in any case the feelings that existed between them were always unequally distributed.[1] He hungered for her love; she put up with his ardor because she valued his friendship. "My God," Turgenev wrote in a letter, "I wish I could spend my whole life, like a carpet, under your dear feet, which I kiss a thousand times. . . . You yourself know that I belong to you" (*P*, 1, 404; original in German). He often seemed happy to think of himself as a slave of love, grateful for the slightest, and most curious, token of affection that a powerful mistress cared to send him: "I kiss your feet for hours. Thank you for the dear fingernails" (*P*, 1, 410; original in German).

Even allowing for the conventions of nineteenth-century correspondence, Turgenev's letters indicate an abnormal desire to appear submissive. But desire can be part of a strategy as well as a constant and uncontrollable impulse. It is worth noting that he sometimes played a traditionally dominant role with other women, especially peasant women, with one of whom he had a daughter. Indeed, though his relationship with Viardot was his most significant erotic tie, it does not necessarily provide the best grounds for understanding his views of women: much of the evidence, in particular her letters to him, is unavailable, making it very difficult to chart the emotions that ebbed and flowed over several decades. By contrast, some remarks of his that were recorded by Edmond de Goncourt provide an absolutely exhaustive commentary of another erotic encounter (though, to be sure, the very exhaustiveness raised difficulties of its own). Goncourt describes attending a lunch at Flaubert's apartment in Paris, at which Theophile de Gautier and Turgenev were also present. The conversation turned to the question of love, and Turgenev related the following anecdote:

> In my past I had a lover—a miller's wife in the outskirts of St. Petersburg. I saw her when I went hunting. She was marvelous— white-skinned, with shiny eyes, the sort to be met quite often in Russia. She did not want to take anything from me. One marvelous day she said, "You must make me a present." "What do you want?" "Bring me some soap." I brought the soap. She took it and disappeared, and then returned, blushing from confusion, and whispered, extending her sweet smelling hands: "Kiss my hands as you kiss the hands of those ladies in St. Petersburg drawing rooms." I threw

---

1. The most illuminating study of the relations between Turgenev and Viardot is in April Fitzlyon, *The Price of Genius: A Life of Pauline Viardot* (London, 1964).

myself on my knees before her. And believe me there has not been in my life a moment that could compare with that one.[2]

Turgenev wants to show the utter simplicity of high passion. In a bucolic setting, away from the empty conventions of St. Petersburg drawing rooms, he can find the proper release for his emotion. But, in the event, passion turns out to be anything but simple: the symbols of purported innocence and naiveté become instruments of deception, tokens in a complex game that turns feeling into an aspect of power. The giving of the gift of soap radically transforms the structure of the relationship, almost as a magic talisman might.

By finally persuading the woman to accept a gift, Turgenev manages to make visible what was previously only implicit; his superior social role, and also his ultimate control of this affair. But the gift is not of course merely a payment, making the woman realize her dependent position; it has the reverse effect also, of masking the woman's dependence. Indeed, both participants in the encounter enact roles that are the opposite of the ones that society sanctions. Instead of expressing obligation, the woman assumes a stance of full control, demanding homage in the form of having her hands kissed; and Turgenev finds a release for his most fervent emotions by throwing himself at the woman's feet, happily submitting to her claims of power.

Nothing has actually happened that should alter their relationship. The gift itself is paltry, lacking any economic value or emotional connection with the lovers' past together. The only meaning the soap has is the one Turgenev and the woman give it during the encounter; it is an excuse to reverse their accustomed roles. But though the reversal of roles is temporary and self-conscious, it brings genuine pleasure. To his friends gathered in Flaubert's apartment, Turgenev described the moment of acting against the grain of expected behavior as one of his most memorable erotic experiences. For him, love depends on a strenuous manipulation of circumstances, an imputation of power which he knows the woman really lacks. His behavior reflects his persistant uncertainty about women, which began with a love-hate relationship with his mother; but it has more than personal implications. As we shall see, even in

2. Edmond and Jules de Goncourt, *Journal des concourts* (Paris, 1908), v, 26.

erotic matters—which are presumably the most private of matters—Turgenev in his own life recapitulated the attitudes of *obshchestvo*, translating political beliefs into individual psychology. The status of love in Russia in the post-Crimean War period is a constant concern in the novels. The most obvious sign is Turgenev's strikingly sympathetic treatment of forceful female characters, a characteristic noted by many critics.[3] In his fictive worlds, women, more often then men, act decisively. Dobroliubov, in his essay "When Will the Real Day Come?," noted this feature: "The fact is that the main character in *On the Eve* is Elena. . . . In Elena the best aspirations of our current life are reflected, and in her surroundings all that is mean in that life stands out sharply."[4] In the years immediately following the publication of *On the Eve*, two articles in leading journals remarked on the importance of women in Turgenev's fiction. Pisarev in "Woman Characters in the Novels of Pisemsky, Turgenev and Goncharov" and Ostrovsky in "Concerning Woman Characters in Several Stories by Turgenev" advanced various reasons for Turgenev's singular ability to portray strong women, but they agree on one point: Turgenev's treatment reflected a change in the actual condition of women in Russia.[5]

Though the statements of contemporaries regarding the status of women were often extravagant, there had indeed been some change. If one event may be said to have altered traditional attitudes, it was the Dowager Empress' decision to form the Sisters of Mercy, who would treat the casualties of the Crimean campaign.[6] At first, the idea of women in field hospitals provoked outrage, but the courage of the Sisters of Mercy mission turned public opinion decisively in their favor. In the period after the Crimean War, the more

3. An early and influential critical work that makes that point is K. Chernyshev, *Lishnie liudy i zhenskie tipy v romanakh i povestiakh I. S. Turgeneva* (St. Petersburg, 1896).

4. N. A. Dobroliubov, "Kogda zhe pridet nastoiashchii den'?" *Sobranie sochinenii* (Moscow and Leningrad, 1961), VI, 120.

5. A. Ostrovsky, "Po povodu zhenskikh tipov v nekotorykh povestiakh," *Sovremennik*, XCII, No. 5 (1862), 136. D. I. Pisarev, "Zhenskie tipy v romanakh Pisemskogo, Turgeneva i Goncharova" (Moscow, 1955), *Sochineniia*, I, 192–231. For an extensive treatment of the condition of women at this time, see Richard Stites, "The Problem of Women's Emancipation in Nineteenth Century Russia," unpublished diss. (Harvard, 1967).

6. The Sisters of Mercy in the Crimea were under the leadership of Pirogov. His account of the mission is in N. I. Pirogov, "Pis'mo k baronesse Raden," *Izbrannye pedagogicheskie sochineniia* (Moscow, 1952), pp. 548–569.

relaxed intellectual climate encouraged women to assert themselves more in Russian society. Women of the upper classes began to appear in public places unescorted, and some began to audit university lectures.[7] Two literary events symbolize the new era, events hardly conceivable even a few years earlier: the translation by M. L. Mikhailov of John Stuart Mill's "The Subjection of Women," which took the position that the biological "disadvantages" of women would become irrelevant in a properly organized society; and Evgeniia Tur's angry attack on Jules Michelet's *L'Amour*, a book that had confidently defined woman as alternately child and invalid.[8] Both these literary events met with broad public approval, which is proof that many Russians at least wanted to entertain an image of themselves as progressive on the woman question. Indeed, the role of woman became increasingly a crucial part of the *obshchestvo* political strategy. As Mikhailov put it, in language not extreme for the period, "Only a radical transformation of woman's condition can save society."[9]

Of course, Mikhailov's comment, though it attributes a vast potential to women, simultaneously implies the lowliness of their actual status. Russian women were in a markedly disadvantageous legal position, and where law did not oppress them, tradition did. The unhappy marriage of Elena's mother in *On the Eve* neatly illustrates the situation. Elena's father freely indulges in adultery, while Elena's mother hardly remonstrates, let alone threatens action. Legal grounds for divorce did exist—and adultery was technically one of them—but social pressure and custom effectively blocked most women from pressing a case.[10]

A daughter was even worse off than a wife. She was continually

---

7. V. V. Stasov, *Nadezhda Vasil'evna Stasova. Vospominaniia i ocherki* (St. Petersburg, 1899), p. 58, remarks on the increasing appearance in public of unescorted women of the higher classes. For an extensive survey of women's education in Russia, see E. L. Likhacheva, *Materialy dlia istorii zhenskogo obrazovaniia v Rossii* (St. Petersburg, 1888). For developments in the post-Crimean War period, see II, 3 ff.

8. The translation of Mill's *The Subjection of Women* appeared in *Sovremennik*, LXXXIV, No. 11 (1869). Tur's attack on Michelet was in "Zhenshchina i liubov' po poniatiiam G. Mishle," *Russkii vestnik*, XXI, No. 6 (1859), 461–501.

9. M. L. Mikhailov, "Zhenshchiny, ikh vospitanie i znachenie v sem'e i obshchestve," *Sochineniia* (Moscow, 1858), III, 371.

10. An extensive contemporary account of the legal situation of women can be found in M. Fillipov, "Vzgliad na russkie grazhdanskie zakony," *Sovremennik*, LXXXV, No. 2 (1861), 523–562, and No. 3 (1861), 217–270.

subject to parental power and oversight, the extent of which can be judged from the restriction that parents could not force their children to commit illegal acts. Within that limitation, parents enjoyed near-total control, including even the right to jail disobedient offspring. For a male child escape into military or civil service was possible; for a female the sole hope was marriage, and that technically required parental consent. The scene in *On the Eve* in which Elena asks her father's forgiveness for marrying without consulting him shows graphically how a parent could retain his legal powers long after he had abdicated all claims to emotional authority.

But if woman's estate was so low, how could she possibly be the agent to transform society? More specifically, how could Turgenev imagine—and his readers credit—a heroine as forceful as Elena, particularly as he also included in the novel many allusions to the oppression of contemporary woman? Russians in the 1830s and 1840s would have looked for an answer to these questions in the Romantic myth of women: she was a creature on intimate terms with the cosmos, her lowly status disguising a magical strength. In the post-Crimean War period, *obshchestvo*, instead of glossing over woman's actual condition, tried to transform her handicaps into an advantage.

Obshchestvo began to explore the potential that lay in social degradation. Russian man was generally constrained and corrupted by the existing order. Russian woman was at least in a different position—perhaps, despite appearances, it was a better position. Pisarev summed up the *obshchestvo* social strategy regarding women in the course of discussing Turgenev's characters: "Man is dependent on social circumstances, woman on private circumstances, on separate individuals, on a father, an older brother, on a lover or a husband."[11] For all his apparent condescension, he is not trying to prove woman's inferiority. In fact, he notes that men, who are in contact with social circumstances, suffer even greater humiliation. They are forced into one of two equally sterile alternatives: "One man comes to terms with social circumstances, another announces his protest." That is, men either acquiesce in evil or rebel futilely. Women, for all the seeming inferiority of their status, are at

11. Pisarev, "Zhenskie tipy v romanakh Pisemskogo, Turgeneva i Goncharova," p. 212.

least absolved from facing this hopeless dilemma, with all its diminishing consequences.

Obshchestvo assumptions were revealed with special clarity by several writers who invoked the period's favorite rhetorical schema, the serial listing of occupations. In applying the device to woman's role, they introduced a significant alteration. The usual contrast was between an individual's inner qualities, cultivated in some place of safety, and the demands of the corrupt existing order: "man as such" as opposed to the dilettante. When the device was applied to woman's role, she was made to represent—despite the shift in gender—the ideal of "man as such," while man became fully a creature of the world:

> What is man in our time? A scholar, judge, legislator, doctor, always a specialist and rarely something more. Only a woman can combine poetry and prose, work and spiritual pleasure. Why is all the attention of our time turned to woman, why is it that the more educated a nation, the more respect surrounds woman? Because the world understands, however vaguely, that only through woman can a new way of life be reached, a life where truth, goodness, and beauty will reign.[12]

Women's power is visible by contrast. A narrow intellectual life and circumscribed area of activity have not suddenly acquired worth in their own right; but in the light of the newly perceived threat of the world at large, such a condition appears relatively benign. Woman is at least freed from engaging in the prevailing corruption. One historian has pointed out in another context that virtually every Russian possessing a certain level of education believed that his proper occupation was service in the government—"except alcoholics, cripples, the decrepit, and women."[13] That is not pleasant

---

12. A. Kh——va, "Pis'ma k russkoi zhenshchine," *Zhurnal dlia vospitaniia*, 1 (1856), 307. Cf. Mikhailov, "Zhenshchiny, ikh vospitanie i znachenie": "In demanding education for woman equal to man's, I, of course, do not wish to see every woman a scholar, philosopher, historian, mathematician, etc., and still less a diplomat, politician, merchant, or administrator, in the current meaning of the word" (p. 391). One "current meaning" of "administrator" tied the occupation directly with the corrupt existing order: "Baburin [in Turgenev's "Punin and Baburin," S, XI, 75] was acquitted by the court. ... However, he was exiled to Siberia by administrative process [*administrativnym poriadkom*]." Cited in *Slovar' sovremennogo russkogo literaturnogo iazyka* (Moscow and Leningrad, 1950), I, 54.

13. M. Aleksandrov, *Gosudarstvo, biurokratiia i absoliutizm* (St. Petersburg, 1910), p. 107.

company to be in; but it may be better than belonging to an apparatus which, though it awarded social status, destroyed one's moral fabric.

The definition of woman's special role put her in a precarious position.[14] Russians who were eager to perpetuate the *domostroi* tradition of total male dominance found that they could use the definition to their advantage by insisting that woman's privileged position meant only that she should discharge her domestic duties exactly and conscientiously. Even more revealing than blind prejudice is the behavior of Russians who genuinely believed in women's rights: they solemnly saluted the importance of women but occasionally attacked them with a viciousness that belies respect. Apparently, to these writers, if woman did not fulfill her potential, she would be left not the equal of man but vastly his inferior. Even a committed supporter of women's rights like Dobroliubov could exclaim, when disappointed with women's educational progress, "Many observations have shown that the brain of a woman weighs ¼ to 1/6 of a man's. This is completely in accord with her intellectual development."[15]

The reason for such unexpected exasperation had less to do with bad science than with *obshchestvo* political strategy. If woman could enact the positive aspects of the strategy, she could also expose its uncertain ones. The pictures of woman's position in society suggests a very precarious perch: she could fall off into two equally bad directions. First, her removal from the corrupt world could

14. One indication of the very uncertain attitude concerning women in this period is the scandal caused by the journal *The Century*. In reporting a certain woman's public declamation of Pushkin's *Egyptian Nights*, including, of course, Cleopatra's offer of herself for one night in return for the man's life, *The Century* had allowed itself a tone that was construed by some as suggestive. The affair occupied the press for months and ended with the journal being forced to shut down. A society that reacted so extremely to innuendo (and indeed the editor of *The Century* claimed total innocence) could hardly have felt secure in the significant claims it made for women. See P. I. Veinberg, "Bezobraznyi postupok *Veka*," *Istoricheskii vestnik*, No. 5 (1900), 472–489. Veinberg was the editor of *The Century* at the time of the episode.

One example of the antiwoman sentiment, which gives a feeling of its spirit, is reported by M. L. Mikhailov, "Zhenshchiny v universitetakh," *Sovremennik*, LXXXVI, No. 4 (1861), 505, who states that some university professors had begun maliciously to stress sexual detail in physiology lectures attended by woman auditors.

15. N. A. Dobroliubov, "Organicheskoe razvitie cheloveka v sviazi s ego umstvennoi i nravstvennoi deiatel'nost'iu," *Sobranie sochinenii*, II, 444.

make her not merely innocent but ignorant, wholly out of touch with urgent issues. As Pisarev, another fervent supporter of women's rights, remarked, "Women in our society often remain children into old age. They do not know life, since they never confront it."[16] Remarkably, the statement appears in the same essay in which Pisarev speaks glowingly of the advantages that women gained from living at a distance from Russian society.

The second danger is described by Pirogov. His "Questions of Life" was widely interpreted as the first published argument for the betterment of women's condition in Russia; nevertheless, the opinion of women that is expressed in some sections of the essay is devasting. To Pirogov, a man who failed to live by humanitarian principles would ultimately admit the fact and try to change; but "a woman would arm herself with deceit to the end."[17] Such a woman was no better than a doll, devoid of true feeling and committed to the tawdry and transient things of the world. In this view, woman, instead of being a carrier of vital new values, is the most submissive servant of the prevailing corruption. The attitudes expressed by Pirogov and Pisarev indicate what an exquisitely measured distance had to be maintained if women were to become the agents who would transform Russian life.

One type of social figure seemed to bring the conflicted view of women into special clarity and, hence, was much discussed. That was the *institutka*, the woman who received her education in a so-called closed institute. These institutes had first been established in the reign of Catherine II by her Minister of Education Ivan Betskoi. Strongly influenced by contemporary European pedagogy, which was often based on a naive reading of Locke, Betskoi viewed students as passive receivers of stimuli. The job of education was to regulate the impressions that students were exposed to, providing them only with models worth emulating. That was best accomplished in a controlled setting; hence the need for the closed institute, with its year-round residence requirement, minimal visiting privileges, and rural location.[18]

16. Pisarev, "Nasha universitetskaia nauka," p. 138.
17. Pirogov, "Voprosy zhizni," p. 83.
18. The history of the closed institutes is examined at length in Likhacheva, *Materialy dlia istorii zhenskogo obrazovania*, I, 100 ff.

Though empirical philosophy was largely out of fashion in Russia by the middle of the nineteenth century, the closed institutes, especially for women, still existed. The rationale justifying the closed institute had to arouse *obshchestvo* interest (indeed, most of the institutes were under the authority of the Dowager Empress, a figure closely connected with *obshchestvo*): the closed institutes, it was felt, would permit women to develop their best instincts by removing them from the general corruption. In her famous memoirs, Elizaveta Vodovozova, who attended the Smolny Institute, showed why the institutes were necessary; her picture of Russian life is lurid as a nightmare, but probably accurate:

> The pre-Emancipation period, before the liberation of the serfs, was a time when the passions of many landowners, which had become unbridled by long-standing tyranny, were expressed in terrible immorality, when in the homes of many landowners there were whole harems of serf girls, when banquests were accompanied with incomprehensible debauchery, drunkenness, brawls, vulgar cursing, when from the stables one could hear the desperate screams of serfs being whipped. By separating daughters from such parents, the institute saved them from moral death.[19]

But, as it is Vodovozova's main point to show, the closed institute was not perceived as an unqualified good. Though it protected its students from evil influences, it could also foster excessive innocence. The girls, who after all had eventually to leave the institute's sheltering walls, were often unfit to deal with the society from which they had been assiduously kept apart. A debate arose about how to mitigate the deficiencies in the system while retaining the advantages. Some proposals that were put forward—such as granting the students vacation periods away from the school—were aimed at introducing the women to Russian society slowly, like deep-sea divers undergoing decompression. One writer ingeniously proposed to redecorate the institute with replicas of rooms found in the world outside, as a means of acclimatization.[20] In fact, no proposal was likely to explain away the sense of contradiction, since the very concept of a closed institute in post-Crimean War Russia was part of

19. E. Vodovozova, *Na zare zhizni* (Moscow, 1964), I, 477.
20. M. Appel'rot', "Obrazovanie zhenshchin sredniago i vysshago sostoianii," *Otechestvennye zapiski*, LXVI, No. 2 (1858), 660.

a social strategy that defined women contradictorily as both innocent and ready to confront the world.

The figure of the *institutka* had an obvious attraction for writers of
fiction. When innocence is suddenly exposed to corruption, the
results are likely to be dramatic, if not always edifying. There were
two distinct treatments of the *institutka*, reflecting the two dangers
that Pisarev and Pirogov had alluded to in describing the role of
woman in general. Approached from one angle, she was a character
whose ignorance of reality led to sterile gestures of rebellion. The
epynomous heroine of Khvoshchinskaia's popular *The Girl from the
Institute (Pensionerka)* grows disenchanted with love and declares
herself a nihilist. In *Is She to Blame?* Pisemsky notes the heroine's
institute background in the course of describing her decline into
immorality and early death. Leskov's *No Exit* has an institute-
educated heroine who participates in a disastrous experiment in
communal living. All these heroines rebel futilely and aimlessly.
Approached from another angle, the *institutka's* upbringing leads
not to rebellion but to total obeisance before social norms, with no
allowance for personal morality or true feeling. Turgenev knew this
tendency especially well, since he translated *Institutka*, by the Uk-
rainian writer Marko Vovchok (in *Otechestvennie zapiski*, No. 1,
1860), the heroine of which perfectly exemplifies the rampant insensitivity that results from an education that is distanced from concrete
reality.

In his own novels Turgenev is sensitive to the question of education when describing his heroines. A single pattern recurs in the
novels. In *Rudin, Nest of the Nobility,* and *On the Eve* the upbringing of the heroines is characterized by two facts. First, it is largely
unsupervised. Natalya in *Rudin* is for a long time virtually ignored
by her mother and allowed to follow her own instincts. In *Nest of
the Nobility,* "Liza had turned ten when her father died; but he had
been little concerned with her . . . he could not stand, as he put it, to
be a nanny to some squealer." Liza's mother "in truth did not concern herself with Liza much more than her husband did. . . . While
her father was alive Liza was in the care of an old maid governness
from Paris . . . she had little influence over [Liza]" (*S*, VII, 239).
Elena in *On the Eve* is allowed to run free from an early age, and
soon rejects altogether any attempt at supervision: she despises her

father, feels "a cold sympathy" for her mother, and scorns and ignores her governess. "From the age of sixteen," Turgenev takes time to tell us, "she was completely independent (S, VIII, 34-35). In no case does education constrain the heroine.

The second fact that Turgenev stresses is that the heroine's upbringing takes place at home. About none of the heroines' families can it be said that they promote or exemplify a set of admirable rules for living. But the home as Turgenev depicts it does provide a place for untrammeled development. His treatment reflects a reawakened Russian interest in the advantages of an education in the home. Russian educational law had always permitted it and there was a long tradition of tutorial education of the nobility's children. In the 1850s domestic education acquired a specifically political significance, an aspect of *obshchestvo's* search for a focus of values that was set apart from the corrupt world yet was also—and here the home seemed an improvement on the closed institute—in touch with contemporary life. Turgenev is very sensitive to the need to locate education at a point of optimal efficiency. In *Asya*, a novella that depicts still another forceful heroine, the title character *is* educated in an institute, but Turgenev takes time to add this information about her earlier upbringing: "At the home of her father she enjoyed complete freedom. . . . He did not spoil her, did not constantly look after her" (S, VII, 94). Commenting on Asya's institutional education, her brother remarks, "Contrary to my expectations, she stayed the same as before" (S, VII, 96). A proper home education, unsupervised but structured by domestic values, can resist *even* the unfortunate influences of the closed institute.[21] In the novels, Turgenev also suggests that an education which is correctly located, regardless of its other qualities, can yield tremendous rewards.

Turgenev's pedagogical themes are always tied to a more general issue: the need to escape Russia's general corruption without succumbing to the extremes of either moral insensitivity or naiveté. Turgenev's readers were aware of the topographical dilemma he was

21. Cf. Pisarev's comment on *Asya*, "Zhenskie tipy v romanakh Pisemskogo, Turgeneva i Goncharova": "Asya does not suffer from the close supervision which transforms a healthy girl into a well-mannered marionette, which stifles free movement" (p. 249).

grappling with in the depiction of his heroines. Of Liza, Annenkov wrote: "There are highly moral personalities who are *born* or at any rate grow up inexplicably. They form themselves without the aid of upbringing, example, laws or directives. . . . They can appear in the midst of complete spiritual darkness, at the core of the most completely depraved circumstances. . . . Only one thing is certain: that sometimes the most meager spiritual sustenance is sufficient for the development of their moral life in all its amazing brilliance."[22]

Turgenev's heroines are remarkable achievements because he acknowledges the implacable evil that is abroad in Russia, corrupt and corrupting, yet persuasively shows that it can be avoided. The heroines are fully Russian, not fantasies or saints; but they find a "core" in Russian life where they can develop their moral sense.

Of course, Turgenev's portrayal of his heroines raises a serious literary problem—one that mirrors a troubling aspect of the general conception of woman's role: How was it possible to conceive of an individual as morally forceful if the individual is confined to an environment whose only virtue is safety? The "core" itself is valuable only because it is set apart from Russian society; as Annenkov remarks, it does no more than offer "the most meager spiritual sustenance." Turgenev found a mode of representation that met the difficulty. His heroines seem to exist in a state of suspended animation. For long periods they *do* nothing. Instead, they concentrate their energies on their inner lives, nourishing their moral sense by contemplating their own beings, like a hibernating bear that lives off its own flesh. Of Natalia in *Rudin*, Turgenev writes: "She spoke little, listened, and looked about her attentively, almost fixedly—as if she wanted to give herself an account of everything. She often remained motionless, letting her arms drop when fully in thought. At these times her face expressed the inner workings of her thoughts. . . . She felt deeply but secretly" (S, VI, 279–280).

Natalia's silence and motionless posture are sympathetic because the reader sees that her moral sense remains active. She has an inner life that is so meritorious that it bodies forth even when she does nothing. The description of Natalia's tacit power could apply to Turgenev's other heroines as well. "However much [Elena] tried to

22. P. V. Annenkov, "Dvorianskoe gnezdo," Russkii vestnik, No. 8 (1859), p. 515.

hide it, the anguish of her turbulent soul revealed itself in the very calmness of her appearance" (S, VII, 35). "[Liza] had no 'words of her own,' but she had her own idea and she followed her own path. . . . She was charming without knowing it. Her every gesture expressed an involuntary, slightly awkward grace" (S, VII, 242). These heroines project strength, even while remaining essentially inactive, because their inner development never ceases.

Turgenev's achievement is interesting in itself—it is the literary equivalent of a blank canvas that nevertheless expresses meaning—but it is more important for its cultural implications. His representation of his heroines suggests a resolution to the contradictory demands of *obshchestvo*. Russian women were to exist *apart* from society, but they had to learn to act *upon* society. The heroines in *Rudin, Nest of the Nobility,* and *On the Eve* utilize the freedom of their circumstances to cultivate their moral sensibility, but otherwise they tend to ignore their surroundings, which offer few opportunities for significant action. When they do at last act—and they all make important practical decisions—it is with the force of a carefully nurtured personality. Their acts are the spontaneous overflow of who they have discovered they really are.

Turgenev does not stop with this symbolic justification of the culture's ideal of woman. Typically he moves to scrutinize that which he has justified. If he shows how the *obshchestvo* view of woman can be rationalized, he also exposes its serious flaws. He took up this double task most conscientiously in *On the Eve,* the third of the four novels he wrote in the years 1856–1861.

On the Eve begins with a scene that is quintessentially Russian. Two friends, Bersenev and Shubin, lounge by the Moscow River, shading themselves from the summer heat under a lilac tree while they discuss the ultimate questions of existence. Their conversation mixes banter with philosophy, expressions of easy friendship with intellectual concerns of the most strenuous order. They discuss the meaning of the natural world. Bersenev remarks that nature evokes feelings of both unease and pleasure: pleasure because it is satisfying to contemplate the self-sufficiency it projects, unease because man is made to feel his own flaws much more acutely in its presence. Shubin cuts short these speculations. If you want life to have shape, he says, you must shape it yourself. That is why he has become a sculptor; in that activity he can reduce everything to forms. As he puts it, "I am a dealer in meat, sir; my job is meat, to shape meat into shoulders, legs, arms; whereas here [in nature] there is no form, no endings, everything spills out in all directions. . . . Try and catch it!" (S, VIII, 9).

The intellectual opposition between the two men is sharp, admitting of no resolution and even little mutual comprehension. The conversation proceeds erratically as each man makes his points for their own sake rather than with any expectation of persuading his companion. And yet for all that, the encounter shows an engagement of passions of the kind we are used to in Russian literature even when the topics are abstract. The reason is not only that Bersenev and Shubin are close friends, though that is part of it, the abstract discussion is animated by true feeling because Bersenev and Shubin love the same woman.

At first they do not mention Elena; they speak of love theoretically. Their attitudes on the topic parallel perfectly their dissimilar views of nature: Shubin wants a love of sensual gratification; Bersenev believes love entails a giving up of the self to a transcendent force. But now a means for resolving their differences exists. Both men sense that the one who wins Elena will have his vision of love, and of the world in general, sustained. From this first scene in *On the Eve*, woman's approval becomes energetically solicited.

Though Elena feels attracted to both Bersenev and Shubin, she ultimately chooses the Bulgarian revolutionary Insarov. It is a reasonable decision, given the logic of the book. Directly before she meets Insarov for the first time, she returns home, after discussing philosophy with Bersenev and flirting with Shubin, to sit by the window, look at the moon, and weep with frustration: Bersenev and Shubin both leave her with merely tantalizing intimations of the ideal. Insarov appears right to her because he possesses some of the best qualities of the other two suitors. He has Shubin's taste for the concrete without the accompanying frivolity, and he has Bersenev's commitment to humanistic values without the accompanying vagueness.

On the Eve is the story of Elena's choice, and also, more generally, of the process of a Russian woman choosing a man to love. The title, which struck many readers with its political overtones, also signals the passage of a young girl into a woman who suddenly realizes that love is a form of expression, perhaps the only one available to her.[23] Once Elena chooses Insarov, she permits nothing to deter her from joining him, not her parents, nor social proprieties, nor even Insarov's reluctance to entangle her in his uncertain destiny. Her disgust for a life without prospect gives Elena a sense of urgency and purpose. In a scene unusually graphic for the times and especially graphic for Turgenev, Elena escapes her parents' surveillance, goes to Insarov's apartment and accepts his passionate advances. "Well, take me, then," she says (S, VIII, 131). The consummation is not merely erotic. When Elena gives herself to Insarov she not only attains sexual freedom after years of binding social conventions but also comes to the end of an intellectual quest. Insarov is the man who will help her fulfill her desire to better the human condition.

Ironically, Elena's gesture of greatest purposefulness is to give herself to a man who she believes will best be able to realize her ideals for her. *On the Eve* thus presents an ambiguous narrative line. Elena is at the center, but since her main role is to endorse someone else, there is a vacuum where one expects substance. The male characters also seem shadowy figures. They continually look nervously to Elena, hoping she will certify their existence; till she chooses, they wander about erratically, each uncertain that the values he espouses really are worthwhile.

Even Insarov, for all his apparent self-sufficiency, requires Elena's approval before he can assume his full stature. Though he comes on the scene heralded by Bersenev as a hero, the other characters refuse to honor him. Heroism for them implies not brave acts but the capacity to invest behavior with moral value, and they see no reason to grant the gruff and unsophisticated Bulgarian such an accomplishment. Turgenev stresses Insarov's unpersuasive appearance by having Shubin sculpt a successful caricature of him, showing all seeming strengths as actual deficiencies—persistence becomes stubborness, restraint becomes conceit, passion becomes

---

23. Dobroliubov's essay, "Kogda zhe pridet nastoiashchii den'?" *Sobranie sochinenii,* VI, 96–140, was particularly emphatic in drawing political inferences from Turgenev's novel.

mere enthusiasm. Even Bersenev, who calls himself Insarov's friend, pronounces the resemblance apt. Nor does Insarov's physical courage alter the prevailing opinion of him. When a picnic outing of Elena's relatives and friends is interrupted by a group of rowdy German officers, Insarov picks up the loudest offender and throws him into a pond. Though the party is first elated, there is something in Insarov's abrupt aggressiveness that disturbs them. Going home in their carriages, they do not discuss the event; a mood of vague unease takes hold, as if everyone were awaiting an explanation of Insarov's state of mind. The only comment is Shubin's mocking remark to Bersenev, "And is he not a hero now: throwing drunken Germans into the water" (*S*, VIII, 79).

But Elena's decision to unite her fate to Insarov's dispels all doubts concerning his merits. She does not instill goodness in him, but by her love she persuades the rest of the world that Insarov's inherent qualities were already good, that his visible actions are aspects of fully rounded individual. Her love is a form of accreditation, the raising of one man over others; and it is felt as such by the other characters. After Elena has left with Insarov for Bulgaria, Shubin says of her, "If we had real people [here in Russia], such beautiful souls would not escape" (*S*, VIII, 142). The love of Elena for Insarov is not a marriage made in heaven but the result of a passionate process of elimination.

In tying the idea of love so intimately to that of choice, Turgenev exposes an ambiguous element in the *obshchestvo* view of woman. Though power was imputed to her, it was never made clear how her power could be used for social change: woman, after all, was confined to a circumscribed area apart from the general corruption— that was, indeed, the source of her power. The *only* role she could possibly play was to encourage man, endowing him with the purposefulness he lacked by himself.

Turgenev acknowledges that such a relationship between man and woman makes sense in Russia, but he also shows that making woman an enabling instrument for man risks tremendous anxiety. A nervous equilibrium of strength and weakness, of control and submission, takes hold. Woman requires man to enact her ideals for her and man requires woman to sanction his efforts. The desperate mutuality may create a love of passionate intensity, but it may cause disaster if the delicate balance is disturbed. Thus, though the union of Insarov and Elena resolves the main issue of the first part of *On the Eve* (whom will Elena choose?), it raises problems of another sort. The courtship and marriage of the hero and heroine produces few moments of joy. Their meetings are always tense, conditioned by premonitions of disaster; their declarations of love evoke pictures of extreme hardship:

> "Yes, Dmitri, we will go together. I will follow you. That is my duty. I love you—no other duty do I recognize."
> "Oh, Elena," Insarov exclaimed, "What unbreakable chains each of your words lays on me." [S, VIII, 128]

Insarov and Elena are not simply accommodating each other, as lovers do. Their comments express true bewilderment about the emotion holding them together. They eagerly surrender power to each other, for each has something to gain from a strong partner. Elena galvanizes Insarov to action by her words of submission; Insarov accepts the unbreakable chains that Elena lays on him because he knows they will inspire his most energetic activity. It is, in fact, to the lovers' advantage not to consider their relationship precisely: it is like some magical dance in the air, the spell of which could be broken by cool rationality. At one point Elena says to Insarov, "Everything is bright in the future, is it not?" and he replies, "You are my future, it is bright for me" (S, VIII, 123). Insarov equates Elena with the totality of experience; no set of single facts or discrete attitudes can be discovered which will account for her attractiveness. That view expresses Insarov's great love, and it simultaneously ensures against any attempt to analyze the provenance of Elena's power.

The fragile balance they must maintain is very soon upset. And though the coda of their love is sounded by a brute physical fact—death from tuberculosis—Turgenev shows that in a sense Insarov deserves to waste away. The disease that finally overwhelms him as the lovers journey to Bulgaria, ravaging his muscles and forcing blood up through his mouth, is the symbol of his misplaced reliance on Elena. Unable to get the strength he sought from her, Insarov weakens and dies. When Elena writes to her parents, "Who knows, perhaps I killed him" (S, VIII, 165), the reader is not shocked.

The event precipitating Insarov's decline is a clear consequence of his love. Going about in the rain to secure a false passport for Elena, in case they have to elope, Insarov catches the cold that will develop into fatal disease. Though Elena cannot be held accountable for the weather, or Insarov for his susceptibility to a virus, the scene indicates their joint responsibility for the final tragedy. The quest for the passport proves to be a test of Elena's symbolic power, which both lovers have tried to establish. Insarov visits a disreputable "retired or dismissed" prosecutor who has access to forged documents; the prosecutor's rooms are dank and soiled, his manner vulgar and leering. In effect, Insarov's ideal vision of Elena is suddenly exposed to coarse reality. The prosecutor's interest in the prospect of a young woman traveling with a man not legally her husband is undisguisedly lascivious. Sniffing tobacco from an ostentatiously displayed "snuffbox that was decorated with a figure of a full-breasted nymph" (*S*, VIII, 115), he suggestively describes the ease with which his false passport will allow Elena to elude the authorities: "Who knows whether [she] is Maria Bredikhina or Karolina Vogelmeyer," he says, invoking German women's reputation for loose sexual behavior.

Insarov withdraws in disgust. But his image of Elena has already been damaged, hence his image of himself as well. The delirium that he falls into on the following day has a psychological as well as physical cause. He dreams of Elena contaminated by the influence of the prosecutor:

> He lost consciousness. He lay flat on his back as though crushed and suddenly had the impression that someone was quietly laughing and whispering above him. . . . What was that? The old prosecutor stood above him, in an Oriental silk gown belted with a foulard, as he had seen him the day before. . . . "Karolina Vogelmeyer," the toothless mouth muttered. As Insarov watched, the old man grew wider, swelled; now he was no longer a man, he was a tree. . . . Insarov had to climb its lofty boughs. Something catches at him and he falls chest downward against a sharp rock, while Karolina Voeglmeyer sits on her haunches, like a street vendor, and babbles, "Pasties, pasties, pasties,"—and there blood now flows, and sabers flash unceasingly . . . Elena! And everything vanishes in a maroon chaos. [*S*, VIII, 117]

A grammatical connection is missing at a crucial point in the passage. The ellipsis before Elena's name makes it uncertain whether Insarov unwillingly regards her as linked with Karolina Vogelmeyer or whether he sees her as the figure who can resist the prevailing degradation and chaos. But such uncertainty is an important concession. Elena's power must become problematical the moment it is called into question; its only source is Insarov's uncritical willingness to impute it to her. When his picture of her becomes ambiguous, Elena's influence immediately declines, and Insarov himself becomes passive and helpless.

Elena ministers lovingly to him during his sickness. The factors that make her wonder if she is responsible for his death are never made explicit. They cannot be, for the crux of the book is that these characters cannot face who they are and what they do for each other. To the last the lovers maintain the illusion that Elena is Insarov's sustaining force; they know of no other way to give their lives purpose. But if the characters never fully understand their distortion of women's role, Turgenev permits the reader to see its unwholesome effects: Because of Insarov's worsening illness, the couple stops in Venice while on their way to Bulgaria, and to pass the time they attend a performance of *La Traviata*. The role of the doomed Violetta is played by a young and naive actress, not very pretty and totally unable to exploit the theatrical effects. "But," Turgenev remarks, "In her acting there was much that was right and disingenuously simple" (S, VIII, 153). The actress' performance recapitulates the double aspect of woman that is hinted at throughout *On the Eve*. An actress usually resorts to gestures not her own; she makes her impression by assuming aspects. But Violetta in this performance disdains the arsenal of effects which the theater puts at her disposal. She instead makes her own person the standard of judgment, and she succeeds. At the critical moment of the opera, Turgenev remarks (putting the phrase into italics), "she *finds herself.*" Not convention shapes her performance, but only the sense of who she actually is, slightly adjusted to meet the demands of the role.

Though the performance charms Elena and Insarov, it also reflects ominously their own situation. When Elena remarks approvingly of the way the actress enacts Violetta's death scene, Insarov replies, "Yes, she is not joking: she smells of death." Elena draws back, for Insarov's comment evokes his own certain fate. In watching the opera, Insarov has had the flash of knowledge that it might be better to consider women for what they really are, that something is lost when they are forced to play symbolic roles. But he cannot bring himself to apply the insight to his own life.

Elena and Insarov are trapped in the psychological mechanism they have assiduously built. Potentially of great efficacy, it can turn on its creators, sapping their energy. As the lovers ride a gondola along the Grand Canal and back to their hotel, they contemplate with anxiety the beauty of Venice that Turgenev described in the opening passage of the chapter. The city has taken on the aspect of Insarov's malaise:

> He who has not seen Venice in April can hardly know the indescribable beauty of the enchanted city. The mildness and softness of spring suit Venice, as the brilliant summer sun suits magnificent Genoa, as the gold and purple of autumn suit the grand old fellow Rome. Like the spring, the beauty of Venice touches and awakens desire; it oppresses and torments the inexperienced heart, like the promise of a happiness that is not so much enigmatic as mysterious. Everything in it is bright, comprehensible, and everything is enwrapped in a dreamy haze of love-stricken silence; everything in it is feminine, beginning with the name: not for nothing has it alone been given the name *The Beautiful*. The huge masses of palaces and churches stand light and splendid, like the shapely dream of a young god; there is something fabulous, something enchantingly strange in the green-grey gleam of the canal, in the noiseless gliding of the gondolas, in the absence of harsh city sounds, of coarse banging, rattling and uproar. . . . It is useless for a man at the end of his life, who has been broken by experience, to visit Venice: it will be bitter for him, like the memory of unfulfilled dreams of his earliest days; but it will be sweet for him in whom strength still seethes, who feels himself fortunate: let him bring his happiness beneath her enchanted sky and no matter how radiant it may be, she will gild it still more with her never fading aureole. [S, VIII, 154]

Venice is feminine, Turgenev stresses, and, like a woman, the city promises satisfaction for the men who encounter it. The city, may also, however, promote enervation and confusion. For just as with woman, the source of the city's power proves difficult to locate. Venice presents itself for inspection, "bright, comprehensible," yet its ultimate meaning lies beyond its visible contours. The "masses of palaces and churches" may be only the "shapely dream of a young god." No wonder that its essence is "indescribable"—not merely "enigmatic," which would be elusive enough, but "mysterious."

Trying to describe this complex of shifting meanings, of visible signs that tend continually to yield priority to seductive but vague implications, Turgenev decides to emphasize the city's habitual epithet: *"The Beautiful."* Such an insistence on a name, to the point of italicizing it, is one way to fix and hold Venice in mind, a safeguard against the tendency of its meanings to fly off into a "dreamy haze." Indeed, even those facts about Venice which may be described with some precision prove less observable qualities than the absence of qualities—the lack of "banging, rattling, and uproar." Finally, it is unclear if Venice is anything apart from the meanings that the viewer assigns to it. Venice is always on the verge of being not what it presents but what it is made to represent.

By the end of the passage, however, the ambiguity surrounding Venice is largely resolved, in a way that minimizes the city's power but introduces a bracing air of reality. It is now made clear that Venice cannot after all generate ennobling emotions in all those who view it. Venice is not a magic instrument to grasp new meanings, it is only itself, and as such it can only give back to those who consider it that which they already are. If the man who visits Venice is strong, Venice will enhance his powers, but it can do nothing for those who are weak. Men must look within themselves for sustenance, instead of constructing elaborate psychological mechanisms that would impart strength from without.

That, of course, is the burden of the book. Elena is only a woman, no less but also no more. She cannot impart power to Insarov, for finally she has no more power than he does. All that is left is the hard business of everyday life. The book's concluding pages, after Insarov dies and Elena decides to proceed alone to Bulgaria, are taken up with references to burial preparations, travel arrangements, and explanatory letters—all expressive of attitudes that are more subdued than had moved the characters earlier but also that are much more levelheaded. Love is dead, the world must be attended to. Or to put it more generally: the vision of *obshchestvo* that would make woman an instrument to provide men with purpose has been exposed for the extremely fragile mechanism it is. A more prosaic means of dealing with the pernicious circumstances of Russian reality will have to be found.

It is possible, I should add, to extract quite another view of love from Turgenev's works than the one that I have just offered, and it is likely that Turgenev would have preferred the alternative. In his letters he often spoke of love as a unique experience, a transcendent force whose onset can be neither explained nor resisted. That view makes the connection of the issue of love with Russian society in 1856–1863 appear tenuous at best. Nevertheless, perhaps despite himself, he allowed even this most private of all emotions to assume a general dimension. Indeed, his intensely personal work, the autobiographical *First Love*, is also the work that most clearly reveals the *obshchestvo* view of the social role of woman.[24]

Sixteen-year-old Volodia is spending the summer in the countryside near Moscow, preparing for the university entrance examination. He studies erratically; the random and marvelous sensations of the natural world bombard him continually, giving him a pleasurable but unfocused feeling. Then, abruptly, his life becomes focused. Returning home from shooting crows, he spies through the woods his new neighbor, Zinaida. He is transfixed by what he sees:

> Several steps from me—in a glade, among the brush of unripe raspberries, there stood a tall, well-built girl in a striped dress and with a white handkerchief around her head; around her there crowded four young men, and she slapped each of them, in turn, on their foreheads with some of those grey, smallish flowers (whose name I do not know, but which are well known to children . . .). The young men so eagerly presented their foreheads, and in the gestures of the girl there was something so entrancing, authoritative, caressing, humorous, and kind that I almost shouted from amazement and joy, and, I think, would have immediately given anything on earth if these beautiful fingers would slap at my forehead also. [S, IX, 11]

The moment transforms Volodia's life. Where previously he had been confused, now he has a purpose. No longer do his thoughts run randomly, without meaning; no longer does he respond to nature with a merely passive wonder. Zinaida preoccupies him fully, and whatever he looks at is shaped and given meaning by the image of

---

24. Cf. the reported comment of Turgenev quoted in S, IX, 460: "There is only one story that I reread with pleasure. That is 'First Love.' In the remaining ones there are—though not many—things that are invented; in 'First Love' are described actual events without the least adornment; and in rereading it, I see the characters as if alive before me."

Zinaida's being. She becomes the touchstone of all his experience. Since Zinaida is four years older, she and Volodia tacitly agree that physical love is out of the question. But that limitation only puts into sharper relief the emotions that bind them. Volodia submits to Zinaida not for a visible reward, but in the hope that she will bestow a purpose on his life.

That first encounter between Volodia and Zinaida establishes the symbolic nature of their relationship. Their meeting has no context; it follows from no history. Volodia abruptly comes upon a group of individuals engaged in a strikingly unusual activity, but he resolutely refrains from guessing at an explanation for what he sees. He is content to contemplate the drama of submission and power for its own sake. Indeed, such details as might detract from the central aspect of the experience are quickly shunted aside. Turgenev, usually so meticulous in his nature descriptions, here simply does not bother finding the correct name for the flower Zinaida wields—since it is only an instrument of her power, its name does not matter.

Throughout *First Love*, Turgenev depicts man's impulse to submit to woman not as blind masochism but as a strategy to acquire a sense of purpose. Zinaida, though she tolerates no breech of respect from her admirers, knows they will not be satisfied merely to grovel at her feet. She therefore establishes an elaborate rivalry among them: any moment of attention one of them receives is given the form of a choice, an indication that he is at least temporarily preferred to the others. Zinaida initiates Volodia into the complex mechanism of selection and rejection as soon as they meet formally. As Volodia watches enviously, another admirer is allowed to kiss Zinaida's hands as a sign of her affection. But as Belovzorov bends to claim his reward, Volodia notes with happy surprise that "while he was kissing [her hands] she looked at me over his shoulder" (S, IX, 19). Her conspiratorial glance makes it unclear to whom Zinaida is granting her attention at the moment, whom she has chosen as her favorite and whom rejected; but the glance allows Volodia to realize that Zinaida sanctions rivalry among her admirers, and that implies the possibility of sometimes winning.

Zinaida, unlike Turgenev's other heroines, is highly self-conscious of her relationship with men. She treats her imperious style as part of a game, and makes the men aware of the roles they are playing. The game is very serious—Zinaida is ruthless when she fails to receive her due, and when she exiles one of her admirers from her presence, he is sincerely despairing—but she has an irony about her that also calls the game into question. Indeed, in the moment of her greatest power she herself exposes the props and pulleys of the intricate psychological design.

One evening, when "The whole company is present, in its full complement" (*S*, IX, 52), Zinaida declares that each individual will tell "something absolutely invented." Zinaida's own story is "absolutely invented" yet utterly realistic: A beautiful young princess gives a magnificent ball in her castle. She summons many guests, of whom all the men are in love with her. Her admirers crowd around her, showering compliments. In telling this story, Zinaida, of course, mirrors her own situation—and she emphasizes the parallel by interrupting herself to issue haughty demands to the admirers crowded around *her*. Her story, with its references to castles and glittering diadems and brightly lit ballrooms, intensifies reality; but at the same time its artificiality and mock emotionality brings reality into question—by repeating in the form of a silly tale the relationship that exists between her and the men around her, Zinaida discloses its tenuous nature.

Zinaida's story ends with the princess drawn away from the ball by a mysterious passion. She goes to keep a secret rendezvous "near a fountain, near the splashing water, with him whom I love, who rules over me" (*S* IX, 54). With these words Zinaida conclusively destroys the sham court with herself as princess and the men as her submissive subjects. As the men (except Volodia) have suspected, Zinaida is in fact enthralled by someone outside the company. She is not a ruler but is herself ruled. Everyone has put that knowledge aside so that the game of submission and domination could continue. Zinaida's story makes it impossible to continue ignoring the truth. Lushin, one of her admirers, says, "And what would we do, my friends, if we were in the ranks of those guests and knew about that fortunate man by the fountain?" (*S*, IX, 54-55). Reality has thoroughly enveloped the game: the strategy of imputing power to Zinaida in order to gain accreditation from her in return—that devious short-circuiting of emotions—must collapse.

The reality that intrudes is particularly distressing to Volodia. The man that Zinaida loves is his father. At first, Volodia tries to suppress the emotions that must follow the knowledge that his father has won the woman he has sought. When he observes his father headed for a rendezvous with Zinaida, he refuses to comprehend what he sees. And when he is forced to acknowledge the obvious, his judgment is surprisingly mild: "Against my father I had no ill will. On the contrary, he seemed to have grown in my eyes" (S IX, 67). In its broad outlines, Volodia's reaction is a representation of a universal problem, the way a son measures himself against his father, and the emotional tricks he must resort to if civility is to continue. The autobiographical basis of *First Love* makes the psychological drama more compelling. But the work's illumination of universal emotional problems and of Turgenev's particular relationship with his father does not keep it from casting light as well on the social role of love in Russia in the 1850s. If *First Love* is about the Oedipus complex, it is an Oedipus in the clothes of the nineteenth-century nobility.

Indeed, *First Love* represents the swan song of Russian *obshchestvo*, at least as regards the issue of love. The hope that imputing power to woman would allow her to confer purpose on man, who would then battle prevailing evil, is exposed as fraudulent. The first touch of reality turns that sort of love into disaster. Thus Volodia suffers more than the loss of Zinaida. When he sees her as actually powerless, utterly submissive before someone outside the circle of her sham court, he becomes helpless himself. In a remarkable scene, Volodia witnesses from afar the last encounter between Zinaida and his father:

> Suddenly before my eyes there occurred a remarkable event: my father suddenly raised his riding crop, with which he had been knocking dust from his jacket—and there was heard a sharp blow against an arm that was naked to the elbow. I hardly could keep from shouting out, but Zinaida shuddered, silently regarded my father and slowly brought her arm to her lips, kissing the crimsoning bruise that was on it. [S, IX, 70]

The remainder of *First Love* is informed by attitudes that are startlingly flat and unfocused. Volodia expresses no regret, jealousy, or anger. The dismantling of Zinaida's power has emptied him of all purpose. When at the conclusion of the story, four years after the main events, Volodia learns that Zinaida is dying in a seedy hotel in unhappy circumstances, he can only say, "I gave myself my word that on the very next day I would visit my one-time "passion" (*passiia*)" (*S*, IX, 74). The foreign epithet suggests how little he now feels for Zinaida. Indeed, "business" intervenes, and he does not see Zinaida before she dies. The bitter irony is that in a sense Zinaida is responsible for the dessication of Volodia's emotions, which has kept him from offering her a final kindness.

Volodia's dim awareness of the reasons for his cruelty accounts for the curious last paragraph of *First Love*. Though he has not taken the opportunity to see Zinaida on her deathbed, two days subsequently Volodia is present—"through some irresistible attraction" (*S*, IX, 76)—at the death of a poor unknown old woman. The woman has previously not received a word of mention in *First Love;* but the description of her pathetic demise, after an existence apparently completely unhappy and deprived, provides a fitting end to the story. She is woman in her realistic aspect, shorn of all magical powers that man would impute to her. The stark realization that man cannot rely on such a figure to invest him with meaning makes Volodia cry out the story's last line, with its surprising last words, "And I remember that here, at the deathbed of the poor woman, I became terrified for Zinaida, and I wanted to pray for her, for my father—and for myself" (*S*, IX, 76).

Turgenev's novels describe a culture that was pervaded by contradictions. It was not seen that way by contemporaries, who continued writing and arguing passionately. The inconsistencies of their beliefs were often hidden by a terminology of elaborate redundancy that gave the feel of purposeful argument. Like any other man, Turgenev rarely got outside the excited swirl of assertion and hope that constitutes a culture, but his novels often cast a bright light on the main problems.

Obshchestvo privileged the inner man, but at the cost of permitting a maelstrom of erratic judgments. *Obshchestvo* forestalled mere dilettantism by insisting that work had to be invested with humanistic values, but in consequence rendered the idea of work most abstract. *Obshchestvo* elevated the status of woman, but finally only to serve, and to serve ambiguously, as an enabling instrument for man. *Obshchestvo* was a flawed, irrational, precarious, political phenomenon. Yet Turgenev also showed that it was better than anything else that could be conceived at that moment in Russia's history. His own personality was a measure of the efficacy of *obshchestvo:* when the personal flaws that previously had left him feeling helpless were construed as aspects of *obshchestvo* politics, they became issues that could be understood and confronted.

9.

Fathers and Sons
and Russian History

The Emancipation Act was signed by Alexander II on February 19, 1861, a little less than five years after he had openly declared his support for the abolition of serfdom. The publication of the new act was delayed until March 5, which was an ecclesiastical holiday, in the hope that religious feeling would temper any anger or disappointment. In the event, the public was mainly confused. That was partly because the Editing Committee that wrote the final version had allowed the Metropolitan of Moscow to introduce inspirational language into some of the passages, obscuring the legal issues without making anyone feel better. But understanding the act would have been difficult in any case. In its effort to please all factions, the Editing Committee produced an immensely complicated document. The rules governing land settlements and the continued obligations of the peasantry varied from region to region, depending on local conditions. More important, the Editing Committee had to meet the contradictory purposes of the government: a liberalized economic system, which meant a mobile labor force, and a restrictive political system, which meant that the labor force should not be allowed to develop into a rootless proletariat.[1]

Despite the many confusing resolutions, some of which were not cleared up for decades, one thing about the Emancipation Act was clear: it was not the momentous document that had been dreamed

1. Terence Emmons, *The Russian Landed Gentry and the Emancipation of 1861* (Cambridge, 1966), pp. 321 ff. I. A. Vinnikova, *Turgenev v shestdesiaty gody* (Saratov, 1965), discusses Turgenev's politics during this period.

of five years before. Though it abolished personal ownership of the peasant by the landlord, the act perpetuated the less visible injustices of the old system, using both economic leverage and administrative control to keep the peasant oppressed. Existing social arrangements were pushed about a bit but not significantly altered.

To the more radical members of *obshchestvo*, the Emancipation Act was both a disappointment and a hope. It was a disappointment because it failed to confront the country's basic inequities, a hope because it would make Russians from various classes see that there was no relying on the government to promote change, and that revolution was the only alternative. The Emancipation Act also revised the outlook of the more liberal members of *obshchestvo*. Some saw it mainly as the end of an outmoded feudal economy and, eager to take advantage of new commercial opportunities, moved closer to the government. Others, genuinely disappointed by the political inadequacy of the reforms, edged toward the radicals. In all, the Emancipation Act caused a crisis in *obshchestvo*, or, more accurately, it intensified the strains that had been in *obshchestvo* from the start. One of the main assumptions of *obshchestvo*, its belief that it could be an influential autonomous force in Russia society, was cast into serious doubt. Though important social reforms continued to be introduced up to the middle of the 1860s, bringing improvement in such areas as the legal system and local government, the Emancipation Act made clear that the government would permit no weakening in its hegemony.

Turgenev saw vividly that the old political alignments were in doubt. Nevertheless, he remained faithful to the *obshchestvo* ideal, hoping to salvage its best elements and to keep it a viable force. His position at the beginning of the 1860s was neatly expressed in his polemic with Herzen: for Herzen was one of those who most dramatically renounced the *obshchestvo* vision, moving emphatically to the left once the effects of the Emancipation Act became clear. In a series of articles in *The Bell* entitled "Beginnings and Endings," which consisted of letters directed to Turgenev, Herzen forcefully described the corruption of European politics as proven by the events of 1848, and claimed that the terms of the emancipation set Russia on the same path. The restrictions on the peasants' allotments, along with the financial redemptions they would be forced to make, would create a nation of small landowners and petty capitalists, with disastrous results. As Herzen put it, "The rule of the bourgeoisie—this is the consequence of emancipation without land."[2] It was necessary for Russia to avoid aping the West and to develop a particularly Russian social structure based on the potential of the peasant masses, as evidenced in the artel and the commune.

The attack on European civilization had to anger Turgenev, since it was his most passionate hope that Russia might someday achieve Western standards of culture. He wrote, in his reply to Herzen: "we Russians belong by language and by species to the European family, *genus Europaeum*, and consequently according to the most inalterable laws of physiology we must follow the same path. I never heard of a *duck* that, belonging to the species of *duck*, could breathe with gills, like a fish" (*P*, v, 67; italics in original).

Turgenev was not returning to the abstract Westernizer opinions he had held in the 1840s. He was now committed to finding answers to Russia's concrete problems. He objected to Herzen's emphasis on the peasantry not because he thought it smacked of sloppy philosophizing—he admired Herzen as a hard-headed thinker—but because it seemed a foolish political strategy. The peasantry was essentially conservative and self-serving, hence could not be an active force for change. Turgenev wrote to Herzen: "The *narod* before whom you bow are conservatives *par excellence*, and even carry within themselves the embryo of a bourgeoisie, in their tanned sheepskin coats, their warm and dirty huts, their bellies eternally filled to the point of heartburn and their feelings of repulsion toward any civic responsibility or institution" (*P*, v, 52).

Contrary to what Herzen believes, the peasantry is *already* comparable to the bourgeoisie, already an aspect of the general corruption. To succeed, political action must find a focus that is set apart from the existing forms of Russian life; only after a sense of independent purpose has been nourished, can evil, including the condition of the peasantry, be confronted.

Turgenev's disagreement with Herzen crystalized around the issue of the *Zemskii sobor*.[3] Herzen, as well as some of the radicals, urged the convocation of this long dormant body, with representa-

---

2. A. I. Herzen, *Sobranie sochineni* (Moscow, 1954-66), XVI, 141.
3. Emmons, *The Russian Landed Gentry and the Emancipation of 1861*, discusses the campaign for *Zemskii sobor*, pp. 385-393.

to be chosen from a nationwide pool and with no restrictions
ed on social status. The plan had the danger that the more aristo-
tic members of the nobility would gain additional influence, but
Herzen was willing to take that chance in the hope of gaining support from other estates, particularly the peasantry. Turgenev was
adamantly against the plan. Including the aristocracy or the peasantry, or both, in the opposition alliance would only dilute its
strength, as well as multiply the points of conflict with the government. The image of a circumscribed force, neatly focused and coherent, informed his most energetic objection to the *Zemskii sobor:*
"Our main disagreement with O[garev] and H[erzen], and Bakunin
also, consists in the fact that they, while scorning and trampling the
educated class in Russia into the dirt, assume a revolutionary principle in the *narod*—when in fact it is just the opposite. Revolution
in the true and vital sense of the word *exists* only in the minority
educated class—and this is enough for its success" (*P*, v, 49).

Turgenev wrote *Fathers and Sons*, his greatest novel, while directly under the influence of the crisis caused by the Emancipation
Act. His first reference to the project that became the novel was in
the summer of 1860, and he finished writing in July or August 1861.
When the book appeared, it immediately provoked bitter controversy. Because Turgenev had created characters that could be
placed on a recognizable political spectrum, every one of their false
steps seems an ideological judgment. What is remarkable, however,
is that *Fathers and Sons* was attacked from all sides. Liberals, radicals, and conservatives alike found the book politically deficient, not
merely in a few details but at its heart.[4]

Contemporaries mainly argued about one question, ending with
widely divergent conclusions: was Turgenev too respectful or too
scornful of his hero, the radical medical student Bazarov? Several
years after the height of the controversy, Turgenev stated that he
endorsed his character's views on all matters except art, which
Bazarov disdains. It is certain that even if Turgenev had declared his
position earlier, debate would not have cooled; the proof is that the

4. Isaiah Berlin, *Fathers and Children* (Oxford, 1972), gives a good account of the
disparate critical reactions to *Fathers and Sons*.

effort to define Turgenev's attitude toward Bazarov persists to the present day.[5]

It should be obvious that the degree of sympathy that Turgenev feels for his hero was always an irrelevant issue. If that were all that was at stake, radicals who disliked the book could have dismissed Turgenev's treatment as prejudiced, while dissatisfied liberals could have declared that what they perceived as an overly respectful characterization of Bazarov was Turgenev's attempt to curry favor with the younger generation. And that would have been the end of it. But even after such judgments were made, the controversy continued. In fact, the fascination of *Fathers and Sons* is the result of Turgenev's having made his hero more than a spokesman—or even a vivid exemplar—of a narrow ideological position. On the most important level of the book, Bazarov represents all of *obshchestvo*, liberals as well as radicals. What made *Fathers and Sons* a scandal is that Turgenev shows that Bazarov's very virtues contain the seeds of his destruction. *Fathers and Sons* is simultaneously an endorsement of some of *obshchestvo's* most cherished beliefs and a proof of their illogicality.

The opening scene, which depicts Arkadii Kirsanov returning home from the university, bringing his friend and mentor Bazarov with him, shows that Turgenev intends to use the same narrative structure as in his previous novels. The main action is set on a provincial estate; contemporary social and political forces will be only implied, not directly described. In *Fathers and Sons*, however, these forces clearly threaten the stability of the enclave as never before. The time is announced in the second sentence of the book: it is the spring of 1859, and the emancipation of the serfs, with all its uncertain consequences, is only two years ahead. In the short space that it takes to describe how Arkadii's father meets the two young men at the posting station and escorts them back to the manor house, Turgenev manages to suggest a world on the brink of extreme change. Even the seemingly prosaic exchange between Nikolai Kirsanov and his valet, as they await the arrival of the coach, becomes permeated by ambiguity. The valet, like all the other

---

5. For a summary of the more recent arguments see Zbigniew Folejewski, "The Recent Storm around Turgenev as a Point in Soviet Aesthetics," *Slavic and East European Journal*, VI, No. 1 (1962), 21–27.

characters, moves in a society where traditional relationships have been put into question:

> The valet, in whom everything—his single turquoise earring, his pomaded hair of various shades and his studied gestures—announced him as a representative of a modern and more perfect age, stared superciliously down the road and deigned to reply, "No sir, there's no sign of them." [S, VIII, 195]

One social order is dying, but a new one has not yet been born. Nikolai thinks of himself as a progressive and liberal, and he has granted his peasants improved working and financial conditions before the emancipation would require it. Nevertheless old attitudes and interests die hard. Nikolai's tone when he speaks of the peasants does not altogether hide his sense of superiority, and he is not above assuring himself of a profit at their expense: he has astutely sold off in advance the timber from land that will shortly pass to the peasants' possession. For their part, the peasants regard their new lot with great uncertainty. They treat all the concessions Nikolai has made them, both altruistic and self-serving ones, with suspicion. At times they seem on the verge of open rebellion: horses are being stolen, ploughs sabotaged, rents left unpaid.

Bazarov is a political animal, highly sensitive to shifting balances of power, and he is eager to channel the peasants' resentment; but he is not a blind ideologue. Turgenev immediately establishes his shrewdness about human relations. When Arkadii's father begins to insinuate traditional values by reciting Pushkin's poetry and rhapsodizing about nature, Bazarov breaks the sentimental mood by abruptly asking for cigarettes; he does not itemize an abstract program but rather shows its correlatives in everyday life.

Throughout the book Bazarov absorbs politics into psychology. He relies on the aura of his presence to persuade others; his politics are an overflow of who he is. He says to Arkadii, "As to the times, why should I depend on them? Much better that they should depend on me" (S, VIII, 226). In fact, Bazarov's imperious claim of self-sufficiency is indisputable; but it proves to be the very quality that leads to disaster. Turgenev neatly illustrates the ambiguous consequences of self-sufficiency by contrasting two of Bazarov's encounters.

Bazarov's argument with Arkadii's uncle Pavel—a "battle royal,"

Turgenev calls it—range over a wide variety of subjects, from art to philosophy to politics. While Pavel argues for an ameliorative humanism, Bazarov accepts only practical activity. He even believes that science is an abstract category that makes no sense until filled by precise experiments. For all the ideological points that get made, however, the argument is primarily a psychological confrontation. It is Bazarov's ability fully to comprehend Pavel's attitude that gives him the upper hand. He never bothers to refute Pavel point-by-point; indeed, he always appears on the verge of giving up the argument altogether in order to pursue tasks he insinuates are infinitely more rewarding, such as dissecting frogs. Pavel, who guesses Bazarov's opinion of him, can only sputter angrily, like a punctilious duelist who finds his opponent has abruptly decided rules governing the confrontation are ridiculous.

Pavel insults Bazarov, calling him a Mongol who does not understand civilization, but the charge is inaccurate. It is significant that Bazarov always leaves it to others to describe his position as "nihilism." Though he favors the destruction of much of contemporary Russian life, he is no unthinking destroyer: he has a precise knowledge of the attitudes he wants to abolish. At one point, Bazarov observes to Arkadii, "Nature is not a temple, but a workshop, and man is a worker in it" (S, VIII, 236). The remark expresses an extreme form of positivism, a disdain of beauty in favor of science. But its epigrammatic style—and Bazarov talks in epigrams continually—has the gracefulness of poetry. Indeed, no character in *Fathers and Sons* except Bazarov could have made the point so neatly. In general, Bazarov has worked through the positions he opposes and comes out the other side. He resolves the dilemmas that hobbled Russians in the middle of the nineteenth century by the sheer force of his personality.

By the end of the book, Bazarov has fallen from the lofty position he occupied in his confrontation with Pavel, brought low by his love for the beautiful widow Anna Sergeevna Odintsova. But, as in *On the Eve*, Turgenev does not portray love as a blank, elemental force: the relationship between Bazarov and Odintsova is a vehicle for exposing the traps that lie in wait for someone who believes in the philosophy that self-sufficiency will carry the day. They become acquainted when Bazarov visits Odintsova's estate. The "excellent, wonderfully furnished house,' with a lovely garden and conservatories" (S, VIII, 271), "not far from a yellow stone church with a green roof, white columns and a fresco above the main entrance representing the Resurrection, painted in the 'Italian' manner" (S, VIII, 273) provides a luxurious and idyllic setting for their conversation. As always in Turgenev's novels, however, bucolic peacefulness is mixed with a sense of practical urgency. The great world threatens to intrude, and men and women feel compelled to define their basic beliefs. Odintsova soon asks Bazarov, in tones insistent enough to appear inquisitorial, "What goal do you wish to attain? Where are you headed? What is your aim? In a word, who are you?" (S, VIII, 297). These are the questions put to all Turgenev's heroes, the demand that they prove themselves by displaying their inner as well as their outer lives.

Bazarov replies, "I have already informed you that I am a future district doctor" (S, VIII, 297). The terseness of Bazarov's remark reflects an important tacit assumption: an extreme focusing of energy must inform all activity. Since Russian reality offers no occupation commensurate with great individual talent, Bazarov will take up a constricting role, hoping to stretch it to fit his extravagant spirit. Odintsova grasps Bazarov's meaning and reinforces it. She declares that "district doctor" is too paltry a job, even temporarily, for someone like Bazarov. His great capacities (which she assumes without evidence) guarantees him a significant future. He should insist on the importance of his inner qualities. Though Bazarov remonstrates, "I am not in the habit of speaking freely about myself" (S, VIII, 297) Odintsova insists: "I do not see why one cannot express everything in his soul." She persuades him to behave in such a way that "your tension (*napriazhennost'*), your restraint will vanish" (S, VIII, 298).

Bazarov is easily persuaded. A view of personality that privileges the inner self is one he already holds, though he has never made it explicit. His superior attitude toward Pavel sprang from his high esteem of his own potential, his belief that his inner qualities would shortly flower into significant action. But what was effective in that antagonistic encounter proves disastrous in love. Judgment that is based on what men and women *are*, on the merits of their essential selves, instead of on what they *do*, makes union unlikely. There is no way to bridge any gap that may exist between individuals; love is either instantaneous or impossible. As Odintsova defines her ideal, "A life for a life. You take mine and give me yours, without regrets and with no turning back. Or else it is not worth it" (*S*, VIII, 294).

Bazarov declares his love in a form that he hopes will meet Odintsova's expectations. "Well, let me tell you then. I love you foolishly, senselessly. There, that is what you have forced out of me" (*S*, VIII, 299). He agrees that his truest qualities must be "forced" to the surface. He comes before Odintsova not as man with political beliefs and plans for social activity, but as a bundle of suddenly exposed instincts. Of course, once he has revealed his inner self, he has exhausted his suit. He can only stand silently, awaiting Odintsova's reply. Unfortunately for him, his revelation of his essential self has reminded Odintsova of her own. She decides she must live alone, nourishing purely personal desires and interests. "No," she says to herself after rejecting Bazarov, "God knows where that might have led, it's no joking matter. A quiet life is better than anything else in the world" (*S*, VIII, 300). Though he knows that Odintsova is attracted to him, Bazarov grumpily leaves her estate on the following morning. There is no way even to begin to overcome the impasse that the principle of individualism has created.

Ironically, Odintsova has both admitted that Bazarov possesses an impressive strength of personality and proven how easily that strength can be ignored. That is a poisonous judgment, since the dismissiveness is wrapped in praise that Bazarov cherishes. To counter the ill effects of his visit to Odintsova, Bazarov decides to refuse to play any role that is not clearly commensurate with the grandeur of spirit he believes is his. Whereas before he believed that any occupation could be stretched to fit his personality, now he needs something that brings immediate acknowledgement of his inner qualities. Politics, which in Russia entailed dealing with peasants who traditionally refused to recognize an intellectual's good intentions, seems an especially poor prospect. Resting on a haystack with Arkadii on his parents' farm, Bazarov provides a striking image to justify his new lethargy: "But I've developed a hatred for that 'every peasant,' that Philip or Sidor, for whom I must crawl out of my skin" (*S*, VIII, 325).

Bazarov's great glory is that he refuses meekly to acquiesce in his lethargy, though he sees its logical necessity. He accepts the principle of individualism, describing himself to Arkadii as "This atom of myself, this mathematical point where blood flows" (S, VIII, 323). But he still wants to get beyond himself, to make contact with others. "One wants to deal with other people," he says, "if only to swear at them, or to be bothered by them" (S, VIII, 324). From this deadlock arises the most striking moment in Turgenev's novels—because it is dramatic in itself, but also because it marks a logical conclusion of Turgenev's intellectual development. Disdaining all social roles as a diminishment of his inner self, Bazarov tries to find a pure representation of his being: he lunges into behavior of a different, almost metaphysical, dimension. Signaling his state of high anxiety by a surprising and abrupt playfulness of tone, he suggests to Arkadii that they wrestle, and quickly puts his hands around Arkadii's throat:

> Bazarov spread his long and wiry fingers . . . Arkadii turned and prepared, as it were in jest, to defend himself. . . . But the face of his friend appeared to him so sinister, he sensed such an unjoking menace in the crooked smile of the lips, in the enflamed eyes, that he experienced an intuitive fear. [S, VIII, 327]

Only the unexpected appearance of Bazarov's father deflects his murderous impulses. Arkadii has in fact done nothing to merit such treatment, but that is just the point: Bazarov hardly cares about the object of his hatred. Lashing out against the threat of inertia and isolation but lacking the means for sustained and purposeful activity, he indulges a blind and unbridled aggression, ready to inflict pain with the sole aim of imposing himself on the world.

Much of the rest of the book is a record of Bazarov's aghast reaction to what he has found himself capable of. He adopts a style of great restraint, keeps himself in check by assuming postures that will not call his essential nature into play. When he returns to the Kirsanov estate, he immerses himself in his scientific work and stays in his laboratory as if it were a haven. When he chances to encounter Pavel, he is always correct, giving no offense, provoking no arguments. Altogether, he puts himself on a short leash.

The one occasion when he does permit his personality to assert itself as of old is when he flirts with Nikolai's mistress, Fenochka, whom he comes upon in the garden. The result is disastrous, and drives him back immediately to his strategy of a purposeful neglect of natural inclinations. Bazarov's flirtation appears to be only an innocent exuberance in the presence of fresh beauty, and even the kiss with which the scene ends has no lascivious intent; nevertheless, Bazarov concludes that his impulses have again carried him in a direction he did not want to go: "He felt both ashamed and contemptuously annoyed. But he immediately shook his head, ironically congratulated himself 'on his formal entry into the ranks of woman-chasers' and marked off to his room" (*S*, VIII, 346).

The self-stylization that is expressed in this passage reflects a mind at bay. Seemingly, only an escape from who he is can bring Bazarov any relief. His path, so logically curved toward despair, signals the end of an ideal: the reliance by *obshchestvo* on the inner self apparently leads to the isolation of man from man, to a constraint on activity and finally to a loss of self-confidence.

But this is only one aspect of *Fathers and Sons*. From the beginning, alongside Bazarov's compelling drama, Turgenev has drawn another line of development: the theme of a home apart from the corrupting world. When Odintsova rejects Bazarov's love, hers is simultaneously a decision to remain within the confines of a sustaining domesticity, the strategy that Turgenev endorses time and again in his novels. In almost acceding to Bazarov's overtures, she "had brought herself to a certain limit, had forced herself to look beyond—and saw there not merely an abyss but a void . . . or shapeless chaos" (*S*, VIII, 300). The theme of the family is embodied in the actions of Nikolai Kirsanov, Fenochka, Odintsova, and, most tellingly, Arkadii and Odintsova's younger sister Katia. The family ideal they all strive for is presented as a form of tacit rebuttal to Bazarov's emphasis on individualism, and as a way to avoid the "shapeless chaos" his actions invite.

But, ever skeptical, Turgenev also shows that the family ideal entails difficulties of its own. Almost as soon as Arkadii and Katia discover their love, they elaborate a set of guiding rules. The rules are not insisted upon—to have done so would have been to transform marriage vows into a declaration of armed truce—but they bind nevertheless. Sitting in a bower, walking through a lush garden, or enjoying the weather, Arkadii and Katia urgently test each other's willingness to make sacrifices, and each other's determination to insist on individual needs. They fix to their mutual satisfaction the rights and limits of the parties in a matrimonial union. Arkadii happily learns that Katia has no money of her own and lives off her sister's generosity, for that means she will have less right to threaten his domination. Katia smugly notes to herself that she will soon have Arkadii at her feet. On the other hand, alongside their willfulness, both Arkadii and Katia indicate a readiness to yield control to the other. Katia sums up the delicate arrangement when she says to Arkadii, "I am prepared to submit, it is only inequality that is hard to bear" (S, VIII, 367). Katia envisions a curious situation where submission does not weaken self-assertion.

Underlying that illogical formulation is the desperate need of *obshchestvo*. The individual's strength should not be curtailed, since it is needed to fight existing corruption; but individuals giving free vent to their impulses can never blend into true harmony. A social entity is required that will acknowledge diversity while keeping it in check. The family seemed an especially attractive possibility: within the family there are fewer diverse urges to consider, fewer egos to confront at one time. In truth that is no logical resolution of the problem, only a scaling down of it, much like hoping to weaken the laws of mechanics by removing some of the colliding atoms. Nevertheless to *obshchestvo* it seemed that if the members of a family were all equally eager to avoid strife, the worst problems of individualism would be solved.[6]

To such an intricate mutuality Bazarov is alien. Though the achievement of Arkadii and Katia suggests an answer to his overriding problem, he must reject it: as Katia says of him at one point, Bazarov is "undomesticated." The family ideal goes counter to his most enduring quality. Though he has forced himself to explore a variety of artificial roles, he has done so in full self-consciousness; in the family, as represented by Arkadii and Katia, the participants cannot look too closely at what they have fashioned, for it is a structure kept in place very largely by wishful thinking.

---

6. The connection between egoism and the family was recognized as a key issue in the works of several writers. For example, Shchedrin's "Family Happiness" (1864) was read by the critic N. Strakhov as a specific rebuttal of Fourier's claims that smaller groups would allow for a harmony of disparate passions. See S. Borshchevsky, *Shchedrin i Dostoevsky* (Moscow, 1956), p. 89.

One other character shares Bazarov's disdain for domesticity, though he arrives at the attitude along a totally different path. That is Pavel Kirsanov. The most important experience in Pavel's life, one that still consumes his thoughts after more than twenty years, is his love for the Princess R_____. Her name is never given in full; that detail accurately reflects the mystery and extravagance of the relationship in general. "Pavel met her at a ball, danced a mazurka with her, during which she did not say a single sensible word, and fell passionately in love with her" (S, VIII, 200). From her deathbed, after years of brief frenzied meetings and abrupt departures, the Princess sends to Pavel the ring with a sphinx depicted on it which he had given her. "She had scratched in the image of a cross over the sphinx and had ordered that he be told that the cross was—the answer to the riddle" (S, VIII, 202). In fact, the gesture solves no riddles; it only intensifies the overtones of mystery and extravagance. Such attitudes, which Pavel still cultivates, cannot fit into a domestic structure.

When Pavel challenges Bazarov to a duel after he sees the flirtation with Fenochka, he is only superficially attempting to defend his brother's honor; nor does the resemblance that Pavel sees between Fenochka and Princess R_____ fully explain his action. The duel, ethically grotesque and historically anachronistic, is Pavel's effort to create a structure that will contain his feelings, since the world he lives in does not offer one. Indeed, for Pavel the duel is totally satisfying. It answers his needs so exactly as to leave in doubt whether the delirium he falls into after being wounded is not actually an ecstasy of spiritual fulfillment. The surge of friendship he feels for Bazarov as he lies bleeding in his arms, though unexpected, makes sense, for Pavel is experiencing finally the great pleasure of a release in concrete ritual for feelings that have long been pent up, and he is grateful to the man who has helped to make this release possible.

For Bazarov the duel solves nothing. He sees it as an empty charade. The example of Pavel's fatuous joy only confirms him in his deadlock more fully than before: he, Bazarov, is a man who requires a structure to contain and check his errant impulses, but who refuses the only structures that seem available. His return to his parents' house after the duel, his efforts to continue his scientific exper-

iments, his desultory participation in his father's medical practice—
these are the actions of a man going through the motions. Even
Bazarov's death, as Turgenev depicts it, is not so much a biological
event as an illustration of how even this ultimate act loses all meaning for a man lacking any abiding confidence in who he is. Though
the death is caused by a typhus infection contracted during an au-
topsy, it is the utter carelessness with which Bazarov tends to his
disease which guarantees his fate. He is a man totally unable to focus
on his own best interests. The final words he speaks are to Odintsova, who has been summoned to his bedside: "Blow on the dying
light and let it go out," he says, and in their extravagant Romanticism, they are very far from the sort of words that came from
Bazarov at the beginning of the book: they are the words of a man
crammed into a mode of expression not his own, and for that reason
—rather than for their immediate purport, which is melodramatic—
they attain a certain pathos.

The last chapter of *Fathers and Sons* presents a culminating
image for each of the two main lines of narrative development—
Bazarov's and that of the family theme—and the two images are
mutually illuminating. They illuminate as well Turgenev's intellectual and creative progress. These last words in the last novel
that Turgenev wrote during the period before emancipation stand
forth with the power of a logical conclusion, though it is a logic
informed by great feeling. The process that Turgenev began with
Notes of a Hunter here finds an end, a tense balance of real hope and
pessimism.

At the beginning of this chapter Turgenev describes the double
wedding of the Kirsanovs, father and son:

> A week ago, in the small parish church, quietly and almost without
> witnesses, there took place two weddings, Arkadii to Katia and
> Nikolai Petrovich to Fenochka; and on the same day Nikolai Pet-
> rovich gave a farewell dinner for his brother, who was going to
> Moscow on business. . . .
> Exactly at three o'clock everyone gathered at the table. Mitia [the
> son of Nikolai and Fenochka] was also brought in and seated; he had
> already acquired a nanny in a brocaded headdress. Pavel Petrovich
> enthroned himself between Katia and Fenochka. "The husbands"
> arranged themselves next to their wives. [S, VIII, 397–398]

The last paragraph of the book describes Bazarov's grave.

> In one of the far corners of Russia stands a small village graveyard.
> Like most of our graveyards it appears dismal: the ditches surround-
> ing it have long been overgrown by weeds, the drab wooden crosses
> sag and rot beneath their once freshly painted gables. . . . But in their
> midst stands a grave untouched by any man, untrampled upon by any
> animal: only the birds at dawn perch and sing on it. An iron railing
> fences it in, two fir trees have been planted there, one at each end; in
> that grave Evgenii Bazarov lies buried. Often from the nearby village
> a tottering old couple, man and wife, make their way here. Support-
> ing each other, they walk with heavy steps; on reaching the railing
> they fall down upon their knees and weep long and bitterly, and
> yearningly they gaze at the mute tombstone beneath which their son
> is lying; exchanging a brief word they brush the dust from the stone,
> set straight a branch of the fir tree and then resume their prayers,
> unable to tear themselves away from the spot where they feel them-
> selves so close to their son and their memories of him. . . . Can it be
> that love, sacred and devoted, is not omnipotent? Oh no! However,
> passionate, sinful, and rebellious the heart hidden away in that grave,
> the flowers that blossom there look at us unrebelliously with their
> innocent eyes: not only about eternal tranquility do they tell us,
> about that great peace of "indifferent" nature; they speak as well
> about eternal reconciliation and of life without end. [*S*, VIII, 491–492]

In the one scene there is conviviality and joy, in the other bleakness and breavement. But the contrast between the two passages is
in fact less than straightforward. Thus the reference to Pavel's departure at once introduces a slight dissonant note into the cele-
bratory proceedings. It is as if the transformation of the place the
peasants call "Bachelor's Farm" ("*Bobylii khutor*") into a site of
domestic bliss were too delicate a process to withstand the presence
of a single disharmonious element. Pavel must be ejected, albeit
with ceremony and honor. The narrative style suggests the fragility
of the community that is being formed. The remarkable attention to
seating arrangements and the precision of schedules suggests a constraining formality, as if the feelings of the participants were being
held in check by proprieties. When Turgenev stresses the word
"husbands," he seems to confirm that forms and labels are crucial
here, a necessary adhesive to individuals not naturally inclined to
band together. Turgenev omits any reference to states of mind. All

evidence of diverse urges has been muffled. We are shown things as in a tableau, a careful grouping that suggests affection but offers no hint of emotional complexity. And as in a tableau our attention is precisely focused, all extraneous confusion screened out or put into abeyance. Turgenev refers to the world beyond ("going to Moscow") in order to dismiss it, so that we can concentrate fully on the representation of the properly cultivated family.

The bleak characterization of Bazarov's grave suggests the ultimate futility of his life. Unmourned and unremembered except by his parents, Bazarov seems to have made no lasting effect on the world. But just as Turgenev had managed to insinuate the limitations of a domesticity that seemed at first glance altogether idyllic, he manages now to recapitulate a logic to Bazarov's failure which in part redeems him. In death Bazarov regains some of his original power, which the events of his life after meeting Odintseva had undercut. Significantly, though Turgenev describes a most emphatically circumscribed area, he manages to suggest considerable movement, and especially in comparison with the scene of the double wedding. The main characters in the first passage were free to move, but the scene was static; the main character is here fixed, but the scene is fluid. The narrative focus shifts rapidly and energetically, from the graveyard to the path and to a suggestion of a nearby village, and then finally to Bazarov's grave. There is an acknowledgement of the world beyond the immediate setting ("Like most of our graveyards") which suggests that Bazarov's fate may have wider meaning. In general, the space referred to in the second passage seems more expandable than in the first.

By the same token, time in the second passage seems more repeatable. The description of the family dinner suggests a snapshot, as if only an instantaneous rendering could capture the diverse impulses of the subjects. The description of Bazarov's grave shows an occasion that will be duplicated many times. The demands of the plot have something to do with the differences between the two passages, but the crucial influence is the different emotions in each. That pathetic moment when Bazarov's parents kneel in prayer indicates a grief that will extend and enrich itself for a long time to come. The happiness of the Kirsanovs, on the other hand, requires a finely adjusted context not likely to be easily secured again. In all, though he is dead and his grave isolated, it is Bazarov who projects the possibilities of greatest energy and purpose.

In the very last lines of the novel, the narrator is swept along by the pathos of Bazarov's fate, His style overflows with great feeling: the syntax careens out of control and meanings are blurred. That, in fact is a duplication of Bazarov's dilemma during much of the book. Feelings too powerful to find an embodying structure become dissipated. Bazarov's spirit, the narrator remarks, escapes the bleak grave and mingles with the universe; but the universe is "indifferent." Bazarov's strength has led him to renounce the supports that those more timid than he cling to, but the consequence is utter failure. In the indifferent universe, Turgenev more than once made clear, every atom pursues its own goal, so that individual purpose is inconsequential and success both accidental and unlikely. The last chapter of *Fathers and Sons* presents an uneasy choice: to be a strong individual, who is necessarily homeless and thus lacks the support that would allow him to impress his values on the world at large; or to be a part of a community that sustains its members, but at the cost of forcing them to restrain their natural impulses.

The ending to *Fathers and Sons* raises a major question about Turgenev's political achievement. Did he help Russians to conceive of their world more efficaciously or was the vision he offered merely one of elaborate stalemate, helplessness disguised by a complexity of emotions? The only way to answer this question is to consider the course of Russian history.

In stressing the role of the family, Turgenev clearly indulged in a great capacity for wishful thinking. In Russia as elsewhere, the family remains an arena for repression and domination. Indeed, Turgenev never was able to detail a theory for overhauling its structure; in his novels, members of families accept constraints with very little struggle; hence the families appear as sad and spiritless communities. But the *idea* of the family, of a mediate agency between a rapacious society and the individual, is exhilarating in the context of Russian history. Turgenev always treats the family not only as an actual social arrangement, but also as a symbol of the desire to escape pervasive corruption. Because he wrote at a time when Russians were still unclear what form the escape could take, he gave the family a hovering meaning—a representation of an empirical fact and a blueprint for an ideal. As a result, even after the family had been dismissed as a potential focus of opposition to the existing order, Russian progressives continued to discuss the issues Turgenev raised: the relationship between a small group and the country at large, the means of establishing harmony within the group, the difference between social and political institutions.

Turgenev did not introduce the theme of the family into Russian literature—no literature of a civilized country could have ignored the theme altogether. Still, it is remarkable how little attention was paid to the family by early nineteenth-century Russian writers. In the masterpieces of the 1830s and 1840s, by Gogol, Lermontov, and Marlinsky, there is almost nothing of the drama of courtship, marriage, and domesticity that abounds in European prose of the same period. Pushkin's *The Captain's Daughter* (1832) is something of an exception, though the Grinev family is presented as a ramshackle structure, its values insignificant in comparison to patriotism and romantic love.

In the years immediately preceding Turgenev's novels, the family *did* figure prominently in the literary imagination, though its meaning was very different from the one he would give it. In the 1840s and early 1850s the family was most often represented as a sterile and degraded convention that impeded a life based on true feelings.[7] George Sand, many of whose works endorsed the overriding claims of passion, was widely cited, and the fascination of Russian literature with unfettered expression probably reached its highpoint in the climactic scene of Druzhinin's *Polinka Saks* (1852), which was a version of Sand's *Jacques*. Upon learning that his wife loves another man, the wise husband of Polinka Saks realizes that his marriage is a paltry reason to obstruct great passion, and removes himself from the scene. In Druzhinin's rendering the husband goes abroad, whereas Sand has him commit suicide—which may say something about the different degrees of adherence to principle in Russia and France. But the basic point is the same: conventions

---

7. On the importance of the family theme in Russian literature in the early 1850s, see B. M. Eikhenbaum, *Lev Tolstoy, semidesiatye gody* (Leningrad, 1960), p. 146; also Eikhenbaum, *Molodoi Tolstoi*, pp. 64–66.

invented by society should yield if they are in opposition to natural feeling.

The endorsement of passion is a difficult posture to resist. It implies greatness of spirit, a willingness to put oneself at risk. Turgenev more than once showed he was sensitive to the glories of passion; his story "Faust" (1857), for example, depicts the transforming power of love, a love that overrides all obstacles. But generally he believed that not the intensity of feelings, but where they were displayed, was crucial. In his novels, he showed that a structure like the family must structure feelings if they are not to be dissipated and corrupted in the world at large. A comment by Mikhailov in 1859, criticizing writers like Druzhinin, indicates how well Turgenev had persuaded his contemporaries:

> [They say] "Feeling is free; it cannot be subjected to any arbitrary control; there are no chains that either openly or secretly it cannot break." These thoughts, which have been only half understood, flattered the immaturity of people who called themselves the educated part of society. Taking them as dogma. . . society has fallen into the chaos of naked and unbridled depravity.[8]

To be sure, Turgenev was not the only novelist in the post-Crimean War period who underscored a new role for the family; but his synecdochical perspective, showing the family as a distinct entity that was nevertheless connected with the fullness of contemporary Russia, was groundbreaking. Three major novels of the period serve to situate Turgenev's achievement. In *The Family Chronicle* (1856), S. T. Aksakov describes the Russian family rhapsodically and singlemindedly. The characters have the determination and bravery of characters in an epic, but they live out their lives in a severely circumscribed area. The births of children, the deaths of loved ones, the uncertainties of harvests, and the building of houses mark out the limits of concern. The setting of the novel, near the frontier town of Ufa at the foot of the Urals, further promotes the idea that the Bagrov family is a world unto itself, oblivious of contemporary Russia. In *Oblomov* (1859), by contrast, the family's merit is most visible when viewed in the context of a larger reality. Goncharov

8. M. A. Mikhailov, "Zhenshchiny, ikh vospitanie i znachenie," *Sochineniia* (Moscow, 1958), 111, 370.

describes Oblomovka, the hero's familial estate, in strictly compara-
tive terms. Mountains in most of the world are "Menacing, ter-
rifying . . . they too vividly remind us of our mortality," but in Oblomovka there are easily comprehensible "copies of those terrible
far-away mountains." Similarly, the sea, which generally oppresses
man by its "boundlessness," is in Oblomovka reduced to "a river
that runs gaily, playing and romping."[9] The family implies comfort
and comprehensibility; unfortunately, it also implies a pure ideal, a
realm accessible only in fantasy—Oblomov can reexperience the
pleasures he knew as a child only by conjuring them up in a dream.
In *Family Happiness* (1859), Tolstoi both stresses the inherent value
of the family and links it directly with a larger reality. But he defines
the nature of that link in terms not many contemporaries could
accept. When the heroine at last realizes the importance of her
marriage, she sees it exclusively as an agency of propagation—an
idea, of course, that Tolstoi repeated still more emphatically in the
ending to *War and Peace* (1868–1869). Individuals find contentment
to the extent that they meet the needs of the species; the family,
which is the means the human species has devised to breed itself, is
linked to the rest of the world by its biological function.

The families that Turgenev depicts are not merely the result of a
desire for nest-building or child-rearing or domestic comfort; they
are aspects of a political strategy designed to permit Russians to live
in the contemporary world. The retreat of the Kirsanovs to their
home at the end of *Fathers and Sons* is a politically self-conscious
step; Bazarov's fate shows the foolhardiness of confronting the fullness of Russian life. Turgenev's politics are distinctly limited—
because he never describes a mechanism showing how the Kirsanovs could extend their contentment beyond their own family, it
seems a politics of self-interest. Nonetheless, it is a politics, which
was a great achievement for the times.

One proof of the efficacy of Turgenev's vision is its continued
influence on Russian political life throughout the 1860s. That is not
to say that he was closely associated with the radical tendencies that

9. I. I. Goncharov, *Sobranie sochinenii* (Moscow, 1934), IV, 102–103. I am indebted to Milton Ehre, *Oblomov and His Creator: The Life and Works of Ivan Goncharov* (Princeton, 1973), pp. 173–177, for calling my attention to these passages.

predominated in that period. When *obshchestvo* collapsed at the beginning of the decade, he lost his position of preeminent spokesman of the culture. But it is also true that the radicals of the 1860s grew out of the *obshchestvo* ideal, which Turgenev had helped to develop. They continued to accept his synecdochical view of the world, his insistence that individuals construct a realm that was distinct yet connected with the whole; they also, however, began to search for a mechanism explaining how the part could alter the whole.

Chernyshevsky's *What Is to Be Done?* (1863), virtually the bible of progressives in the 1860s, stresses the importance of the family no less than Turgenev had. In fact, the novel, for all the revolutionary meanings that contemporaries attached to it, at times suggests a guidebook for newlyweds. Can either partner in a marriage enjoy privacy if the couple lives in a small apartment; should one partner's zealous study habits irritate the other; do marriage vows imply love or only affection?—these are the issues around which the plot revolves. Nor can the fact that the family in Chernyshevsky consists of *raznochintsy* rather than members of the nobility in itself serve as proof of a political aggressiveness lacking in Turgenev; politics depends on action, not social pedigree. It is only when the heroine Vera's first husband steps aside to allow her to marry her true love Alexander Kirsanov (his last name is, of course, no accident) that the novel's landmark purpose becomes clear. *These* Kirsanovs, Chernyshevsky insists, can extend their happiness beyond the limits of their own family. At the conclusion of the novel, Vera's first husband reappears under a pseudonym, remarries, and with his new wife settles in rooms adjoining the Kirsanov residence: the two couples "visit each other like relatives" and "live in harmony and amicably, in a gentle yet active fashion."[10] Chernyshevsky's language reflects his view that since individuals are basically selfish, increasing the size of a group is a most delicate step; nevertheless the harmony of Vera and Alexander has been extended, to one more family at least. Presumably it could continue to be extended in the same way, family by family.

10. N. G. Chernyshevsky, *Polnoe sobranie sochinenii* (Moscow, 1950), XI, 636.

The insistence on a step-by-step subversion of the status quo was the radicals' emendation of Turgenev's vision. Dobroliubov stated their program most explicitly:

> The question of so-called *family morality* is one of the most important social questions of our time. We will even say that it is significantly more important than all other questions because it enters into all the others and has a meaning more *internal*, whereas the remaining ones are generally limited by external circumstances. Our literature, recently occupied with these external social questions, has almost forgotten about family relations, about the meaning of women in society. Some even wanted to find some kind of natural contradiction between family and social relations, whereas this opposition is purely artificial and extremely absurd. No matter what is said about different means to improve the life of society, these always have their beginnings and ends in the relations within the family, understood not only in the sense of marital bliss but in a meaning much broader. In the family there is achieved the most complete and natural fusion of personal egoism of others, and there is set up the foundation and basis of that brotherhood, that solidarity, the creation of which alone can serve as the lasting bond of a correctly organized society.[11]

Dobroliubov stresses the importance of the family by contrasting its "internal meaning" with those social phenomenon issues that are "limited by external circumstances." Though the family may raise issues that are less vital than, say, serfdom, they are issues that the government does not directly control. Dobroliubov's argument recapitulates the strategy of *obshchestvo:* action in a circumscribed sphere is more effective than action in the world at large, which is fully in the control of the existing political order. But, Dobroliubov adds, change within the family *leads* to general change; though the family is "in natural opposition" to society, it can exert a critical influence on society: "The means of improving life in society... always have their beginnings and ends in the relations within the family." To organize each family's life in accordance with humane principles means to subvert a corrupt society's awesome power step by small step, but nevertheless decisively.

A committment to what Dobroliubov calls "internal meanings" dominated the radical movement during the 1860s. After a flurry of propagandizing among the peasantry, workers, and army at the time

11. N. A. Dobroliubov, *Sobranie sochinenii*, II, 234.

of the Emancipation Act, radicals turned their attention to their own condition. Though they never lost sight of their goal of eradicating injustice in Russia generally, they intended first to nurture their own powers. The creation of "new men" and "new women," of "critically thinking individuals," was their shibboleth. Debate centered on such issues as the relationship between hierarchy and power in small groups, the logic of mutual cooperation, the role of women. Recruitment to the cause continued, but it was mostly among individuals predisposed to progressive principles, like university students; the rest of the country took on the aspect of an incomprehensible Other. A foremost historian of the period neatly sums up the dominant form of organization: "Bodies which came into being independently, which took action consistent with their own strengths and their own ideas, which tried to join up with those that had similar tendencies . . . but which had little real chance of development."[12]

The radicals' attention to defining one's own capabilities and one's relations with those who were similar in outlook made the family an obvious area of interest, and experiments with new domestic arrangements were widespread, including several communes that achieved notoriety because of alleged licentiousness. Even when the traditional family was not the immediate target, the values that the radicals associated with an ideal family continued to play an important role. Members of Peter Ishutin's "The Organization," which was very influential, subjected their private life to the severe discipline of the group, cultivated a common ascetic style that gave them a sense of unity, and used all personal wealth for the promotion of their ideas.[13] A similar spirit of sacrifice for the good of the group pervaded the various commercial communes, self-help corporations and mutual loan banks that sprang into being.

Though these projects required various sorts of expertise, the vision informing them all derived from Chernyshevsky's *What Is to be Done?*—itself an elaboration of Turgenev's novelistic achievement. Russian literature of the period acquired a status in the 1860s that is often claimed for it but rarely achieved: it altered the way

---

12. Franco Venturi, *Roots of Revolution*, trans. Francis Haskell (New York, 1966), p. 469.
13. Ibid., pp. 331–353.

individuals thought and acted. It is therefore not surprising that when the strategy based on "internal meanings" broke down, one sign of the change was the displacement of the Turgenev type of novel. With the beginning of the 1870s, it became clear that Russian progressives would have to go beyond their own small groups and explore the political potential of the rest of the country. A politics based on carefully structured organizations with explicit programs and tight internal discipline was declared outmoded; the Populist ethic gained ascendency. Shchedrin, who was a Populist earlier than most, clearly stated the consequences for literature:

> It seems to me that the former basis of the family has been lost at that moment when the idea of the family (*semeistvennost'*), and all that pertains to it, begins to change its character. The novel (at least in that form in which it has appeared till now) is for the most part a work about domesticity (*proizvedenie semeistvennosti*). Its drama begins in the family, does not depart from there, and concludes in the same location. [It may be] in its positive sense (the English novel) or negative (the French novel) but the family always plays a primary role in the novel.
>   That warm, cosy, well demarcated element, which gave a substance to the novel, is vanishing before everyone's eyes. The drama [of the novel] begins to demand other motifs; it is born in the expanse and ends there. No matter from what point this expanse is illuminated, everything in it seems cold and dark and uncomfortable. No perspective is visible; drama seems sacrificed to happenstance....[14]

Shchedrin put the theory into practice himself. His novel *The Golovlovs* (1872–1876) shows a family that is no alternative to the world but only a more compact arena for the expression of selfishness, mendacity, and tyranny.

Increasingly as the new century approached, progressives sought new means to cope with evils of the existing order—but the part-whole perspective on the world which *obshchestvo* fostered never lost its potency entirely. Even the Populists' strategy, though a rejection of that perspective, was built on the experience that *ob-*

14. N. Shchedrin, *Polnoe sobranie sochinenii* (Moscow, 1936), VIII, 312. Shchedrin had earlier attacked the idea that the family could serve as the basis of a political strategy. In the ironically titled "Family Happiness" (1864), he had insisted that the "family union," far from being "the seed of civil (*grazhdanskii*) union," is, in fact, a means of perpetuating the general corruption. See *Polnoe sobranie sochinenii*, VI, 420.

shchestvo had provided. By the 1890s, after Populism had failed, Marxists were again stressing the need for the rigorous organization of vanguard groups, though now combined with a more thorough understanding of objective conditions in the country at large—a sense of "internal" meanings balanced by a grasp of Russia's institutional structure.

To most of his Soviet critics, Turgenev is a representative of the liberal tradition that failed to comprehend the country's needs. Most of his Western critics place him in the same tradition, but voice regret that the country failed to understand the merits of liberalism. Whether a misguided fool or an unheeded prophet, Turgenev appears as a voice crying in the wilderness. From this point of view, it makes sense to ignore his politics altogether, which indeed is not an uncommon approach.

But I believe there is no need either to stigmatize or to fantasize about Turgenev's political position, for it was in fact very much in the mainstream of Russian history. It is true that Russia had no room for amelicrist dreams: that some individuals achieve contentment is not a reason to assume, as Turgenev often did, that contentment will spread. In omitting a description of the mechanism for social improvement, he exhibited a distressing political tentativeness. Russian life clearly required a more purposeful wrench than he cared to contemplate. Nevertheless, in conceiving of an area apart from government hegemony where individuals could control their own destinies, Turgenev established the basis for much of the progressive political activity of the late nineteenth century.

In his novels Turgenev proceeded with hesitation, with constant self-correction. Ideas and social forms that are endorsed are also fiercely scrutinized. Even if his contemporaries had read him with perfect sympathy and understanding, they would not have learned of a program for changing Russia; his novels raise more questions than they answer. Nevertheless, the novels did strikingly define the political landscape, which had the effect of making questions purposeful. He showed Russians that they lived in a comprehensible world. Considering the national psychology before he came on the scene, that was a very great achievement.

Index

213

Index

Index

Index

Index

Index

TURGENEV'S RUSSIA

Designed by G. T. Whipple, Jr.
Composed by The Composing Room of Michigan, Inc.
in 10 point VIP Caledonia, 2 points leaded,
with display lines in Caledonia.
Printed offset by Thomson/Shore, Inc.
on Warren's Number 66 text, 50 pound basis.
Bound by John H. Dekker & Sons, Inc.
in Holliston book cloth
and stamped in All Purpose foil.

Library of Congress Cataloging in Publication Data

RIPP, VICTOR.
    Turgenev's Russia.
    Includes bibliographical references and index.
    1. Turgenev, Ivan Sergeevich, 1818–1883—Criticism
and interpretation.   2. Russia—History—19th
century.   I. Title.
PG3443.R5   891.73′3   80-15534
ISBN 0-8014-1294-3